Each book is available to buy separately*

On the Other Hand:
The Little Anthology of Big Questions

Just Around the Bend:
Más o Menos

Louder than a Whisper:
Clearer than a Bell

*E-books are not illustrated.

A Three Course Meal for the Mind is not
available to buy in e-book format.

"This is for the ones who stand
For the ones who think they can
For the ones who need a hand
For the ones who try again."

'Comes and Goes' Greg Laswell

A Three Course Meal For The Mind

Renée Paule

RPG Publishing

A Three Course Meal for the Mind

By Renée Paule

Edited by G R Hewitt

Cover design and artwork by Renée Paule
All illustrations by Renée Paule

Printed by CreateSpace

Written in British English

ISBN: 978-0-9935098-0-3

If we really want to see change in the world,
we must be prepared to make those changes.

My meaning of certain words used in this book

Humanity
Each and every one of us as a *whole*.

One
All that is, was or ever will be.

Ignorant
To ignore.

Intelligence
Independent and radical thinking.

Society
The world we've created for ourselves to live in,
with all its complex mechanisms.

Belief
A personal preference.

Hope
Waiting for a future event that may never arrive.

Fear
Dreading a future event.

Spiritual
Thinking outside the box and searching inside
ourselves for higher meaning.

For your convenience there are blank pages
for notes at the back of this book.

On the Other Hand

Just Around the Bend - 107

Louder Than a Whisper - 197

On The Other Hand: The Little Anthology of Big Questions

Originally published in France by RPG Publishing 2013

Standalone ISBN: 978-2-9546811-7-7

Questioning everything raises consciousness
and this will change our world.

Thank you

Godfrey for every day you helped.
Chris for Sundays.
Al.
Mike … for going out of bounds.
Louise … for staying within them.
Anne for scrutiny.
'little red ball'.
Hazel.

"Success is the ability to go from one failure to another with no loss of enthusiasm."[23] Winston Churchill

M any years ago, I began my autobiography. Not long into this project I realised the degree to which I'd refined my thinking meant, rehearsing the past would serve minimal purpose. However, some insight into my life is necessary in order that you may know the background processes leading to this book being written. What follows is a relatively brief synopsis of what's gone before.

~~~

Despite having two living parents, I was placed in an orphanage at the age of nine months; my parents *apparently* went their separate ways. My foundation was lost long before I could build it. My time in orphanages was not pleasant or loving. That footing led me to characterise the outside world as a hostile, selfish, violent, confusing, dishonest and unfriendly place - a world with which I was unable to interact. I was afraid of the frightful images that appeared both in my dreams and during my waking state.

At twelve I was marched into the matron's office and introduced to a woman I was quite casually told, was my mother. I'd always been told she was dead. I remember running out of the room but can't tell you where I went as I've no memory of it. I've around twelve year's amnesia and a few openings where snippet memories, like this one, remain intact. The incident was the hardest blow of my childhood that I can remember. Because of these blows and being forced to deal with them at such a young age, I've been able to cope with other difficult situations in my adult years. I've also been able to let go of conditioned beliefs.

This painful upbringing led me to stumble and fall a great deal in my earlier years. I wavered between feeling; despair, hatred, self-hatred and self-pity. Emotions more damning to the purity of a child's mind and ones I couldn't share. My childhood was brutal and left me with little appetite for the challenges of adult life.

I learnt some difficult lessons in the hardest way.

I went to night school and learnt skills like typing, shorthand and communication. I worked as a secretary, temped for a while and became a personal assistant. However, staying too long in one place suffocated me and I could never make sense of petty office politics. Office work was mundane and from the expressions on the faces of other personnel, no-one was particularly happy doing it. I tried many other things including running my own business. I was meticulous and committed but didn't enjoy it or the ridiculous amount of time required on administration rather than actual work. I was incredibly bored which sapped my motivation. Although I earned a reasonable salary, I didn't feel as though I were doing something worthwhile with my life.

I went to university and studied English Literature but it was focused on highly regulated literary criticism rather than author intention. Writers wish others to experience their horizons, not to look down at every stone on the path they want you to tread. Again, boredom set in. I've a sharp and active mind and it needed more positive stimulation. Family Circumstances then led me to leave two and a half years into my studies. The wind blew, yet again, in another direction.

By this point I rather looked forward to the changes that came into my life and was perhaps guilty of triggering them quicker than necessary. I still had no locus and couldn't find anything to love about the world; I'd no idea if I loved anything at all. I didn't enjoy the basics of everyday life - nightlife, shopping, reading, social gatherings, cinemas, holidays, touring or drinking - all these meant little to me. I was a loner but didn't like being in my own company, which made life pretty difficult. I lived without passion for the world and its population, wondering why I existed at all. But somehow, something 'new and exciting' always appeared and led me in another direction. These stepping stones kept me above water, despite often slipping rather dangerously off some of them. Nevertheless, I was still able to reflect, smile and move on.

I never wrapped myself up in a guru or any other mentor. This may be because the opportunity didn't arise or because my sub-conscious told me it wouldn't help. All the blame for the mistakes I made in my earlier life was directed *elsewhere* and I now take full responsibility for all of it; no-one is to blame - it's how it happened.

I've been married four times, six, if you don't include the pieces of paper making them official. In between them, I've entered into several dysfunctional relationships. I've lived in so many houses that I couldn't even try to count them - I can honestly say I've never felt at 'home' in any one of them. Deep inside my subconscious mind I sought my 'home' and this was probably my motive. I can assure you I gave each relationship my utmost attention and devotion (relative to my ability at the time), but my naivety meant I picked the wrong relationships. This was due to 'needing' to be in a relationship and I sought parental guidance, missing from my childhood, from my husbands. I now know I wasted considerable energy in a desperate attempt to nurture what were weak bonds. I'd have saved myself a lot of trouble had I the foresight to discern the difficulties that arose because of my childhood, and left them behind. A blank slate would have given me a better context, a fairer perspective. We don't listen or learn much while we're in 'why me' mode, do we? But life doesn't play fair - our base instincts tell us to participate wholly reliant on personal experience.

The craziest things begin to happen when we start to question our world. I remember once I decided to move (alone) to France. I experienced considerable opposition from friends who said, "You can't just go around doing whatever you want" and I'd reply "Just watch me". I'd made up my mind and I did it, I'm still here to tell the tale and I'm still standing upright after overcoming several hurdles; learning to speak French being just one of them. Leaps of faith are just that. Opportunities have to be taken before you find out what's on the other side. I've always jumped from pool to pool and though sometimes the water can be rather deep, if I could turn back time, I'd do it all again - perhaps with more vigour and gratitude for the experiences.

The most profound and magnificent moment in my life was when I walked one evening along a beach on the Sussex coast in England, watching the most amazing sunset. I stood still for a moment to admire it and I found there was no separation at all. I felt the waves, the sun, the sand, the rocks and the *Everything*. It lasted just a few seconds but it was deep, informed and I was so moved by the experience that I haven't stopped or left my path since that moment. It was another new beginning and the closest I've ever felt to *home*. The more I consider the questions, but dispense with the urge to answer them, the more I make sense of my world.

I now don't watch television, eat at restaurants, go to pubs or any other social events. I do have like-minded friends and love to spend time with them. It wouldn't occur to me to give up; it's exciting, a great deal of fun and for the first time in my life I feel I've found something worth pursuing; something to be truly grateful for, which I am. I now realise that for many years I'd been listening to the wrong voice inside my head - the one that says 'life stinks' and 'no you mustn't' as opposed to the one that says 'life's a miracle'. The notion of writing my autobiography was a sort of 'self-help' therapy, a process of coming to terms with my self. That realisation was central to discovering my *raison d'être*.

Introduction

Life isn't something that happens to us - 'we' happen to life.

This book is the result of my life's experiences, which for many years were accumulated and carried around in a bundle of mental baggage I'd no idea what to do with. My preface covers the underlying circumstances and the substance of the book shows how the contents of our minds can be unpacked through close examination. It's possible to stop baggage controlling our reactions to daily events that bring further conflicts and challenges; for example; from news stories and stresses in our working environments. One way to do this is to examine present circumstances that trigger trained emotional reactions from our pasts. One of the most common of these is that we all want to be liked and if someone doesn't like us, we revert to the emotional state from a past similar experience. Why?

The mind and the ego: What are they? Do we create them? Why has the mind got two conflicting voices? I raise these and many other questions with other diverse but related subjects. By looking into them we can begin to see the world as it really is; an incredible and ingenious illusion that has a disproportionate impact on individual well-being. Questioning the world surrounding us from time to time isn't enough. We have to do it continuously, repeating the same questions in order to discern how we can dispense with societal conditioning that has pervaded our being and influenced us since our births.

Technology has surpassed us and we carry it around as though it were an additional organ; it thinks when we don't. It sees the whole picture and we don't. We look at ourselves relative to the outside world and we don't feel powerful enough to make a difference.

This book is different in as much as it looks at life *now* and the things we're *not* seeing. It looks at what we push aside and don't want to see despite the fact that it's all there, right in front of us. It looks at these things without the influences of dogma or other ingrained beliefs. Humans are funny fickle beings:

- We don't like what we read in the news, yet we still buy the papers,

- We don't like what we watch on the television, yet we still watch it,
- We claim not to like violence, yet we accept it as entertainment,
- We don't like pollution yet we continue to contribute to it.

Why do we do these things? *On the Other Hand* explores these facets with some bold and frank questions that make for uncomfortable reading.

The first chapter *Something's Not Quite Right with the World* examines some of these issues, such as why everyone struggles in their lives. We don't want to give up accumulating material things and we hide in virtual reality worlds and on social media websites rather than seeking our own purpose. We're all powerful, yet we follow trends and celebrities as though they were our gods; we follow their every breath and obey their every 'command'. Throughout this book the reader is encouraged to look at life from another perspective and see that change is possible, if we ask the right questions.

We can change our lives for the better *now*, not in some distant time that may never arrive; we're good at putting things off until 'tomorrow' and tomorrow doesn't exist. But we must be ready to deconstruct every part of the life we've created, leaving no stone unturned. Be prepared ... old beliefs are hard to eliminate and to let go of. I write nothing you have to believe. I ask you to believe nothing. I do try to show you that Humanity created this world and only Humanity can dismantle it.

I've paused, reflected, procrastinated, been interrupted by my schizophrenic mind, jotted down ideas for other chapters, designed six different book covers, written the blurb, weaved a little more text in here and there and stopped to search for appropriate quotes to include. My mind tried to block my progress with this book, but here it is completed, finally. I grew with the book and, despite my search for wisdom, humility and grace, I felt rather chuffed about having finished it. I'm now not the same person and many of my thoughts have changed. I've changed the way I look at myself and my world and I've changed the way I look at *you* - less judgementally.

I can't provide you with any answers to questions, but I can help you find the courage to discover your *own* questions. I say again, these questions don't need to be answered; they just need to be recognised in order that we can distinguish between truths and untruths. We've learnt all we know through repetition and we must *unlearn* it by the same process. This message is reinforced throughout this book for exactly that reason. The questions are far more important than the answers when we begin our journey of discovery; further along the road, we don't need them at all.

If you've ever felt you don't quite fit in the world, wondered why there's so much conflict or why there's no harmony, then this book may be of help to you. Are you ready to change? We're, collectively, the cells of Humanity. We're One and indivisible. There is no 'time', no 'left or right', no 'up or down' and no 'space'. We're the world. We're not powerless. We can remove ourselves from the stream of chaos and make a big difference to our lives. I invite you to see the world through my eyes and share with you my deepest thoughts about the world and its inhabitants.

Something's not Quite Right with the World

"Common sense is a collection of prejudices acquired by age eighteen."[2]
Albert Einstein

It's impossible for a square peg to fit into a round hole. No matter how much we shave off edges to round the peg, we'll never fit in any way that isn't illusory. Trying to be *normal* can be an upheaval and it would be better to be neither round nor square; both shapes have finite boundaries. Why do we pretend to *fit* by keeping quiet about a life that is at best robotic and commercial? There's something not quite right with the world.

Doubtless, like me, you've wondered why the world's not a happy place to live in; why there's so much division, why we struggle and why we just can't seem to get it right. What's holding us back from experiencing our true nature and making us want to argue and fight, rather than love and appreciate each other? What makes us competitive; needing to keep up with *The Joneses* or exceed them? What makes us want the things in the world that environmentally, or otherwise, we're better off without? We claim to care about the world but we choose to ignore it in favour of selfish gain. Something amazing is waiting for us to notice it, regardless of whether we want to believe it or not and, we're part of it. As W. H. Davies so beautifully put it in his poem *Leisure*, "We have no time to stand and stare"[3] at the marvels of our world because we keep ourselves too busy.

When I've spoken to people about spiritual matters and how incredible Humanity is, they'd ask me for proof of it. Yet they'd never had any proof for anything they'd been taught in school or by their parents. We accept most things without question. I find it a little bit odd that we believe everything we're told, particularly as our 'teachers' were taught by *their* teachers … and so on. These same beliefs have been passed down for generations. Our belief systems are founded on what we've been told by highly questionable authorities who decide, for unclear reasons, what our children learn. For example, schools teach our children the 'Theory of Evolution' as an unquestionable fact; but they also teach religious education. When I was at school, questioning or disagreeing with teachers was strongly 'discouraged'. I couldn't accept my questions being ignored and rejected; I'd a great many of them. As a result of this I learnt to doubt everything people tried to teach me and a large part of my school years were spent truanting. My favourite haunt was the Oasis swimming pool in High Holborn, where I would spend hours in the water - I didn't have anything else to do and no-one noticed my absence. Despite the lack of alternative beliefs, most children grow up never to doubt or question what they've been told. They're pacified with toys and computer games and kept busy in and outside school hours. Children lose their individuality and their own unique character as a result of this; it's replaced by a compliant and systematic one. Our *purpose* can't be to lie dormant; each and every one of us must have a worthwhile meaning.

I've no doubt we do! How can such magnificence not have meaning? What could this meaning be? Perhaps it's to see if we can remove the veil hiding our true self before the end of our lifetimes; who can say? You may be perfectly happy to see your life through without a spiritual thought and that's okay. However, as you're reading this book you've started making enquiries about the meaning of your life. Essential to this journey is to doubt what we've read in text books, newspapers or what we've heard on the television. If we doubt any part of it, but choose to believe *some* of it, then shouldn't we take another look at why we're so selective?

Now that the contents of the world have become 'disposable' we've lost appreciation for anything in it. If something we've bought breaks we can easily replace it. Any guilt we may feel for 'waste' is driven away because we're encouraged to take our unwanted things to council 'dumps' and place them in the giant skips provided. We're told these things will be safely recycled and made into something else; few people look further than this. In effect, we're given *permission* to throw whatever we want away and we're encouraged, through advertising, to buy up-to-date replacements. If society says it's ok to do this, we don't give it another thought - we've absolved ourselves of all environmental responsibility and tell ourselves that we personally, can't be blamed. If you're familiar with trips to the rubbish dump then you'll know that no matter what day we take our rubbish there we have to queue to dispose of it; we queue when we buy things and we queue again to throw them away. We don't think too much about where this rubbish goes as it's 'officially' dealt with. We don't struggle to abdicate responsibility or physical clutter, but we do when that clutter is psychological.

Do we care about our welfare as much as recycling waste? Do we care for our children? Do we see any improvements at all in the world? We've seen a steady increase in the violence, gore, sex and bad language in the films we watch. Why are these in films at all? Have we ever given these issues serious thought? If we had, then we would see it's our *desire* for them that brings them into being - we buy them and are therefore, responsible for their production. By changing the way we interact with the world and not waiting for someone else to do it for us, our world will change. More importantly, we can't leave it to people who don't hold high standards or live by their own 'examples' of what's right and wrong. If we didn't buy or watch the films then there wouldn't be a market for them. So why do we buy them and why do we put our trust in the authorities when we all know it's not such a good idea? We always have choices; it's rare we make them.

Multiple choice questions are often the format for exams and this doesn't leave room for independent thought. Have you ever filled in one of those questionnaires in a magazine that tries to 'type' you or tell you who your ideal partner is? They ask you questions such as 'If a man asks you if you want to dance with him at a disco and you don't like the look of him would you:-

- Bluntly say No thanks!' and walk away?'
- Dance with him even if you don't want to?'
- Say you're waiting for someone who's the jealous type?'

What if none of the above answers apply to you? The suggestion is usually to choose the answer which fits the closest. Well it's not true then is it? What if you don't go to discotheques? When you consider the rest of the questions and you choose the 'closest fit' answers how then can the resulting standard personality type, which results from your choices, tell you who you are? We may as well be part of a lucky dip filled with personality types. That's exactly what we become if we fill out the answers and believe the 'results'; a standardisation of mankind by proxy. Who designs these questionnaires anyway?

That the authorities are questionable is not difficult to see. Look at so-called history; were we ever not in the middle of some war or another? We've only to look at media stories about government officials, religious representatives or any civil service departments to see that they can be highly a-moral. When exposed, often few, if any, disciplinary measures are taken and it's all hushed up in the wonderful way we're familiar with and we never question it again. We do, however, take the time to satirise the scandals for long enough to make them 'amusing' and the purpose of this is to 'soften the blow', creating laughter instead of the tears they warrant. Then they dissolve as other scandalous stories take the stage, continuing the cycle. Are these not just the same old stories with another face on them?

These are the same authorities we allow to tell us how to bring up our children. We put our children into their institutions such as schools, so they can be educated in a curriculum based system whose aim is to produce, compliant non-questioning individuals. They remain there for the majority of their most influential eighteen or so years of life. If we want to know more we just need to do a little research and it'll reveal itself; when I say research I'm talking about closing our eyes and just thinking about it ... no book is needed (the best things in life are still free) and you already *know* all you need to know.

Are we, considering the above, fit to bring up our own children? Do we not just pass on to them what was passed on to us by those with no more comprehension or proof about our world than we have? This situation is self-perpetuating and not only do we pass on our experiences to our children but new ones are passed on to them from authority figures and family members who haven't managed to improve their own lives. If I'm given any advice, one of the first things I do is look at and listen to the person talking and ask myself if they live by their own convictions. To me this is the only *qualification* we need to give advice to anyone else.

One consequence of this society is a decline in the health of an already 'sick' and corrupt system. Another consequence is that children grow up insecure and never quite *fit in* because they've not been given a stable foundation to stand on. This has resulted in an unhappy world where most people hold grievances, loathe themselves, live in fear and spend their lives in front of the television. We don't care much for anything that sounds like self-development. We generally prefer not to make efforts when it's perfectly acceptable to push the button on the remote control and change channel. This is not too different to turning over in bed, pushing the snooze button on our alarm clocks and going back to sleep. We look to others for images of what we *ought* to be like, usually on the television, because we're unhappy with ourselves. Next time you go to a supermarket slow down a little, take a look around and try to find a happy face in the crowd.

Think for a moment about 'self-help' books. We need help when we're in trouble, right? Well, I invite you to take a look at how much self-help is available; we're in *big* trouble. I searched for 'self-help' on google.co.uk and got 1,600,000,000 results and I got these results in 0.28 seconds[4]; what exactly is the world concentrating on? How many different ways can there *be* to help ourselves and if they're any good why aren't we seeing the benefits? Another search revealed the first self-help book was purportedly written in 1859 by a man named Samuel Smiles and it was called *Self-help*, but the concept goes back a great deal further. In *The Great Learning*, written around 500 BC, Confucius said "The ancients who wished to illustrate illustrious virtue throughout the kingdom, first ordered well their own states. Wishing to order well their states, they first regulated their families. Wishing to regulate their families, they first cultivated their persons. Wishing to cultivate their persons, they first rectified their hearts. Wishing to rectify their hearts, they first sought to be sincere in their thoughts. Wishing to be sincere in their thoughts, they first extended to the utmost their knowledge. Such extension of knowledge lay in the investigation of things."[5] That sounds like self-help to me.

Why do we still need it? Why do we need it at all? If society's healthy then surely we would all support and discuss things with each other? Why has Humanity not advanced psychologically? Technology, commercialism, social media and the like have advanced. Why has Humanity been left behind? The main reason is because we're not willing to tackle this question or even accept the question exists. We just roll along with it all and occasionally complain. What does it mean to complain? We see the advancement of technology as our own advancement. Among other unhealthy past times, we eat junk and spend too much time in front of the television or inside virtual reality games. With such a huge demand for self-help, it's obvious there's a need in society we're not fulfilling. Why aren't we paying attention to this need? Could it be that the morale of Humanity is too low to care?

Humanity follows influential figures like sheep, whether it be through soap operas, so-called Hollywood celebrities, promising politicians, sporting stars, pop stars or anyone else who can apparently not only survive but are able to thrive in this 'system'. The chances are they're not any happier than you or me and the stories we find in the media 'confirm' this. We follow the lives of these people and mimic their behaviour by following their fashions and we follow them on social media websites. We wait for celebrities to announce the names they've chosen for their new babies and often, if the timing is correct, give our children their names; why is it important to us?

Think about following *trends* for just a moment. We buy goods like 'lift and separate' bras, tight fitting trousers to show off our bodies and we even cut our hair according to latest fashions. We're given a string of orders which we follow such as; hems up, hems down, g-strings, baggy trousers, chains, piercings, tattoos, torn trousers, falling down trousers, flares, hoods, bras on, bras off, red dress, black dress and it goes round and round ... but the pattern never changes. We always do as we're 'told' and wear whatever uniforms are handed out, often looking down on those who are *so* 'last year'. Corporations name the game and we rush in obediently like a tsunami buying up their stock because we, or our children, *must* have the latest craze.

There isn't a person alive who can state categorically that they haven't asked themselves 'What is this life all about?' or 'Who am I?' at some point in their lives. Everyone, without exception, has suffered in some way in this 'world' and continues to do so, regardless of whether they admit to it or not. Humanity and the environment are 'sick' and we're not nursing or even paying attention to it. There are some of us who attempt to bring these questions to the surface, but as we try to encourage others to take a look at the situation we're shut off and labelled as 'insane' or 'deluded' and so it goes - this pattern has been repeated throughout history. Why are these issues not discussed in the media? When my mother was diagnosed with cancer, my brother decided to give 'McMillan Nurses' a try for some support. He told me his first thought was whether he could stand the company of those 'do-gooders' and that made me think. What does that make those who make such claims? Do-badders? I asked him this and he saw my point. The nurses helped my brother a great deal and were wonderful all round and I recommend them to anyone seeking support.

~~~

I don't, as such, believe in the past or future but I write it that way for clarity. This is a good place to state that I *believe* in no-thing at all; not that the world is a sphere, flat or even a planet; belief is not the same as *truth*. I want to make this quite clear before going on. For me, based on current knowledge, I'm lost in some sort of space and am on my way 'home' - I'm obliged to use familiar terminology in order to make myself understood. I do *know* we're all connected and that everything each one of us does affects Humanity as a whole.

This I can say is a truth.

As I walk around a supermarket a few things catch my attention and I stop and ponder these thoughts:-

- The many types of perfect toothpaste - why do we still need dentists?
- Why is there such a thing as 'luxury toilet paper'?
- Why, when technology has advanced so much, have I been using the same brand of hair removing cream for forty years (though the name has changed)? Even the smell is the same.
- Why is there a sell-by-date on bottled water? It's been around since the world began! Why is it bottled at all?
- When will televisions be big enough and flat enough?
- I'm standing here holding on to my trolley and … I've seen all this many times before. Where am I? How did I get here? What am I doing here?

Most people search books like these for answers but they'll never find them amongst the pages. There are no short-cuts and no-one can tell us what we must 'realise' for ourselves. Books can guide us but we must ask our own questions. If we don't follow through by giving the issues arising from our enquiries our total and personal attention, actually thinking things out, then we're going to go round and round like a hamster on his wheel and it'll never stop turning, no matter how many books we read. Our search must be genuine; if it isn't we're lying to ourselves. The only important question is 'Who am I?' If we look for answers in books to questions we can't be bothered to ask ourselves then like the hamster, we won't get far.

I'd like to explore some of these issues further with you and I ask you to keep an open mind about everything, as I will. As I write this book thoughts stream in and out of my mind solidifying my beliefs about something or another; or knock them on the head, so to speak. I may change my views as we progress - this happens when we question everything and nothing makes sense any more. What's important for me is in recognising the title of this chapter, *Something's Not Quite Right with the World* and my next one *Open-mindedness*.

Open-mindedness

An open-mind can have no fence around it.

Being open-minded isn't about appreciating other people's rights to do what they want, or accepting their sexual preferences. It's not about accepting that comedians often tell hurtful, biased and demeaning jokes about others. It isn't about accepting everyone as a friend regardless of their political persuasion and it isn't about remaining comfortable in familiar territory. So what do I mean by keeping an open mind? What is an open mind? It questions everything no matter how silly it may or may not seem; it questions the answers too. For example, the question 'Who are you?' Most people will give you their name when you ask this question or tell you what their profession is, like; a secretary, a lawyer or a writer. But is it who they really are? Are you 'Jenny Jones' and if so, who were you before your parents named you? I took ten days to officially name one of my children - who was she during those ten days?

It's just a name. It's an identity we invent to function in this reality. For example, we need a name when we go to school, get a job or to open up a bank account, but it's *not* us. If we're adamant about being Jenny Jones then we're not open-minded at all. If we give it some thought and imagine a time when we didn't exist we'll find it extremely difficult; even impossible. Close your eyes and imagine yourself 'dead' or 'not existing'. Can you do it? I haven't succeeded. We'll always exist in some form or another, physical or otherwise. Therefore we can't categorically state we're Jenny Jones. Try to prove it? You can come up with paper proof but what proof is that? If we question the answers every time they present themselves then eventually, we run out of questions and we run out of beliefs.

The only 'proof' of our existence, other than on paper, lies in this so-called five-sense-reality. As Morpheus says in the first of *The Matrix* trilogy movies "What is real? How do you define real? If you're talking about what you can feel, what you can smell, what you can taste and see, then real is simply electrical signals interpreted by your brain."[6] All of these senses can be and often are deceived whether it's through our eyes by optical illusions or our ears when we may hear a voice behind us calling out our name. How about an amputee who can still feel pain from a missing limb? I can sometimes smell things from my past, like liquorice, and there's none in sight. The smell must come from part of memory or I wouldn't be able to recognise it. I can also taste it when I think about it. There's plenty of research on this subject and a lot of interesting examples on the internet. We've more than five senses; intuition and a sense of danger are just two of them.

It's not my intention to use this book to continuously quote others but it *will* happen as intertextuality is unavoidable. One consequence of this is that proof of anything at all is near impossible to find because peoples' books and ideas are always copying, referring to, quoting, arguing with or analysing each other. Literary criticism prevents clarity and can't know an author's original meaning; we can't see through the eyes of another. People rarely agree and frequently argue with each other. Perhaps it's always been this way? We can't agree with *ourselves* so how can we agree with others? Have you ever spent ages deciding what to wear to a party? Confusion comes from conflicting ideas and those ideas come from excessive criticism of something *original*, thus dividing it. Before you know it, no-one knows the origin or truth of anything; or if you prefer, where to find the 'needle in the haystack'. Literary criticism is not open-mindedness; it's the creation of confusion. It fragments author intention and those fragments tend to remain apart.

It's not the purpose of this book to convince you of anything and I shan't even try to as I know it isn't possible. This book serves two purposes; it clarifies my own thoughts and maybe it'll raise a little doubt and curiosity in someone else's mind about the world they live in. Intertextuality is not only unavoidable from book to book - it's entirely unavoidable. Everything we know (or think we know) has been told to us from Day One of our lives by our parents or some other authority such as; a person, a film, a book, a song or a memory of some other kind. Therefore, we can't avoid referring to something from the past and we can't state anything that's not from memory whether the memory is from a few seconds ago or from an experience many years earlier. Any thoughts we have are plucked out from our memories. Would we know what tastes sweet if the word hadn't been introduced to us? How would we see the colour red if it hadn't been repeatedly pointed out? Are we doing anything other than parroting when we speak to one another? Do we not take on traits from our parents, celebrities and authority figures? Why do we mimic others, albeit unintentionally?

If we put together the paper proof I mentioned earlier with the information about our senses then we're memory on paper, which for all intents and purposes is a book and as paper is not part of 'us' then we can't be anything but memory. In other words we're a story and it's the story of our lives. It's the story of our egos, surreptitious and *invisible* to most people. This thought is worth giving our attention to and we should think about it with an open mind starting from scratch? That we're memory is *obvious* to me now but when I first thought about it I couldn't accept it; it was *far* from obvious. It does become this way and if you give it enough time you'll see it too. We've been recording data since the day we were 'born'. Everything must have a beginning whether it be; a tape recording, a television programme, the first brick laid to build a home, or even the alphabet. From these beginnings evolve a symphony, a film, a house and a book.

Open-mindedness could mean believing in *nothing;* to believe in something, whatever it is, must by definition, be fixed. Unless we can see options or choices we're not open-minded. Is '1 + 1 = 2' fixed? Is it really? Are two apples the same as two pears? Is it the same two? If we ask many questions and don't accept standard responses, we then begin to see and feel all possibilities. It shouldn't matter how foolish the question may seem. Question whether you existed yesterday or that you'll exist tomorrow and, if you're serious about the question, interesting thoughts arise. The important thing is to question *every* single thing with the incredible abilities we've been given to do it with. For example, what is a dog? A name we've given it, or to be exact a noun, which are names we've given to 'things' but is it what they *are*? The world can be dismantled by removing the words that created it. We've come to treat these words as though they were solid but nothing new is created when we create a new word for it. If we rely on adjectives to describe our world then we're missing a sensual beauty that words can never describe. If we question absolutely everything, without a dictionary, we'll see more marvellous things about the world than we've ever seen before.

Consider the age old question 'Which came first; the chicken or the egg?' How close have you ever been to solving this question? Is the question or the answer important? Consider this also. When we were born we knew nothing at all … then we opened our eyes and began to learn about everything around us. Information streamed in at such a phenomenal rate that we couldn't, knowingly, comprehend it. It was the beginning of our memory of this life. When I ask myself a question, I question the answer I get; no matter how foolish it may seem. Let's look at the first part of that sentence and think about the words, 'When *I* ask *myself* a question'. What's going on here? Who's the 'I' and who is the 'myself'? When we begin to question our beliefs the mind puts up arguments because it's not used to it. The habits of the mind are so ingrained that it'll take some time to break them and to take back the power we gave it; just how long it'll take, is up to us. But if we persevere, we regain our control and then find ourselves behind the steering wheel instead of in the passenger seat. As we begin to see the world in a different way through constant questioning our consciousness level increases, as does our intelligence. It's a 'process of unlearning'. When we ask ourselves a question, where do the answers come from? I remember my father used to say to me "I've taught you all I know and now you know nothing". I never got the chance to find out if he understood what it meant but I suspect he'd no idea.

To erase our beliefs is not a fast process; a great deal of personal effort and total dedication to the enquiry is needed. It's a bit like floating in outer space in as much as there's nowhere to go and no ground to stand on. The process removes everything familiar, comfortable and secure that we've kept close to all our lives. It's a process achieved by constant questioning of *everything* we've ever been told by our five senses from the moment we were born. We can't consciously remember that far back, but the foundations are still laid. It takes a lot of searching, for every skeleton in every little closet no matter how well we've hidden them. Then we must face them courageously, until we can see they don't really exist. For example, I can think about my childhood and recognise it as an experience and then I recognise the experience was an illusion. It can't be located anywhere, therefore it can't exist other than in my memory.

The experiences we have in the world have nothing to do with who we are. In my childhood I'd fret about why my father didn't care for me and I used to believe I was lacking in some way. It could make me feel quite bitter towards him if I ran it through my mind enough, as I often did. By learning to watch these thoughts, they disappear as though they'd never existed. Thoughts come and go so fast that we can't follow them. If we hold on to them they can haunt us and if we let go, we set ourselves free. If we fret over something long enough, even if it isn't true, we make it true and set it in stone. I used to have many thoughts troubling me during the nights and they often led to the nightmares I suffered with for so many years. The more I learnt to watch these thoughts, the more they dissolved and didn't trouble me any more. Now, the nightmares have ceased.

The mind argues with us and it's a formidable foe with a firm grip on our 'reality', to say the least. It'll tell us everything is real and important and that we should be angry and do something about some issue or another. If we comply, it then contradicts itself and tells us we shouldn't have done it. Society encourages and reinforces this behaviour and it's not an easy wall to penetrate. It'll tell us life's not fair and that 'so and so' should be punished for what he or she once did to us. It'll come up with anything to stop us being at peace. The mind doesn't let go easily and it's negative; it's up to us to change ourselves by recognising how our minds work and changing the way we think. Changing the way we think can be likened to changing our shoes. We have to take the old pair off before we can try on the new. We can't stretch new ones over the old pair. The dilemma here is that one part of us wants to try the new shoes on, but the other half refuses to take the *tried and trusted* pair off. Perhaps it would be more fun to walk through the middle of the argument, barefoot.

How come we've two voices and why are they at odds with each other? We can't defeat the mind and by trying to we only succeed in strengthening it. We can't lose the mind and we can't destroy it. We can become aware of how it works and begin to know ourselves better. We can take control of ourselves by getting rid of all the nonsense; we've never stopped dumping our rubbish and we love to rummage around, just in case we need the contents one day. As you read this book your mind may be telling you that it's all rubbish! My mind told me that when I thought about writing it. The mind always tells us things like that and it can be likened to us playing 'piggy in the middle' with our two voices. If the 'piggy' sits down or walks away and stops running after the two voices they tend to get bored. This results in the silence so many of us are afraid of. Being aware of how our mind works is an ongoing process and mine often wanders elsewhere with its favourite distractions, but I tune it in again and it wanders less and less. If we get rid of the doubter, and we can, we'll feel much happier. The mind is the biggest doubter we'll ever encounter and it's keen to discourage us.

I've said this journey or path is a tough one and takes a great deal of effort but results come straight away if we're willing to completely let go of all our ingrained beliefs, right here and now. For most people, including me, the process is a gradual one. It's far easier to reject these thoughts than to believe them or even to think about them. It's easier because staying with what's familiar to us doesn't rock our worlds and tip us overboard where we'll struggle and get bumped around a bit at first, but we'll survive and be stronger for the experience. We tend to stick our heads a little out of our shells, see something new and think 'EEK' and scurry back to the safety of our familiar comfort zones. To jump into the Sea of Possibility involves a whole lot of responsibility and for a change; it's to 'us'. We often get more involved with other people's problems than we do with our own because we can see how to help them - this is a tactical move by the mind and often the advice we give to others, applies to us too. We all have a responsibility to discover our true nature.

We're born and shown the basics of survival in this world by our parents, we're educated, work hard to strict regimes in order to pay the bills and then, often earlier than the retirement we've been heading towards all our lives - we go to our graves. I accept there are variations to this but are they real or important? The only choices we have are limited to things like 'which toothpaste to buy' or 'what flavour of ice cream' - this is an illusion of choice, already made for us, and we can't see it. It's a bit like saying we can have a black, yellow or red car; but not telling us it could be green. There are many ways in which we're distracted from asking serious questions about our lives. We tend to think of these as a way to make life more bearable and we make the most of them while we're here. But what if there's something we're missing along the way; something important. There's something far more wonderful that most of the world's population is blind to and distracted from by a variety of entertainments.

Most entertainment is provided by the media and breweries for the purpose of appeasement. This has become known as 'bread and games', a term alluding to one first coined by the Roman poet, Juvenal (1st and early 2nd century AD) - "The people are only anxious for two things: bread and circuses."[7]. In other words, we're kept occupied and tranquil with trivia and worthless things while the governments and elite do what they want without any threat from the 'proletariat'. By worthless, I mean the pleasures we get from them are immediate and serve no long term lasting good purpose that can improve the morale of society.

Television and magazines entertain us with; recipe programmes, soap operas, home improvement shows, game shows, bad news, gardening, celebrity news, trivia, reality shows, sports and most importantly ... *advertising*! We want bigger televisions screens to watch them on and more 'friends' on facebook and we want to spend our lives twittering celebrities and each other. We want iLives and the big companies know this and give it to us at great cost to ourselves and our children; not just in monetary terms. We may not agree we want these things, but then we'd have to accept we tolerate them. How does this work? Think about how we *share and declare* our lives and the lives of our friends and family on social media? Is this not like an open and online private and business diary? Everything we do we plaster all over social media including photographs, family disputes, births, deaths and marriages. Life is digital and life is information.

When I registered on a professional social media website it wouldn't accept my own email address, but it did accept one of the big cloud group email addresses which I shan't name; it insisted in copying all my personal contacts and there was no opt out choice. I've noticed this happening on more and more social media websites and as long as we're willing to share information with them, they'll be willing to collect it. Have you ever wondered why they ask for this information about us? Why are these social media sites being pushed hard on to us and our own websites? I'm not against these sites, as such, as they're a nice way to share creative ideas and get to know other people around the world. However, they're often used to hang out our 'dirty laundry' and for family or business disputes. This can create an unhealthy environment on what has become the *Cloud* of Humanity; I'll talk more about this later. There's a tremendous amount of personal information out there. Do we still have any privacy? Do we care?

I once asked a lady if she ever just sat down to think about life. I asked her because she watched a great deal of television and it blared in the background - all day long. Her reply was "Oh no ... I don't like to think about things like that!" Well that's why the world's the way it is because everyone's thinking in automaton mode as dictated by the media, in its many forms. Everything is provided on tap and there's no need to go to the trouble of thinking. The lady mentioned above does not sleep well at night and suffers with chest pains ... the kind we have when we live in fear. I can relate to these pains because I did the same for many years and I used to call them the 'dreads' and I've to be honest here; I've no idea what I dreaded. I suggested she leave the television off ... she wouldn't hear of it.

I once visited a friend in Australia who'd four televisions in her house; they were all on all day long, because she didn't want to miss anything when she went from room to room. Her conversations were mostly limited to information about celebrities, the news, politics, the weather, game shows and soap operas. It was as though she wanted to be the first to know the latest news. She also spent a great deal of time online looking for her perfect partner. She was hypnotised by the media and believed it kept her informed. No matter what this lady did, in the background she absorbed more information than she would believe possible and she'd blurt it out at everyone she spoke to. This lady was never calm and suffered with low self-esteem and severe backaches. I never went again.

Life can be likened to a traffic jam. People are kept in jams in order to prevent them from having any 'free' or 'spare' time. By using these terms we kid ourselves we're *partially* free? Are we ever free? I know many people who, when I call them and ask 'how they're doing' their first response is, "I've been so busy. I've not had a minute to myself" and they never stop being busy or having to go somewhere in a hurry, every day of the week. We check the internet for traffic problems that may prevent us getting somewhere on time and we search for alternative routes so we're not late; but there are always traffic problems and it's just a question of the degree. The rush hour is no longer limited to just work days; roads are congested at the weekends too as we rush to shops and DIY stores that stay open every day of the week to cope with consumer demand. Whereas we could once estimate arrival times if we were visiting friends or family on Sundays, we now arrive irritated and bothered from the journey. Why haven't these traffic problems been solved? It's easy to solve them by providing a decent free efficiently run public transport system, for *our* benefit not the benefit of corporations or governments. We need the free time to enjoy it, not just to perform a function that supports our work and shopping schedules. The world's problems are easy to solve if Humanity cares to solve them. Humanity created these problems. Humanity perpetuates them.

Individuals blame governments but it's not their fault. It's our fault because we allow it to go on. For example, despite being told about the dangers of certain household products we continue to buy them and flush them down our drains. Where do we think they go? We're not forced to buy them. We do these things because it suits us to have sparkling bathrooms, glistening kitchens, 'whiter than white' clothes and germ free toilets. We give no thought to the consequences; then we blame someone else when we're told the oceans are polluted. Governments are made up of human beings, just like us, and they have the same weaknesses we do; they can't improve our lives for us. We're all the government; we're One. All the complaints we put in are about things we've created and then tolerate. Did you know that 'complaint' is an anagram of ''compliant'?

People can't choose what they want to do with their lives without first considering how they're going to pay their bills. We're taught the value of money at an early age when we're given pocket money. We can't buy anything without it and learn fast what we can and can't afford. Money becomes increasingly important when we start working and doesn't stop being that way until we die. It's difficult for most people to live without debt and our children, if they don't have wealthy and supporting families, are forced into it if they go into further education; often before they find their first job. Their lives are 'pay as you live' and their children's lives will be the same but more extreme with larger debts. We're charged for water, which is the most abundant substance in the world - this is madness. Money is an abstract concept but it's the energy that drives the world we live in.

We look to money to solve the problems it has created and this is why it won't change unless we do. It doesn't matter if we drop £1 into a charity box or £10,000, it won't make a difference to anything except the way *we* feel and we *feel* much better for having done it. Money won't solve any of the world's problems. As Albert Einstein said "We can't solve problems by using the same kind of thinking we used when we created them."[8] Until we change this 'kind of thinking' the only thing that'll change is that life will become more and more expensive; success is already measured by, among other things, wealth. In order to begin changing our lives we must first see it for what it is and recognise the futility of it.

Recognising this hits you straight in the face and when it happened to me I collapsed; luckily I'd a friend close by who took me up to my bedroom to rest. I'd recently been through my fourth 'official' marriage breakup after my twelve-year-old stepson tried to stab me with a knife and my alcoholic husband thought it nothing but a childish prank, which it most definitely wasn't. Life had become pointless for me. It was about 4.30pm and my head felt so heavy I couldn't lift it off the pillow. Everything I'd ever thought was real could not be seen, heard, felt, tasted or smelled and I felt disorientated. I couldn't use the word God any more and I didn't know who to direct my prayers to, if anyone. I'd no idea who I was. I'd been *dumped* and I was alone in the world without direction, faith or hope. I fell into a deep sleep until the next morning. The following day I felt as though I was walking on the earth again for the first time. I'd no choice but to be open-minded after this incident; I'd now have to find my own truth.

As I became more aware of being part of a greater whole and that Humanity is focused on transient unimportant and destructive things; I saw life as 'pointless'. Sometimes I'd arrive at a supermarket, stand in the car park with my trolley in hand waiting to go in and my feet would become heavy and fixed to the ground. I'd feel overwhelmingly that I was stuck in a loop. It all felt unnecessary and it was all happening in a repetitive cycle. The same feeling would come when I filled my car up with fuel, cooked dinner or even went to bed at night. All I could think of was 'I don't want to be here' anymore. It wasn't a depressing suicidal feeling, but more of a scream to "get me out of here" and I went out into my garden one day and yelled it at the Universe. Though this felt frustrating, it was also uplifting because I felt free from my chains and free from fear. However, I didn't know what I was supposed to do with my life now. Something happened to me but my ego told me it was all pointless and because I gave it this label, that's what it became.

I felt there was nothing between me and death, like being in a waiting room with nothing to do and nothing to read and it was boring. I didn't want to be here feeling pointless for the rest of my life. I now see this as having been a shift in awareness - a point where I let go of control and trusted that life would now bring all I needed - I was tiny in the universe; a humbling experience. It was a point where I no longer felt afraid or concerned about death and felt a strong need to find something purposeful to do with my life.

If we stand back and take another look at the world. If we remove ourselves from it and just become aware of it as a 'whole', then it looks very different. We can see how we rush to the sales to buy things we don't need, we can see why society is sick and when we listen to the *news* we see it in a whole new light. If we watch documentaries about past wars, if we ignore the homeless, if we continue to want more 'things', if we continue to amuse ourselves with trivia and trinkets, if we prefer to feed electronic pets than the starving in third world countries, ignore warnings printed in books like these, put sparkle into household appliances and fittings rather than ourselves, if we pretend the things I've mentioned aren't true, then we're not at all open-minded and we might as well walk around with paper bags over our heads.

Interaction

There's no such thing as good luck ... only a good attitude.

E very day we come into contact with other people in one way or another. Usually, we don't give them a second glance. When we do it's often in passing judgement relating to their social status, physical appearance, dress code or some other critical observation. Sometimes these observations are kind; sometimes not. Why do human beings have difficulty interacting with each other; particularly with strangers?

What does it mean to be human anyway? There's an air of decency implied in the expression 'human being'; it doesn't quite fit with the way we behave. When I think about Humanity on the *whole*, the arising thoughts are disturbing. We come together in times of need such as when there's an earthquake or a big charity event to 'save the world'. I can't think of much more that doesn't require a crisis to spur us into 'action'. There's a regrettable need for this in society and if we want to rid ourselves of it, we need a sea change on the inside of each and every one of us. Charity is born from suffering: why do we allow it in our world? These actions place plasters that don't stick, on wounds that don't heal. However, they do show we're capable of incredible humanitarian feats when we *connect* for the common good. In general we're; vain, violent, aggressive, ignorant, greedy, jealous, self-centred and a whole lot more and few of us ever recognise or admit to these traits in ourselves. Our personal problems are bigger than anyone else's and they occupy us all the time. Human beings are pretty strange.

Ever since I can remember, I've been watching people interact with each other. When we moved to our current home, we met a couple who live in the next closest house on the same road, about half a mile away. The husband had warm eyes and a friendly disposition, but his wife was hard and unmoving and I knew we wouldn't become friends from the way she scanned us; well maybe it would take a few years. Sometimes when I've passed their home and they were in their garden, I said "Hi" and invited them for a coffee. I always got a sharp and abrupt "we haven't got the time" from the wife. I've noticed her several times rushing into her house as I approached their home on my way back from shopping, so she wouldn't have to say hello. That's such a pity. Why are we unfriendly towards each other? It's a wonderful thing to meet new people. Why don't we take the time and trouble to get to know them? Can we do this?

When we look at another person we're seeing a part of ourselves. So if we take a dislike to a person we need to look at ourselves to find out why. It's always because it reflects a part of us we don't like. The lady up the road keeps busy with her duties and family and she doesn't wander far afield. When we first moved in, I told her we live solitary lives and that we're spiritual people; her expression became one of disapproval. This feeling didn't come from us; rather it came from inside her, from a fear of hers she wasn't ready to face. Whatever this fear was, it's deeply hidden and I doubt if she realises it or has ever questioned her likes and dislikes. We tend to accept our predicaments and limitations and rarely challenge them preferring to live within their protective shield.

We can make changes to the world and even if they're small ones, they make a big difference. Why not try smiling at the cashier next time you go to the supermarket and see what response you get? Sometimes I get a grimace in return and the same from a passer-by in the street, but I persevere regardless. The message I get is "Can't you see I'm miserable and don't want to be cheered up". However, several members of staff now smile back at me and that's got to be worth something - perseverance pays off.

We hear stories all the time about people living and dying alone and the chances are there's someone who's lonely living close by to all of us. We don't want to know. We may see someone walking past our window or pass them in the street on a regular basis. We may know them by sight as 'the old biddy', and 'the grumbly old man' but we've probably never spoken to or considered visiting them even for a few minutes just to see if they need anything. Why aren't we more proactive in reaching out to people? Have we become too suspicious of each other? Is it an innate fear of rejection or do we fear being accused of having ignoble motives? Whatever our reasons, we leave their care to the authorities; though we know it's often not adequately provided. However, because it *is* provided, we tend to choose this as a preferred option for caring for others. Because we all have to work hard and we occupy ourselves with trivia, we don't have the time or inclination to care for people in need. The saddest part of this is that there exists a profession called 'Carer'; how did caring become a profession? Childminders and carers have to be approved, trained and scrutinised and then police checks are made on them; what is this world we live in and why is it so hostile?

We interact less and less with each other while we live out our roles and we've become increasingly divided. Because we've our comforts and we find security in them, we don't mind what goes on outside - I'll talk more about comfort and security in a later chapter. Think about how we behave toward each other on a train or bus in the rush hour; physically we couldn't be closer, mentally, we couldn't be further apart. A person sitting down can avoid the glance of a needy person standing up because they don't want to give up their seat for them; Humanity can be very selfish. We read newspapers, books, do crossword puzzles, play number games, talk on our mobile phones and listen to music, but we'll not speak to another person. It reminds me of children who don't want to listen to something so they stick their fingers in their ears, screw up their eyes and pretend the outside world doesn't exist.

We don't speak to people we don't know. One of the reasons for this is that we've been taught from childhood 'not to talk to strangers', to report incidents and not get involved in certain situations. We've been divided into social groups (among others). A businessman will look at a young lad with a hooded top and because of the media, judge him as some sort of troublemaker; he'll have a low opinion of him and be 'on guard'. The youth sees the businessman as unapproachable and someone who'd look down on him; they're intimidated by each other. The two have pre-conditioned opinions; though they've never met. We also have these conditioned opinions for the homeless, the rich, the poor, the scruffy, a person who drives a rusty banger or a shiny new car - these opinions may be far from the truth. The divisions are ingrained from a young age and children learn about social interaction from films, schools, clubs and their parents. Everyone is in defensive mode; we fear judgement, reaction and rejection.

We think we're better than each other, but on the other hand, we also think we're not good enough. We can't see that the society we've created made us this way. We're selfish and do everything for our own gain, even if it doesn't seem that way. For example we may give someone a gift but we want them to be forever grateful for it, or we think our act of generosity was a 'good deed' but tell other people about it; we don't give from our hearts. We need and search for gratification and confirmation of our own existence. We're Humanity; Humanity is One and it doesn't like itself too much.

I've heard stories about people who are regulars at the doctor's surgery who can't be placated until some sort of diagnosis is given. Do we go to the doctor's looking for a proxy parent to make up for what we believe we lack in our lives? Some of us look for this comfort from alcohol and drugs; I've heard people bragging about how sick they were after being out on a binge with friends *and* the size of their hangover the next day; as though it gave them increased 'street cred'. Why do we do these things to ourselves? Among other reasons, it gives us a false sense of security and self-control - we've done it by our own choices. I remember a girl at school who'd broken her leg - everyone signed the cast so she could keep it as a souvenir. Why would anyone want to keep such a thing? A couple of days ago when I chatted to a friend and told her I'd cut my finger badly she interrupted to tell me about an injury she'd had recently - and one of her boyfriend's too. Our minds aren't too healthy and we too often see our injuries and scars as trophies to be proud of and compared. There are people who can't cope with interaction with the outside world anymore and they withdraw from society. My mother was one of those.

My mother's life became centred on television listings. She never left the house for many years, except for Christmas Day. Human interaction with 'real' people in the outside world came to be replaced with the thoughts and activities of a world created by the media. My mother slept between her favourite programmes and mourned serials that came to an end - not knowing what to fill the free 'slot' with. At her happiest after being diagnosed with cancer; she'd jumped into her own hospital drama; playing the starring role. She never complained about her illness, not even when she was dying. In some odd way she'd been well prepared for her crisis by watching a variety of hospital dramas.

We struggle to solve problems between ourselves and don't often succeed. This is because we need to deal with the causes rather than the symptoms. For example, a married couple can't solve their problems just by talking about them. The problems will never be solved unless the root causes are identified and both parties are willing to find a solution. It's a bit like mopping the floor from an overflowing sink without turning off the tap; the solution is always simple. Problems often persist because the couple want them to; the talks are all part of perpetuating a situation that deep down they don't want to resolve. No-one wants it to be solved; it's the game play. The key to solving our problems is first to 'want to' and then we can identify the reasons for them; this takes thought and a great deal of naked honesty between the parties involved.

We can begin to interact with each other far better when we accept we're pretty lousy at it. Do you find you're often waiting for another person to stop speaking so you can cut in to say what *you* want? Do you listen to what others are saying at all? When we meet up with someone we know we ask 'How are you?' but do we ever listen when they deviate from the expected "I'm fine, thank you" with something more honest like "well, now that you ask, I haven't been too well". Do we really care when we ask the question at all, or is it just an accepted form of greeting? If we're honest we know that what we have to say is more important than what someone else is saying; we *prepared* it while they were talking to us.

Our conversations have been prescribed for us and we rarely talk about anything original or different. We've lost the art of communicating for ourselves. We've lost the art of thinking. We've no spontaneity, no creativity, no imagination and we don't care much for anything except our own stories, ambitions and dramas. We're terrible listeners; have you ever noticed how much we interrupt when we talk to each other?

Have you ever been to one of those parties where people stand around in groups? More often than not they remain in the same group they arrived in for the entire party; no-one's interested in mingling. If we go out in groups and see someone sitting all alone, does it occur to us to talk to them or invite them to join us? Do we offer them a smile? We tend to walk past and not notice them, or think they're weird in some way and that they're on their own for a good reason. Why are we afraid to talk to them? Is it because we don't want to listen to their sob story - perhaps because we're in the middle of our own? We've disconnected ourselves from each other, especially the needy. As a result of this separation we're now connected to a media 'matrix' that decides how we interact, what we want, where we put our personal information and on which latest apparatus.

~~~

We interact through language and language has changed a great deal over the years; we've 'apparently' gone from drawing on the walls of caves to reading complex programming languages like DNA. We now text each other in 'TextSpeak'; it's become the 'shorthand' of the Cloud. One day we won't recognise the symbols written in this book and children already struggle with language from Shakespearean times. We translate ancient texts, such as hieroglyphics; we can't be sure true meaning isn't lost, like in the game Chinese Whispers.

Some children like to bury time-capsules and schools assist them with these projects. They prepare all sorts of things to put inside them wondering if some future generation will learn about our times. What are these time capsules and why do we bury them? My personal feeling on this is that whoever, if anyone at all, digs up these treasures in the 'future', they won't comprehend our languages - we've over 6000 of them.[9] The things they find will be unidentifiable and end up being put in a museum, just like we do with the relics we dig up from ancient sites now. Future relics will be as big a mystery to the next generations as past ones are to us today. Humanity will not make sense of us or our languages. Because our technology is advancing at a phenomenal rate, a lack of discernment is already evident between *living* generations; our children and grandchildren would never have used three and a half inch and five and a quarter inch floppy disks to store information on and they're unlikely to recognise one if they saw it now; they wouldn't be able to read the information on them either.

Over time, the way we interact with each other has changed. Once we were 'out and about' communicating face-to-face with real people or writing letters with a pen. Nowadays we rely on computers and social media sites for these activities and the art of conversation is rapidly losing ground. Whereas we would once sit in our lounges at home and socially interact with family and friends; we now use technology to converse. We can be sitting in the same room with friends or next to each other in the pub and often have a separate private conversation with just one of them via texts - it's a new type of whispering. This is how we connect and interact with each other; how we arrange meetings, organise sporting events or parties. We now send a text message to see if someone's home - when they live next door - before we pop round for a coffee or text from our cars to announce our arrival. The doorbell and calling through the letterbox are becoming obsolete.

We're losing our social skills and life is lived through the screen. Nowadays we don't even need a computer as televisions have become 'smart' and web enabled; mobile phones too have become evermore sophisticated. They've become 'smarter' than we are. If we believe in destiny, then we don't have a choice and all this is 'meant to be'. It's reaching a point where we won't need to go out at all because food and just about any item we can think of can be delivered to our homes - we can and increasingly do, work online. Couples argue and dump each other by text and bosses have fired their staff the same way. We 'check in' to the *cloud* in the mornings and 'check out' at night, often while in bed. We catch up with and discuss news stories and friend's updates on pods, pads, mobile phones, laptops and computers and these have become our priority. Some facebook pages are so frequently updated it can take hours to read through what's taken place while we were sleeping. I know of people who do this while they're at work. It's gossip and we're obsessed with it. It can't be denied that the world is interacting more and more through technology.

Communicating through electronic media can be problematic because there's no body-language involved and we need body-language just as much as we need speech. Instead of body-language we use the crude system of emoticons to try to display the emotions connected to the messages we send. They're not at all accurate and our mood or meaning can be, and often is, misconstrued. Often we don't send the emoticon that matches what we're feeling. For interaction purposes, the internet begs dishonesty and conversations without thought - it's impulsive. It allows us to develop another character and this character can't be a grounded one. We've the ability to proofread, alter and erase our messages which we can't do when communicating face-to-face. What long term effects could this produce in society? Electronic media tells us a great deal about each other and we upload all our thoughts on to it - it's our external hard drive. Mobile phones and now tablet devices have become a new type of body part; we don't leave home without them. They are, in effect, our electronic selves and we prefer them to our molecular ones. Our Mind is in the process of relocating from organic bodies into a cloud!

Everything is in the cloud now; the technological consciousness of us all. Technology is advancing into a superior being leaving Humanity far behind it. I've nothing at all against technology or even interacting through it, but when I see that we're becoming ever more separated from ourselves and evermore dependent on technology rather than our own faculties, I can't help but feel a little sad for future generations. Technology is not being used for the psychological advancement of Humanity - it's doing the opposite.

~~~

Adverts take up the space on most websites and we constantly have to avoid them. Many websites now have more adverts than they do the information we've searched for. As we surf they attempt to force us to listen to auto-play video adverts that boom into action as we hover over them. Increasingly we're being directed to websites that don't give us what we were searching for. Adverts jump, shake, spin and flash around the screen; they follow us as we scroll down the page pestering us, as though we've ignored them. It doesn't matter what websites we go on to. Today I looked up a word on an online dictionary and got 'all' of the above; they distract from our purpose. Have I mentioned distractions somewhere before? Does anyone give in to the temptation and click on them, other than by accident. Anyone living in this world, who can't see something's wrong with it, should look again at the stealth activities and juvenile trickery of advertising. What is advertising?

Adverts *are* interaction. Just about every advert is aimed at what you've shown an interest in or bought in the past. It's not too clever because we've often already bought or found what they're trying to sell. Advertising invades the threads on our forums. If you don't click on them and don't buy from them they have no choice but to disappear … our demands created them. The advertisers are us too and they interact with us by invading our spaces with their personal agendas. It's not just about buying their products; it's about clicking on their links as they're 'pay per click'.

The way society is at the moment we don't need to communicate at all and this is because it's all done for us. We're so involved, with television serials, the internet, the media, gossip, celebrities and the latest technology that we've no time left to recognise the magical world we live in. We copy behaviours, language, fashion, violence and attitude from the television and other media sources and if anyone steps out of line, we ostracise them. If a company wants information to go viral, it only needs to put it on a busy facebook account then just sit back and watch the fireworks. We complain about the bad news on the television and in the newspapers and we think our complaint is enough. We're happy to leave solving the world's problems to governments and because *they* never succeed with it, we don't believe we can either so we just sit back and say "That's life".

We're fragmented and we've become further fragmented by using the internet as the interface we communicate through. We try to put the pieces together but they never fit as they should, because we're not prepared to take responsibility or stand alone and turn away from our personal dramas. We try to squeeze ourselves into what makes us acceptable in the eyes of what we see as a 'normal' society. We've a great capacity to love each other and be creative, but we've also a great capacity to hate and destroy. Are we capable of living in a better world? Only if we want to. Are we destined to ride this rollercoaster? Only if we believe it!

In recognising how we interact with each other we're already beginning to change it. Once we can see, we begin to observe our own behaviour and it becomes difficult to behave in the same way again. It becomes difficult to pass by someone in need and ignore them and harder to judge others by their appearance. When we can shine on each other, life becomes worthwhile. We change what we see in our world when we change ourselves; we can never change anything else.

Does it Matter?

There's more in the mirror than we see at first glance - so it is with the world.

This book invites us to consider thinking about things from another perspective. If we do this with an open mind we've got nothing to lose and much to gain; there's no risk and nothing to fear. If there's something after this life that we're supposed to be striving for; then life matters; too few people care enough about this to give it any thought. Because we don't know what happens to us after we die, we don't want to put effort into something requiring us to look at things we buried long ago and would rather not exhume. We look *forward* to things like; holidays, becoming twenty-one, promotions, retirements or the next episode of a soap opera, yet on the other hand, we've adopted a 'live for today' attitude without a thought for the long term consequences.

After much reflection about the world we live in it's become clear to me that rather than live life, we tolerate it as dictated to. We believe ourselves to be individuals; nothing could be further from the truth. Just like a tree whose branches reach out in different directions, so it is for Humanity. The branches seem different at first glance but on closer examination it becomes clear they're part of the whole. They're like the veins carrying the blood of Humanity and for now, they're rather dry and brittle. If statistics can be believed, there are billions of us. Billions of branches who at our core seek; good health, peace, knowledge, prosperity and harmony, but on the outside we don't know where to find them because we're not looking in the right direction.

To strive for something after our lives is difficult because we can't see *beyond* the finite and solid wall called 'death'. Because of our financial culture we want rewards right now for our efforts; we don't like waiting for them. In other words, we want a guaranteed return before we're prepared to *consider* risking anything out of the ordinary. Would we give up our life for a beautifully wrapped package without knowing what was inside? We're happy to invest in life, but only if the benefits are good enough!

If we're serious in our search we find, without doubt, there are wonders waiting to be discovered; *no-one* can ever take them away from us or put a price on them. They can't be reclaimed by banks or governments; they're our inheritance and they're free; all we have to do is open our hearts to our untapped potential. We already have all we could hope for but it lies beneath the persona we're reluctant to shed. We're wrapped up tightly in our own cocoons and don't have the time, or inclination, to listen to anyone who has other opinions. Inside a cocoon is a butterfly, inside a gift box is a present and inside a seed is the code for creation - what's inside you?

If we can make sense of this we begin to see how separation is the cause of the world's conflicts. Whether you're a tramp living on a park bench or some high-ranking executive, we all have the same opportunities and abilities to find our way; no-one is excluded. There are many philosophical theories on the meaning of life but these are 'theories' and truth can't be a 'theory'. Enquiring within is the only way to be sure of our truth but if you keep looking outside, all you'll find is more confusion. There isn't a single one of us who's better than another regardless of their; age, race, religion, skin colour, cultural background or education. It's important to realise this in order to see how separated we've become from each other. We're Captains of our own ships and there's no co-pilot and no crew. We can remain in this ocean, or navigate our way out of it; which we decide to do is up to us. One way to begin this navigation is to look at some of the charts - the established theories. Some of these I've sketched below.

One philosophical theory about this life is that it doesn't matter what we do with it. The theory says Hitler was treated the same as Mahatma Gandhi when he died. It also says we can do whatever we want including blowing up the entire planet and wiping out its occupants; which is not very intelligent. What's the mindset of someone who'd want to do something like that anyway? Is this life a living film and after having played out our parts we walk off the stage; like children who play 'cowboys and Indians' or 'cops and robbers'? It's a popular theory and can be explored if you think it's plausible. Is it popular because we don't need to think about; what we do with our lives, how well we treat others or feel any remorse for things we may have done in the past? To make this plainer - does it suit us to believe it? Is it convenient? Is it fashionable? Does it let us off the hook? More importantly, is it true? It's a bit too easy to *escape* with this theory and it requires no work whatsoever on our part. For me, it can be likened to sweeping dirt under the carpet, which we tend to do anyway. This theory gives us permission to continue doing what we're already doing.

Another theory is that we're here to learn, but just what we're here to learn is unclear. Should we learn how to get along better with each other without judgement or criticism? If we're here to learn then we don't seem to be learning much. Education is in decline and people are being 'dumbed down'. Television and the internet take up most people's free time with game shows, trivial reality programmes and silly entertainments. The only thing the world is learning is how to keep its head in the sand because we're perfectly happy to go on pretending everything is just fine. If we're here to learn then it follows that we'll 'graduate' in some way after this life and move up to a higher plane; then repeat the process and reach higher still. By experiencing or overcoming certain difficulties we can move on and experience others. If we're learning then we're learning the wrong things like; aggression, violence, disharmony, and complete disregard for Humanity and other life forms. We haven't learnt too much that's worthwhile; we've submitted to empty-headedness. We don't notice the beauty of the world we live in; we live within the shallowness of a prescribed life in return for a few worthless trinkets that can never justify the suffering endured by so many people. We're still at war with each other, using increasingly sophisticated weaponry; I can't see this changing in my lifetime or even within the next few generations.

There are those who think we're dreaming this life. There's a lot to be said for that. Here are just a few questions that have occurred to me about this theory. If it's a dream why do we return to it every morning? Why does it last so long? Why do we dream every night within this dream? Who is dreaming? The list of questions is endless. If it's a dream then we may live from dream to dream. Changes I've made in my life have been reflected in my dreams. Does this mean dreams are a guide to the healthy or unhealthy state of our minds? Dreams are muddled up events, our hopes and fears, which can make them unrecognisable as a reality we can relate to. We can experience walls crumbling around us, driving cars with no brakes, walking on water or flying? How do we create these dreams?

Yet another theory is we die, ceasing existence altogether. This can be likened to organic matter left to decompose in a compost heap and then disappearing altogether. This theory is hard to get to grips with as it's obvious there's more to us than that. I fail to see how life could have been created so we're born to be slaves to a system that values transient and abstract things above all else. Are we here to live in a world riddled with confusion, illness, corruption and perversion? Must we remain desperate for answers to innate questions and watch while the world is at war with itself? No! Something's wrong here. This to me is impossible and it doesn't take much thought to figure this out. Everything comes out of a void. If you plant an acorn and let it grow, the oak tree produces more seeds that have come out of *nothing*. These weren't there before; just the *information* needed to create them. In the same vein, think about a baby ten months before its birth or a word not yet spoken. Where do they come from? What happens to our consciousness after death? Our consciousness is not made of what we consider to be matter; it can't decompose.

Is life some sort of multi-dimensional game? Another theory says we're living in a holographic Universe and this is a virtual reality world. There are many videos and books on this subject. It's not necessary to agree with what they say but it's possible to fit pieces into the jigsaw puzzle after listening to them with an open mind and allowing our *own* thoughts and reason to stream through. Are we here to find our way out of some sort of labyrinth? If this is a virtual reality game within a holographic Universe then I can't exclude the *possibility* that the whole world is *me*; I'd be the player and the game. It would mean everything is coming from inside me including every person I've ever met; making me the entire Universe and multi-dimensional. If this is me then it's *you* too. If this is the case, our own Universes are overlapping or 'masking' each other in some amazing and divine way. The only thing I could be sure exists, is my own awareness. The implications and responsibilities that go with this are colossal. It may also mean no-one would ever find the time-capsules I mentioned earlier because with our 'deaths', the world would disappear just like turning off the television while the programme is still running. However, if we flick the 'power' switch on again, the film is still there. What an incredible thought that is when I allow it to grow!

There are many more theories about the world we live in and it's not necessary to go into all of them. Whichever theory we give credibility to, we owe it to ourselves to examine it and face every question that arises. To follow blindly or believe in it just because it came recommended in a best-selling book is not wise. Along the way we may discover several theories can fit together or at least parts of them - we may even discover a new one.

~~~

We're eternal *beings* who are all connected, like droplets in an ocean. This has become known as *Consciousness*. If there's only one Consciousness, then surely there must only be one Mind. A little research into my own mind - a part of the whole - has raised many questions for me to ponder over and that our true nature is magnificent is beyond questioning. Most of my research was done by watching my own mind and thoughts; a most beneficial exercise - if we watch *ourselves* instead of others we learn a great deal more about reality. What we're doing here in this life is a question most people have given up on, if they've asked it at all. This is why we still have questions after thousands of years of investigation; after all this time we just don't seem to care. We tend to look to science for answers but the problem with this is that science looks at the physical world with measurement and logic. As we're not mechanical beings with mechanical responses, can science ever find truth? Remember, it's the questions that are important!

~~~

For as long as I can remember I've heard words like *eternity* and *infinity*. However, we can't conceive of these concepts because we're locked in space and time and they imply finite boundaries. No-one seems to know where they are in the Universe. Ask anyone *who* or *where* they really are and they'll stare at you as though they've short-circuited; society can't think this way yet. We're waiting to die and making the most of our time here with a plethora of toys, gadgets and entertainments available for us in 'God's waiting room'. Life can be compared to long delays at an airport; we wander around the shops looking for yet more things to buy and occupy us, in order to help us pass the time until we board the plane. It's easy to think nothing matters and that we're powerless when we read the horror stories in the media, but it isn't true. We're hedging our bets on living 'happily ever after' and hoping it'll be alright by the time we reach the last page, as this is what we're shown in so many films and books; especially in the fairytale and fantasy genres.

It can't be denied that we're being distracted from thinking about the *deeper* issues of life and encouraged to occupy ourselves with more trivial and abstract matters. Why don't philosophical and spiritual matters appear on the radar screens of large numbers of people? The subject of 'Humanity' is never discussed in any serious way in the mainstream media or in schools. What exactly is being obscured by these distractions? Why don't good news stories spread as quickly as the bad ones?

We love to listen to bad news and we pass it on and corrupt it further by adding our own criticism and judgement to it. We continue to listen to the news on the television and radio, even though we find it distressing. We know we don't get told the whole true story, if any of it. We listen to the stories about wars and those injured in them, the starving in third world countries, our badly behaved sporting 'heroes', corrupt politicians, and many more. Why do we *need* to listen to these? Why is it considered 'de rigueur'? We listen, we watch, we fret and nothing changes because we don't change ourselves. Why do we continue to do it?

Science makes everything seem out of reach by inventing big numbers and then adding an 'illion' on the end; this makes developments in our lifetimes appear to be beyond possibility. Beyond the 'illions' there's a googol which is 10^{100} and a googolplex which is 10^{googol}. It's so big it isn't even a number we could ever really use. We couldn't count up to it in our lifetime; why are we wasting our time on this nonsense? Don't these big numbers imply a finite boundary somewhere? At what point do we accept infinity? In his series *The Cosmos*, Carl Sagan stated "A piece of paper large enough to contain all the zeros in a googolplex couldn't be stuffed into the known Universe."[10] We think future generations can benefit from all this knowledge, but not ourselves, because the numbers are so big and way beyond our reach. If we can't see these numbers is it any wonder we that can't fathom the concept of eternity? Consequently, we seek comfort in: things; amusements; pleasures, celebrities; films; media and other trivial distractions because there appears to be little point and no encouragement to do anything else. Our children stand to inherit our, knowledge, foolishness, possessions, depressions, traumas and ignorance, just as we did from our parents and we're doing nothing to change it; we can't be bothered. We look at what our five senses perceive and at our own 'survival'.

It's hard to ignore that we, as individuals, must be able to attain our goal within our own lifetime; imagine what we might be turning our backs on by ignoring this? We must find out what we're doing here and without delay if we're to achieve it - none of us knows *when* we're going to die. The goal has nothing to do with a university education, regardless of the grade achieved. If we're eternal beings and can't die then what does this life matter? This is not an easy question to think about. Are we supposed to find our purpose and achieve our goals blindly? Ask 'Who am I?' and don't stop asking it. Don't expect a voice to call out from behind you with an answer but if you do get one; question it. The question is about heart, deep inside us; it's not a question we can answer mechanically like in an 'answer book'.

It's important to remember that all theories - some lasting and some fashionable - aren't *facts*. If anything, I'd say we're more likely here to remember 'who we are' and who we truly are has nothing to learn. On the contrary, the more we're taught the more we have to 'unlearn' in order to find our true self. We need to find our purpose. Our purpose must be to return to where we came from and to leave the body, the mind and the ego behind. They're not who we are and we're far too attached to them; all our anxieties, problems, fears and insecurities belong to them. Are we the sum total of this 'lifetime'? I invite you to ponder this interesting question for a while but look at Humanity as a *whole* rather than yourself as an individual while you think about it. For every question I get close to answering, many more get raised. Why is this?

The truth can be found by each and every one of us. True happiness and joy can be achieved through sheer effort and determination to find them. Look at the trees, a blade of grass, the sun, and a flower. Look long and hard at them; there's real magic waiting to be discovered if we take the time to observe our world and it's not millions of light years away. Can true happiness and joy be handed to us after our deaths without us ever having lifted a finger to find it? Does it make sense or seem likely to you? Does it matter? It does if we want it to. If you believe it doesn't, then why are we here at all? Every philosopher has worked out his philosophy for himself and we can all do it. We don't need a degree or anything else; truth can be found just by sitting on a park bench. You're reading this now because it matters to you; something is driving you to find the questions. Perhaps it matters to you because you want to find your own truth, to prevent yourself from finding it, or perhaps you're seeking to destroy someone else's truth. You may also be denying that you're looking for it at all.

Time

If time heals ... how long will it take to complete the process?

It's a dry sunny day and I'm typing this on my laptop looking outside the window. The tops on the trees are swaying in a gentle breeze and birds are coming to feed from the bird table competing for the food I've put out for them. It's lovely and quiet but despite movement, nothing is obviously changing or aware of the monotonous 'tick-tock' of the clock. If I wait an hour I won't see anything different. I did the same yesterday and I'll do the same tomorrow. I haven't looked to see what the time is, I don't wear a watch and I don't know what day it is. Time has not affected my view in any visible way I can determine and it can't spoil my enjoyment unless I spend it worrying about a past event, future appointment or thinking about whether I should start preparing lunch; each new moment is right now. If I wait a few weeks more flowers will bloom and more will die off but it's all a cycle and a rhythm that has nothing to do with *time*. Time changes nothing but we've created a mechanism for it and slotted it into the natural rhythm of nature. Because we believe time to be 'real' we then have to *fill it* and now we've expressions such as spare time, no time, free time, overtime, quality time, flexitime, save time and *even* a waste of time. But we no longer have the time to watch the sun appearing and disappearing on the horizon and, if we live in a town, we've no *time* to observe nature except perhaps if we go for a walk in the park or look up at a starry sky on a clear night.

Time is how we measure the movement of the universe; we attempt to measure its rhythm and regulate our lives by it. This doesn't work too well, which is why some months have different numbers of days in them; we also add an extra day to February every four years. The purpose of time is to help us 'schedule' our lives. Imagine going to King's Cross station to catch a train and finding out it's already left. How would we make appointments or keep to schedules without time? We need time to keep up with the pace of the society we've created, and that's *all* we need it for. The Universe manages perfectly well without it.

Is turning over to look at the clock the first thing you do when you wake up in the morning? My friends and family get busier and busier as they try to fill in the hours with rituals. These rituals include but aren't limited to work, television, sports, social media, shopping, fitness, cooking and socialising; we fit these in between our other commitments. We keep different time zones and put our clocks forward and backward twice a year. Some of my friends monitor more than one time zone. How many time-pieces do you have in the house including on the oven, mobile phones, watches and media players? How would you cope without them? The flowers in my garden are still blooming without any help or awareness of the seconds and minutes passing by and they're not in a hurry; neither can they be hurried.

If we don't get something done according to a schedule we say we've 'run out of time' or passed a 'deadline'. How is this possible? Why do we have breakfast, lunch, and dinner times; why don't we eat when we're hungry? We need these mealtimes because we have to fit in with the tight schedules of employment, appointments, travel, and television timetables. We *combine* some of these in order to save time such as eating while watching the television, or travel and organising our appointments through the use of computer tablets and mobile phones. I don't believe we're meant to run and rule our lives according to mechanical or digital devices, manufactured with increasing precision. We're obsessed with exactness and technology.

A delayed train or flight can have serious consequences for a tightly-scheduled businessman. It's partly for this reason that webinars have evolved for conferences and presentations and it's more profitable for a company if it doesn't have to put its directors up in hotels and pay for expensive flights. It's not just about saving money either as it saves a great deal of 'time'. Human beings have become mechanised and moulded into shape according to the advancements of technology. We 'function' to the rhythm of the clock. What time do *you* have to get up for work?

The world must remain highly organised if it's to continue meeting its financial and productivity targets. *Self-help* or *self-improvement*, rather than helping us to become happier human beings are becoming concepts designed to increase our efficiency by managing our time better, particularly where work is concerned. Ironically, this means learning how to slow down time so we've more of it in order to cope with the workloads and stresses of our jobs and the higher expectations and demands of our employers or schedules. We need diaries and gadgets that bleep to remind us of our commitments, in order to cope with the demands on our time. We speed up cooking times with microwave ovens and ready meals; we also speed up the growing process of our crops with faster growing varieties of genetically modified foods. Despite slowing down or speeding up time there are still only twenty-four hours in a day; we can't cram in another millisecond. Technology has advanced so much that a mere human being doesn't have the *time* to keep up; we must change in order to accommodate it.

Mahatma Gandhi said "There is more to life than simply increasing its speed."[11] We're getting to the point where the only way to keep up with our busy schedules is to mechanise human beings. We already have robots doing the repetitive jobs in factories that were once done by us; they do them faster and more precisely without the need for tea or lunch breaks; they also don't require 'time off' for holidays or sickness. We get faster and faster at sporting events; Thomas Burke achieved 12.0 seconds in the final of the 100 meters at the first Olympics in 1896. Usain Bolt ran the 100 meter dash (final) in 9.63 seconds in the London Olympics 2012; when will we get it down to under 9 seconds? How? We'll need more than human bodies if we wish to keep running faster and our future athletes will have to be transhuman.

This is not about transcendence to 'higher realms' of spirituality but transcendence of the human body into technology; a merger of the two. This concept is far from new. The concept was 'shown to the public' in the form of *Frankenstein: or, The Modern Prometheus*, a novel written by Mary Shelley in 1818. Later examples include *The Six Million Dollar Man* television series way back in 1973 which was based on a novel called *Cyborg* by Martin Caidin published in 1972. This may seem far fetched but we don't need to do too much research to see it's not far off. Transhumanism, in films and literature, is now accepted without horror or question, whereas the idea of Frankenstein was originally shocking. Other more recent films include *A. I. Artificial Intelligence* and *Bicentennial Man* in which robots want to become human beings. We already walk about with our gadgets and most people couldn't do without them; I've known people to be frantic when they've dropped their mobile phone on the ground or in water. My own opinion is that our 'natural state' is so advanced we've no need for technology. It could be argued that the only war is between the 'god of science and technology' and the 'god of spirituality'. It could also be argued that we're travelling back in time; returning to our *origin*. Is there any way of knowing?

~~~

Have you ever had that 'I don't remember the bit in-between' feeling? For example, when we're driving our cars and realise we've been 'absent' for part of the journey. We've negotiated traffic lights, roundabouts and other obstacles, but have no recollection of doing so. In my experience, sometimes twenty minutes have passed by without my knowledge. What happened to the time? A part of our mind has wandered elsewhere yet we've still managed to drive many kilometres without full concentration or incident. Who was driving the car? How is it we didn't hit a pedestrian, another car or drive off the road? Were we daydreaming or is this some other phenomenon? What has this to do with space and time?

Have you ever sat on a train pulling out of a railway station and felt a little disorientated. Sometimes it feels as though the world outside is moving and the train is stationary; this concept is called 'self-motion'. This motion is caused by us and not by an external action. Similarly, when another train pulls out of the station while the one we're on is stationary, it can feel like the train we're on is moving backwards. We feel this disorientation many times in our lives without realising it; for example, when we walk on land after being on a ship or standing still after spinning on the spot. This phenomenon is heavily researched as it has many uses in the creation of more believable experiences in virtual reality games. I'm no scientist, but if the world we live in is a virtual reality, then we're probably victims of the biggest hoax going and this must have been created by a far higher level of Consciousness. Have we created a 'game' for our own amusement? Is the earth moving or is the universe revolving around us? Is anything moving at all?

~~~

Time is a strange concept. We turn time back when we remember the past and forward when we go to the future; for example, when we've got an appointment to keep. Time is abstract and linear; our minds travel up and down its line; late, early or on-time. We can't *actually* go anywhere along the time-line. Time is a measurement of distance between two places in a similar way to feet and inches. When we travel to work for example, we *measure* the journey from our homes to our place of work in both miles and minutes. But time doesn't necessarily involve a physical journey from place to place. Time also passes when we don't move; while we're waiting for a bus or sleeping. Our obsession with schedules makes time important, but only to us, as the 'natural' world continues regardless.

We've all had days where time drags and it's usually while we're waiting for our working day to finish or when we're bored and unchallenged? Other days, *time flies* and we don't know where it's gone. This is often when we're enjoying ourselves or we've a deadline to meet. Time doesn't feel natural to us; it curtails our more enjoyable and challenging activities and stretches out the dull and mundane ones. What's happening here? Time slows down when we're focused on things we would rather came to an end but, when we're enjoying ourselves we live more in the Now and become unaware of the clock.

We count the days until our next birthday, anniversary, mortgage payment, retirement and other notable dates. Children can become obsessed with time, like when they state their age as twelve and three quarters; they can't wait for the magical transition into their teens ... then they can't wait to get out of them. Coming of age at sixteen, eighteen and twenty-one is all important because it brings *rewards* such as, 'grown up' status, being allowed into clubs and pubs or getting control of our own bank accounts.

~~~

Every thought we have originates from the past; every single one of them. Thought is memory. These thoughts can and do manifest in many ways, like when we remind each other of things we might have said or done twenty or thirty years ago, or we may remember an embarrassing moment that still makes us blush. It's difficult to let go of hurtful experiences; the mind holds on tightly and broods over them, which has a negative impact on our well-being. We go to the past when we look at photographs; think about that. We can never go to the future. We're always here, right Now, *out* of time when we're doing it. If we can't go to the past or future, do time and space exist at all?

Where is Chapter One of this book right now? It's not in the future. We could look for it in the past if we search our memory banks, but we won't find it in the Now. You can never find it in the Now. As you read this paragraph only the part you're reading at this precise moment is in the 'now' and it's so precise we can't pinpoint it because by the time we think about it, it's already in the past. The future can't be located; it can be waited for but it'll never arrive. The past can only be remembered. When we think about the future or the past we're in the Now. We can't go to the future or return to the past. If we're in the 'Now' ... what is time? It's an abstract concept designed to occupy us as we rotate it between work, play, families, stress etc. We can stop the clocks, but we can't stop the rhythm of the universe; we're all a part of it. Time is a 'tool' we use to measure and schedule our lives; like clockwork. The Now exists between thoughts. The Now exists between the past and the future. The only time is Now; but it's been divided into years, months, weeks, days, hours, minutes and seconds.

Time is an illusion obscuring the Now.

Right and Wrong

Perspective is the pen that draws the line between right and wrong.

This chapter is not about what's right or wrong in the sense that to commit a crime is wrong. Rather it's about following the path that's right for us and recognising other peoples' rights to follow their own. This means we don't impose our beliefs on others if we believe them to be wrong. We've been taught right and wrong from an early age, but these standards were based on the upbringing and disciplines of people who were taught by others. In this society we don't live by what we preach; what standards are we following? It's up to us to decide what's right and wrong for ourselves and up to us whether to live without hypocrisy. No matter what path we decide to take it'll ultimately lead us to the same place; it may take a great deal longer some ways and nobody can say which way is the right way. We constantly talk about right and wrong, war and peace, good and bad and it's silly as these concepts are abstract stagnant distractions and they'll remain stagnant until intelligence is born in society.

As long as we look at right and wrong subjectively we'll end up with opposing views and conflict because for the moment at least, we're rarely in agreement. Conflicts arise between us because of these opposing views. As individuals coming from different cultural and educational backgrounds it's inevitable that we grow up with different beliefs and standards. For example, a person may believe that it's right for humans not to eat meat; someone else may believe it's ok to eat it. Neither person is wrong in their own eyes but both are wrong in the eyes of each other. As long as *right* and *wrong* exist harmony can never be found because they cause separation between us. Right and wrong must come into being simultaneously; like 'left and right' or 'malevolence and benevolence'. What sort of world would we live in if these opposite words didn't exist? Perhaps only the fine line in-between can lead to harmony? To make the point a bit clearer, can 'left' exist without 'right', or 'up' without 'down'?

~~~

When I first learnt there was more to life than I'd ever thought possible I wanted to tell the world and I tried hard to do it too. I joined forums where arguments about the world were rife and these forums buzz night and day. Most of the members were regulars and the threads got thousands of views; they discussed the latest political scandals, media stories and different conspiracy theories. I noticed the 'happy' threads too, way down the lists with only a few views. I started a couple of new topics, but they never got anywhere near the number of views the angry and scandalous threads got; they hardly got viewed at all and only two or three people contributed towards them. Someone came on to one of the threads I'd started and said "way too happy in here" and left. I left the forums soon after this incident as I could see it wasn't the place to air my views and I'd waste my time trying to change something that didn't want to be changed. They weren't wrong and neither was I. We were walking along different roads.

On another occasion, I went with my partner to a spiritual group meeting in Brighton. I was excited at the thought of meeting other people on the same path. I fell flat on my face when we walked in; the meeting was already in session and the group were enthusiastically discussing the latest earthquake. I got up to leave and apologised for the confusion about the group's purpose. This didn't go down too well and I got nasty looks from a red-headed woman who wanted to talk about the earthquake; she wasn't happy I'd interrupted her. The group became divided on this subject. I would've got a better reception if I'd turned up as a 'little green man'; as it was I turned up happy and sure of myself and people don't like a happy person too much. The meeting brought no harmony, no peace and no answers; it wasn't for us and we never went again. I'd nowhere else to turn - at least I thought this at the time. People didn't want to know and I couldn't change them. They were more interested in the current news scandals and what was being done about them. I tried to change the world outside of me. I swam upstream and got nowhere. I tossed and turned at night for several weeks but afterwards realised they weren't wrong to want to discuss the earthquake; they enjoyed and found security in the discussions; it wasn't my place to tell them they shouldn't be discussing it. I made the choice never to go again and it was the right choice for me.

I once asked my hairdresser if she ever took quiet time to 'think' because whenever I go to her salon the radio is blaring; I don't think she even knows it's on. She told me she was 'afraid to think'. I found that to be an incredible statement. How can anyone be afraid to think and what *exactly* are they afraid of? The situation didn't invite further conversation and I didn't volunteer any. Again here, it's not *wrong* to be afraid and as her statement made clear, she does this by her own choice. We can't help anyone who doesn't want to help themselves; it's not possible. It took me a long time to accept this.

~~~

Interesting rights and wrongs have evolved with the creation of class systems. In the higher classes, having correct posture and a code of behaviour around the dinner table is expected. These tables must be set 'correctly' and it's frowned upon to use the wrong utensils when eating different courses. I'm not saying it isn't right to live this way but I'm saying that in *my* opinion it's folly - it can't improve the eating experience. However, for people living in 'polite society' it's taken seriously. Though it's not wrong for them to eat this way, it *is* a disciplined behaviour and this means there are rules and regulations they *must* follow. They would frown upon the way most of us eat as families in our homes which is not necessarily around a dining table. This process of comparison comes from our separation from each other. People in 'high society' aren't better human beings than anyone else; they see things differently because they've been the subjects of another type of conditioning. I see their way of eating and behaving as not too different from highly *trained* performers, but I don't see it as *wrong*. A question that arises here is: Who's training them? It would be easy to think the so-called 'lower classes' aren't also trained performers, but would it be true? We've been conditioned to believe we're right and the others are wrong; the result is conflict. This gets more interesting when we realise that we've the same conflicts within each and every one of us.

One of the reasons I never completed my autobiography is that my mind kept arguing with me; the mind is conditioned and therefore, 'trained'. It told me I couldn't write anything that isn't already in the book shops; my little book wouldn't make any difference and nobody would want to buy it anyway. Above all these reasons it told me my family would resent what I wrote about them and it would cause all sorts of problems. I wanted to show people they could recover from their traumas or problems and the only way I knew how to do this, was to write. However, my mind argued and it's still arguing even though I'm writing an entirely different book. I know that no matter what; it'll still argue with me. The difference now is that I'm aware of the process and just *observe* the 'me' that wants to write and the 'me' that doesn't. This type of conflict isn't different and it isn't right or wrong; we can observe from the middle - objectively. On a deeper level it's also possible to observe the middle itself.

~~~

To recognise 'ourselves' in another is a part of the path to Grace. We become more tolerant of the human race and realise that we're all struggling regardless of rights, wrongs or class systems; we're all part of the same picture and we each have a role to play. Humanity has fallen, become fractured and it won't put itself back together again. So as long as there's competition and comparison there'll be no harmony. We're all at odds, not only with ourselves but with each other, whether it's in small groups or in nations; we're shadow boxing night and day. Every human being, at some level knows these things. Can we ever get to the point where right and wrong don't exist; we just are? We just observe without judgement?

The hairdresser mentioned earlier in this chapter wasn't ready to face the part of her that made her uncomfortable; the part she's most afraid of admitting exists. She wasn't ready to confront her own ghosts and may never be ready in this lifetime; her focus was still outside of herself. When each of us is ready we can make a conscious decision to climb out the doldrums and look for something better, but we all decide this for ourselves when the time is right for us. This trip is a solo one and it's through having the courage to be 'alone' with ourselves that we begin to see things differently. I'm not talking about loneliness; it's a wonderful thing to be alone once we're not afraid of it. Living this way won't win any popularity contests but if we care about popularity, then we're not ready to live this way.

I know some people who say they're certain when we die, that's it! They believe it and I don't and that's ok, but I must continue in my own way. The decision to change reaps benefits when we're ready to let go of our self-imposed and inherited restrictions; including the limitations friends and family may try to put on us. This is normal and part of the process to reach a higher level of consciousness. People don't want us to grow and change; they still prefer the way things are and would be happy if we did too. Whatever a person does in their life must be right for them, or they wouldn't do it. Even in the case where a battered wife may stay with her husband, it's right for her. We always choose what's right for us at the time. It's hard to see these things from another perspective and it would be harder still for us to walk in their shoes.

There's something innate that wants to continue with the 'norm' in society. We want to stay put and despite our apparent objections to 'darkness'; Humanity has a strong tendency to lean towards it. We desire; things, money, homes, better bodies, romance and everything else society offers through advertisements and we want them now; we want *entertainment* too. We can't comprehend when someone turns their back on society; if we could we'd be forced to look at *ourselves*. By resisting, we don't have to acknowledge there's a better way to live with each other and we don't have to make any sacrifices in order to change our own lives.

We'll never find inner peace if we look outside or to others for it; it lies within. Until we're ready to look we'll not listen to anyone else's opinions. We reject all they say and think they're nuts, or we want to follow them and read all their books before moving on elsewhere looking for another excuse not to alter our current way of life. We're afraid to find it and not prepared to put in the necessary work searching involves; it'll disrupt our illusions and our schedules. In general, people don't want to be their own masters and they prefer to follow governments, celebrities and guru figures. To look at our shadow and admit to the ugliness contained in it is difficult and often painful but this journey can't be completed without facing it or by holding someone else's hand. It takes a tiny flame to light up a darkened room, but we can't light up anyone else's when they don't want it to be lit - a guru can't do the work for us. There are those who believe we chose our lives before coming here and if this is the case there must be people who chose not to 'wake up' during this lifetime. I don't follow any particular belief but some things are clear.

We're eternal beings. We're pure Consciousness. That we live in this world of suffering for an eternity makes no sense at all. As mentioned earlier, we all have to walk this path sooner or later, but only when the time is right for us. It's not possible to give this information to a mind not in tune with or resisting it. One of the wonders of the world has to be to light the fuse leading another person to the realisation that there's something wonderful and magical about us and our world. Can life be worthwhile if we can't help one another?

There's no right or wrong way; it's subjective. My way is right for me and the red-headed woman's way is right for her. We can't climb into someone else's head and see the world through their eyes. We must see from our own perspectives and our *judgement* can only be based on what we've learnt since the day we were *born*. We must choose our own paths and if that includes living in darkness, then so be it. Some people aren't ready or are unwilling at this moment to consider an alternative to the life they've created for themselves. We live in fantasy worlds of our own creation. If we came into this world with a purpose then I feel certain our *true nature* knows what it's doing.

That right and wrong are subjective can't be argued. Social conditioning has given us *all* different ideas about what is right and wrong and regardless of these beliefs; we believe them to be true. What we do with these beliefs is another matter entirely and for those who say "oh well, I can go and commit murder then"; they haven't been *thinking* intelligently and they're unlikely to in this lifetime. Should we harm another human being or force them to do something against their will? If we have the right to choose, shouldn't other people have those same rights? These questions are for each one of us to think about and to be entirely responsible for our judgements. We have an innate knowledge of what is objectively right and wrong and our only real choice is to choose one or the other - from our two voices. However, is it really necessary to choose at all?

Light Casts no Shadow

A shadow is cast where light has been interrupted.

The shadow is what we hide from and what we leave lingering as we walk through our lives; it resides deep in our subconscious minds. The shadow speaks to us when we look in the mirror but we ignore it because we don't want to hear what it has to say. We prefer to hear lies and create a more pleasing reality for ourselves. Most of my life I've not liked what I saw when looking into the mirror. So I created something else; a world where everyone else was to blame for my predicament - a world in which I was 'helpless'. This avoidance of the shadow allows it to project itself so critically on to others; we can't face the truth about ourselves.

Several years ago, I went for a walk with my partner and as we walked we saw in the distance a mother coming towards us with her overweight daughter. The daughter was raising and lowering her arms by her sides and my first thought was "She'll never manage to take off". I recognised that I was being cruel and later mentioned it to my partner who admitted he'd been thinking the same thing. It was in that moment I realised I'd cast my *own* shadow on to the young girl; I'd opened the door and allowed my *beast* out. Since then I've been self-correcting these thoughts, as and when they arise; now they're less frequent. If we do this repeatedly it soon becomes natural, as opposed to contrived behaviour.

We've to do a great deal of self-reflection in order to accept the things we're not willing to face. Playing victim is a habit; it sticks like glue and the dark self-pitying thoughts leave us believing we're not good enough. If we believe the world is against us we give ourselves an excuse to keep things as they are. We refuse to see that we're responsible for our own predicaments and we refuse to change. We *all* do this and until we see that we're fundamentally the same our problems will continue. We've all suffered in some way and we all focus on our own 'bad story' as though it were the only one in existence. The parts of our nature we're most uncomfortable with are what we see and criticise in others. I wasn't free to fly any more than the young girl who was waving her arms about.

Humanity likes to complain about its crises but the world is this way because we've created it. In every supermarket we see more unhealthy foods than healthy ones. Supermarkets supply us with the products that sell best. There are still only tiny sections in supermarkets stocking organic products; this is because of a lack of demand. Supermarkets now sell just about everything because we want to buy it. We created this consumer shadow. We want these products for our convenience and know they need to be highly competitive in order to supply them at rock bottom prices. Our shadow knows others have paid dearly for this, but in the same way as when we look in the mirror, we pay no attention to it.

A great deal is wasted in this world. We buy to replace just because we want newer versions of things that, if we're honest, aren't significantly different from the old; such as televisions, computers and mobile phones. We change our televisions but the media don't improve the programmes we watch on them. Your average person won't be aware of all the functions on their mobile phones and never do anything with them except make calls and send text messages, yet still, we want the latest version.

We continue to want new things and ignore that our desires create havoc in ways we refuse to look at. As long as we 'want' things like worthless trinkets, ornaments, rave parties, new cars, huge houses and junk food then the world will be filled with them; that's what will be manifested. As long as we ignore that many products are produced in third world countries by under privileged and underpaid workers, we're contributing to the continuity of world poverty in order to satisfy our petty desires. Humanity has cast this dark shadow on society and Humanity is deaf, dumb and blind to it.

Our choices have created this world. We each decide what to put into our shopping trolleys, what we do on the internet, what we fill our minds with and how we interact with each other. When we begin to make wiser choices, when we take *responsibility* for our actions then the world will become a better place to live in. It'll not become a better place if we leave the thinking to governments who, let's face it, have a poor track record when it comes to the welfare of us or the planet. It's easy to sit back and 'tut tut' about the state of the world as innocent bystanders, but we're not; we've not only contributed, but we're the cause. Governments are run by human beings just like us, with the same sicknesses of mind; the minds are the same but the toys we play with are different.

The internet is a wonderful tool for communication, learning and for our interaction with each other. Because of the mindset of Humanity, it's become polluted with our darkest shadows and desires. We're not forced on to websites with pornographic, violent or abusive content any more than we're forced to take drugs or get drunk; they're there because we want them to be there. The internet is what *we've* made it. Why do we choose to look at the more unchallenging and vacuous content when we could put it to much better use?

Science and spirituality take the backstage and few get views on their internet videos, whereas pop stars and celebrities go viral overnight. Society reflects what we feel about ourselves, like a mirror, it's not reflecting anything too bright at the moment. There are many wonderful videos that lie unwanted by the masses. To find personal peace we must search inside ourselves but the problem here is society isn't ready to face its shadow. We don't want to change. Why is this? It takes a lot of effort to change and we're not prepared to put in the work needed to do it. We want to live in the easiest way possible and that's why we choose *convenience*, enjoy lame entertainments and allow governments to go on with 'business as usual'. We've lost interest in 'harmony' and don't strive to better ourselves or ensure we 'leave' this world having done our best to make some sort of positive difference; we don't believe there's any point.

~~~

We know that mobile phones are hazardous for our health. We know third world manufacturers employ poverty stricken workers for a pittance and charge extortionate prices for their goods. We know big corporations make obscene profits. Every year the media trumpets the Rich List. What kind of society brags about who's the greediest? We know our children are kept occupied by television or computer games because we've less time for them. We know we're polluting the atmosphere and water with household products. We know waste is replacing the soil in monstrous landfill sites. We know the Amazon is being destroyed. There's more to us than we think and we can change the world, as individuals and collectively; this has been *screamed* at us from rooftops in many ways including; films, music, fantasy and science fiction. We know all this and much more but we choose to ignore it for no good reason. We complain about things so much that most companies have a complaints department. Why do these companies still exist? We tell ourselves it's not our fault, but there's no-one alive who can hold his hand to his heart and claim they don't know these things. G. K. Chesterton said "It isn't that they can't see the solution. It is that they can't see the problem."[12] Shadows are cast by something blocking the light. We're so busy with our own agendas that we can't see the bigger picture or the damage we're doing. There's a big, dark and ugly shadow hovering over us and it's expanding, fast.

We can change this and it has to be done by each and every one of us. We can disperse the cloud hanging over Humanity and all we have to do is change perspective to see what's happening, together. We can see that we're afraid of horrors and at the same time, see how we contribute to them. We're afraid of death but we smoke and drink despite being told of the damage they cause. We drive too fast and we 'drink and drive' and for every law created by governments there are many people that think nothing about breaking them, which leads to the creation of more laws. Is Humanity a sado-masochist? Humanity is chaining itself up in a prison of its own making and there's no-one to blame. If we continue to behave in the same way we'll always get the same results. Humanity is selfish and self-centred and until it changes, the world won't change because we *are* the world. It's no good waiting for someone else to come and save us … we must save ourselves. We're worth it and we can do it.

Where am I?

"... overcome space, and all we have left is Here. Overcome time, and all we have left is Now.[13]*"* Richard Bach

Ponder the question 'Where am I?' and then ask yourself 'Relative to what?' and some interesting thoughts come up. In order to think about where we are we need a point to start from. If I say "I'm in London" then I'm approximately sixty miles from Cambridge. But, if I say "I'm here", how far away is Cambridge? Wherever I am in the world I'm 'here' and I can measure the distance to anywhere else starting from this point but it always begins 'here'. This may not make too much sense yet, but the world already doesn't make much sense to you, otherwise you wouldn't be reading this. In order to see clearer we must raise our level of vibration and, for the vast majority of us, this is a gradual process. Somehow we've become trapped in space and time and disconnected from our origin. One thing's for certain; there are much bigger things in the 'Universe' than we're capable of imagining while we're in this form. If this life is a virtual reality game then it's probably called *The Trickster Mind*; it's a pretty good and advanced game, don't you think? Would you play it? Who could've created it and made it seem so real? Are our dreams as real; are we still 'here' when we dream?

Where do we go, if anywhere, when we dream? Some mornings I wake up from a deep sleep and find myself in-between the dream and waking states. Are these two different worlds? This can be disorientating and I could argue I'd been dead or perhaps in another dimension or reality. I sit bolt upright and think to myself 'I'm back!' and sometimes it's disappointing, particularly if I'd been enjoying the dream. The world becomes a bumpy and uncertain place when we question reality, but it's more *real* for me than it ever was before and I'm much happier in it.

Am I 'here' when I'm asleep? I've no proof I'm in my bed when I'm asleep. I know I wake up in it but that's not proof; it's only proof I'm 'here' when I wake up. If we're in our beds while we sleep who is in our dreams? How did we create those 'worlds'? Where are we when we're sleeping? What happens to the characters in our dreams? Do they cease to exist? They're real people to me; where do they come from? Who created them and decided on things like hair colour, weight or mannerisms? Who made the scenery? Once

49

I get started on these questions I can't stop. I toss and turn in bed thinking about them as my mind is sharp and alert; often getting back to sleep is not an option. Is it possible to determine where we are at all? My partner says "I know you're in bed when you're sleeping because I can see you there"; I don't go with that idea too much, because if I can't be sure where I am then I can't be sure where he is either. What if we're not in the same space and time? My world feels like it's *my* world alone; will this world still exist after I'm dead or will it *die* with me? There are lots of questions raised here, but as mentioned at the beginning of this book; the questions are *important*. Just as important, is questioning the answers for once we've accepted an *answer* it shuts out further investigation. If we ask the right question it answers itself though maybe not as fast as we'd like and *not* in the traditional sense; it may just point us in another direction. Some of these questions may seem ridiculous but if you can't *prove* something, why believe it?

Am I like the particles popping in and out of existence in the wonderful world of quantum physics? They can pass through solid objects and can be in multiple places at the same time; there's much more to them than this but I'm not a scientist and more than a passing comment on the subject doesn't belong in this book. Perhaps a better question to ask than 'Where am I?' would be 'Where is here?'

'Here' is where I can be found … there can be no doubt about that. How can we be sure where it is? If *here* is on a tiny planet lost and floating somewhere in eternal space - visible in a sun beam - then it's a bit beyond the comprehension of most people, including me. It makes you wonder though doesn't it? If there's that much space out there, where did the concept of measurement come from? Where are North, South, East and West? Something tells me we've never moved even a millimetre. If time and space are abstract concepts then there can be no 'here' either. So are we everywhere? It's amazing how one question can lead to another.

Without getting deeply into science, what are coordinates? The 'earth', or what we think of as the earth, is spinning in outer space in orbit around a sun. All around this action, in every direction, is infinity; it's hard to imagine. There can be no measurements; such as, longitude, latitude, speeds or distance because there's nothing to relate them to. In this case, it isn't possible to know if anything is moving at all. If we left the earth and went far enough away from it, how could we define in *front*, *behind* or *distance*? We would never be able to return; there are no signposts, no coordinates, no landmarks, no sound and no compass points. There could also be no up, down, left or right, except in relation to ourselves. If we're the starting point then everywhere and everything must be relative to us; we must be at the centre. Isn't it possible that outside this bubble of *experience*, what we've come to know as 'physical laws' don't apply? If we're the centre of everything in *outer space* then we must be 'here' as well? Doesn't every part of our lives begin with us?

If the Big Bang happened, a random dot that exploded and is still exploding or expanding, then who or what lit the fuse? Where did the force come from that was the cause of the explosion, where does it continue to come from and most importantly, where did the *infinite* empty space it exploded in come from? What is space? Is this explosion not just in our minds? I began this life as a baby. I'm 'expanding' my comprehension of the world; my world has been expanding since my birth and it hasn't stopped. As I let go of conditioning my world is expanding as my perspective changes - not because of the accumulation of knowledge but with the dispersion of it.

Curiosity and Confusion

I am the product of all my thoughts.

We're set in our ways. We don't like to listen to the opinions of others, unless we want to have a good debate; in which case we're catching a ball in order to throw it back. We do things like sulk, tense up and fold our arms when we don't want anyone else's 'input'; our personal and impenetrable protective shields. What are we protecting ourselves from? Paradoxically, we've spent our lives listening to the opinions of others; which is where we get all our knowledge from in the first place. We prefer artificial beauty and admire our electronic accessories more than a person passing us in the street; we often prefer our pets to other people. None of this makes sense to me. How strange human beings are. How did we become this way?

~~~

We take a great deal for granted in this world. For example, we believe our reflection in a mirror is who we really are, without ever thinking about it. We believe it because we've been told it and spend a great deal of time looking at our reflections; particularly when we're young and curious. I remember opening the door of my bathroom when my eldest son was around seven. I found him standing on the child step, studying himself in the mirror pulling all sorts of silly faces. He was having incredible fun exploring his face and amusing himself with all he could do with it, just like a new toy. Babies explore their bodies this way too. They grab their hands and feet curiously and explore their fingers and toes; everything goes into their mouths. They tug at their clothing and pull their shoes and socks off. Has the baby found itself in a new body/environment; somewhere strange? Are babies honing taste, touch, smell, hearing and sight? Perhaps the baby is protesting against the world it finds itself in. These are strange notions, but when we're pursuing a line of enquiry many unusual questions arise. If they arise it's because we need to think about them. Do babies have more of an idea about who they are than we do? Most of us put the 'Who am I?' question on the back burner because we don't have the time or inclination to think about it.

One of the differences between a baby's curiosity and ours is that we've adjusted to our environment after many years of coaching and supervision. The people who've coached and supervised us don't know who *they* are any more than we do. Most grown-ups shed these questions a long time ago. Our curiosity is rarely resurrected because we've buried it - along with our dreams - beneath life's experiences. G. K. Chesterton wrote "Education is simply the soul of a society as it passes from one generation to another."[14] These things don't change because *we* don't change. We continue to teach the same things and they still don't involve asking questions about our amazing selves. Children find this frustrating because they're curious about everything they feel and see; they're sadly without a voice but only because we're drowning theirs out with our own. We learn through repetition, rather like a horse learns to run faster with the crack of a whip. Education would be much more fun and less troublesome if it were based on what we're curious about; instead this curiosity is suppressed and frowned upon. I've a friend who explained to his ten-year-old grandchild how we don't actually see anything. He told him our eyes are sensitive to photons, we convert them into electrical impulses, optical nerves carry these to the visual centre of our brains and give rise to the images we see. Because this child had lost his fascination with his world and his need to challenge it, he replied; "I knew you'd say something weird".

If we stopped focusing on things like technology and more on ourselves and spirituality it wouldn't take long for the world to become a pleasant place to live in. We all start curious and because this curiosity is discouraged we become bored and discontented. When I was around eleven I wanted a guitar but my father wouldn't buy one for me no matter how much I asked. He said it was a waste of time and that I couldn't make a decent living playing music. More recently in my life, I showed some of my animated gifs to an uncle who commented "They're really nice but I can't see how they could ever be commercially viable". This is what we've become; competitive and ambitious for money; we stifle talent, curiosity and creativity because they're not profitable pastimes. We're encouraged to develop abilities that will prove to be commercial successes; this is a sad - and robotic - state of affairs.

~~~

I've always been fascinated by the development of babies, especially when compared to the fellow creatures sharing the earth with us. Babies are slow to get up on to their feet. Horses can walk the same day they're born, wolves at two weeks, cows after just a few minutes. We're much more intricate and have a great deal to learn such as using utensils, mastering our own bodies, building our world. Other creatures don't need anywhere near so much development to live out their lives. If you look into a baby's eyes they're full of wonder and innocence - they don't know lies, anger, judgement, disappointment or hatred. A baby spends nine months in the womb but that's not the end of its development; it continues for years after; we reach puberty by our early teens! Why do we succumb to being complacent about the miracle of life?

A baby's mind can't cope with the obstacles we place in front of it and they constantly walk into things and hurt themselves. For this reason, we protect them from table corners and other household furniture. Babies struggle with the world we've created, especially when around roads and busy streets. When a baby wants something it just goes for it without regard for its safety or what's in front of it; a baby is continuously 'corrected'. Our environment isn't natural and we have to constantly reinforce the rules and regulations of society before a baby can 'take care' of itself. We make our environment safe from their curiosity by securing them from it; by doing this, we introduce them to 'fear'.

If we constantly correct babies and teach them to be afraid is it any wonder they become confused. We put babies in cots and play pens with sponge balls and squeaky toys and they're not free to explore 'their way' because we put many dangers outside of these enclosures; they don't learn to protect themselves because we do it all for them. Our environment is hostile and alien to a young child. How did we ever manage to look after babies before? Would they adjust faster without a world they must become afraid of and dependent on? Shouldn't we stimulate and encourage all parts of a baby's brain to develop to its full capacity. We train babies to survive and live in the society we created, even though we don't do too well in it ourselves. We also train them to protect themselves from our violence through 'sports' like the martial arts. It's become 'cool' to fight.

Many people have little curiosity about esoteric matters; in some cases, they're concerned more about what's on the television tonight or new postings on social media websites they *need* to 'catch up' on. We're happy to wait until we die to find out answers to questions we've forgotten how to ask. I've discussed this subject with many people and the most extreme reaction I've had so far from one of them, is that he got up and left the room - agitated - as though I were trying to administer a poison. Why do we ignore innate curiosity about what life really is? Is the veil of ignorance also innate? Where do innate questions come from? Why are we content to work, support our families, suffer poverty in some cases, settle for trivial entertainments and then die?

Let's look at it plain and simply for a moment. We've come from *nothing* and have been unceremoniously dropped into an established 'system' that stifles the natural talents and curiosities we were born with. Spirituality is frowned upon by the masses but 'religions' are considered okay as long as we behave the way they tell us to. Hypocrisy is also okay. Everyone is confused on some level, some have buried the questions and some can't; there's a Force that insists the latter explore further. What picture does this all paint?

~~~

Let's get back to the mirror. There are many people who play virtual reality games. I played around for a little while with a character on Second Life. I got bored because it was time-consuming and not *real*; it felt rather like playing in a doll's house. We still look in a mirror when we see the character on the computer screen; the principle is the same; it's a projection of our own creation. We create *dream* characters because they're more pleasing than the way we see ourselves. One problem with this is, when the game's over we return to our 'own bodies' and our discontentment with this life continues; until we login again. The frustrations increase because the characters still exist inside our heads and no matter what we do, we can't become them outside of the game. Creating and playing the roles of these characters serves to make us more insecure. The character I created could be anything I wanted it to be; any shape, height or colour. It could have amazing clothing and hairstyles, limited only by my imagination; it could even have wings and fly. The other characters we encounter are also not real. They're just like us; pretending to be someone more agreeable. Any interaction in these virtual realities is illusory and fake. I didn't stay around the website for long.

I know of a man who plays a character responsible for several war ships in an online virtual reality game and he's more than obsessed with this; it's his life. He gets up in the middle of the night to keep an eye on the virtual situation but doesn't spend any time on himself; preferring to be the game character. This is because it feels safe and can be turned off at any time; there's no threat or fear. In the game, people look up to him and he feels needed and important. Outside the game he's back in the uncomfortable world as the character he doesn't like - *himself*. He doesn't feel confident in his own life; his situation isn't uncommon. We like the character we've created so much we become addicted to it; consequently, we require more and more time online. Likewise, we've become addicted to our bodies, minds and egos and don't want to give them up and from these thoughts come fears of non-existence.

How it all works I don't know, but through constant questioning I know that what I see in the mirror isn't me at all, but rather it's who I used to think I was. For a while I researched this subject but the amount of literature on it was overwhelming and contradictory; it's impossible to read all the books. One book leads to another and they all cross reference something else; I do it in this book too. Determined to find out more about my reflection, I took a large mirror off the wall in my lounge and wedged it between the arm and cushion on my settee. I took my laptop over there and sat working facing the mirror for the most part of four days. This was a daunting and intimidating experience and it was hard to meet my reflection eye to eye at times. I was looking at someone else and I felt like *she* was trying to outstare me. I was being watched and it felt uncomfortable. At the end of the four days I knew for certain the image in the mirror wasn't me. I highly recommend this exercise and you can be certain of results at the end of it; which may or may not be the same as mine.

~~~

Our memories are formed from everything we've ever touched, smelled, tasted, heard or seen. However, despite all our knowledge we still grope for clarity of what life is all about. Our search may lead us to a spiritual leader, believing they can give us answers - but they can't. There are as many answers as spiritual leaders and this leads to further confusion; we end up with a collection of riddles. We hope that by visiting a spiritual leader, something called *enlightenment* will happen, if we remain in their company long enough.

Books can guide us too, but it's easy to get bogged down with the cross-referencing and jump from one book to another in a desperate and futile search for one true answer. What we're doing is avoiding facing our darkest thoughts, often looking for answers where we know we *won't* find them. We don't like ourselves and self-hatred is more common - and more powerful - than most people imagine or will admit to. No-one likes what they see in their own mirror. We see the burden of memory with all its judgements, prejudices, sufferings, guilt and anxieties; not a pretty sight.

The mind is a wonderful puzzle; it's complex and confusing. We've absorbed fantastic amounts of random information; with few connecting links. Every time we discover something new we fit another piece into the puzzle but still can't see the whole picture. We don't like the mind and we don't like what it says about us. It tells us things we don't want to hear and chooses the things that might disturb us the most; it's inclined to look on the dark side of life. The most interruptions I've encountered while writing this book were from my mind - it can be such a nuisance and leads to endless confusion and internal arguments. The mind is a vault of all we've experienced and these experiences have been piled on top of the innate questions we've buried so deeply. There's a lot more to it than we know about or are aware of and it doesn't turn off even when we're asleep. The more I think about these things the more my curiosity is aroused. I see beauty and magnificence in everything.

The man I mentioned who left the room agitated, when I tried to discuss philosophical issues with him, is typical of many people. As soon as there are two people together in a place, with different opinions, there's conflict. We cling vehemently to our beliefs and we're not willing to have them challenged; I was not willing to listen to him either. On some level we know we're avoiding the bigger issues but choose to stay close to what's familiar to us and well within our comfort zone. The thirst for knowledge is still in our minds but we can't reach it. A thought doesn't just disappear; it remains in our memory banks, buried beneath the prejudices, opinions and beliefs we've accumulated. Our stored up unanswered questions, anger, frustrations and bitterness reside there too and this collection of experiences makes up what we are; confused. We don't remember them all but they're still there and affect our daily lives. These thoughts have become our reality and we're not willing to part with them. We're not willing to acknowledge they exist.

Just like conflict arises between two people; it arises between two 'countries' or 'nations'. The people living in them are still in conflict with themselves therefore it's not possible to live as a harmonious unit while conflict is at the core. This creates an unhealthy and volatile force causing wars and hatred. It doesn't take much to set one nation against another and we've all seen this happening many times. The matter then appears impossible to resolve because we believe it to be out of our control - we feel we're just one person and powerless to change anything. Society reinforces those beliefs and therefore, we do nothing but grumble and complain about it. If we don't change who we are we'll remain confused and fragmented; the problem will not resolve itself and the cycle will continue.

This is important so let me clarify it a little. The conflict begins within us. Our mind is always arguing with itself. If you can't sleep at night then you'll know the mind comes up with out-of-date unimportant rubbish and distracts you from what you're trying to concentrate on; it's never silent and seeks to divert our attention with unconnected topics. It's difficult to concentrate when our mind wanders. Thoughts are like waves; as one becomes the ocean, we jump on to another. Our minds remind us about: unresolved issues, appointments, shopping, insecurities and other such irrelevant occupations. It focuses on our irrational thoughts and feelings about others because we don't want to focus on ourselves. For example, if I'm lying in bed thinking about *who I really am*, my mind starts chattering away about something I'd once said in anger. It then recites new scripts for me, polishing and perfecting the scenes it would've preferred me to act out; if I'd wished to claim a *victory*. The mind also prepares us for future events; playing mental chess and running through possible scenarios of what to say or do in certain situations and it predicts the possible outcomes. Does this happen to you too? Is your mind your harshest critic? We all struggle with these internal battles. It's simple, but complicated to resolve because for some crazy reason we like it this way - if we didn't, we would change it and we do each have the power to do that.

~~~

One of the reasons our lives have conflict in them is that we're confused about our purpose. There are somewhere around one thousand professions to choose from - I got conflicting numbers when I tried to find out this information but it doesn't matter enough to search further. What matters is we have to choose one to earn our living in order to pay the bills society puts through our letter boxes. We study something like twelve subjects that can lead us to one of the more 'respectable' of these professions, if our final grades arc good enough. We're swimming upstream in a fast flowing river and the current is getting stronger. The competition is fierce and the territory hostile and few of us climb higher up the employment 'ladder'. When we die, will it matter if during our lifetime we became a lawyer or a dustman?

Few people do a job they love and if we ask most people why, they would say they couldn't make a living at it. A great many people don't know what they would love to do anyway, but we do all have hidden talents. This problem is a direct result of our curiosity, true interests and natural tendencies being stifled in our infancy; we've been taught to think in a linear way and this limits our perception. It's also a result of the subjects we've been taught and no matter how 'professional' we become it's not for the good of Humanity that we do it. The only people who benefit from our efforts are governments and corporations. Were we given this world in order to live in and systematically destroy it?

Esoteric ideas are so far away from what we've been taught in schools; we can't relate to them too well. They're not discussed in the media in any meaningful way and it was the media who labelled the *spiritual* movement of the sixties 'Flower Power' and associated it with mind altering drugs and free 'love' (sex). We're told there's a God but how many of us have found out for ourselves if this is true? Truth comes from *knowing* and not from believing what we've been told. *Believing* doesn't make something *true*; these two concepts are different. One of the reasons there are so many religions is that we can't settle on any one belief that resonates with everyone.

It's important to remember confusion doesn't come from just us; it comes from previous generations too - we've inherited it and it's deeply ingrained. We've been educated with concrete beliefs, so abstract ones are hard for us to comprehend. By the time the notion of spirituality reaches our ears, our mind is already full of confusion it can't accept the concept of a question not having an answer. It's difficult to visualise a 'directionless' journey that's *not* physical or methodical because we're surrounded by an abundance of signs directing us to places, telling us how many miles to go, dictating strict rules such as 'Keep Left' or 'One Way'.

We look to books and media for information, maps for directions and television for weather reports. We also have the radio turned on for the latest updates; we check traffic and accident reports to ensure we're not delayed on our journey. In effect, we've opened ourselves to receive information from all these sources without questioning its influence on us or the authority of those who provide it; we accept this information, verbatim.

We don't think about the process of the transmission and reception of this data; all information must be transmitted and received. How does this apply to us? It's all there wherever you go. Next time you're out and about think about all the information being transmitted and received around you; it's an invisible world but it's there and you're transmitting and receiving it too. I'm transmitting this information to you through words on a page and you're receiving it. It's all a bit alien to us. We don't know where to turn or which books to read and there's no 'logical evidence' to prove anything anyway. When we let go of the framework holding our lives together we find ourselves without support and that's a major difficulty to get over before we open the way for a new kind of thinking. If what we've always believed is not true then in order to see something new we must let go of the crutch we've held on to; the support structure we built for ourselves.

Our beliefs are so ingrained that we won't *listen* to the possibility of a non-physical journey because there aren't any 'visible' signposts to guide us. My mother used to say she believed in *something* after this life, but on the other hand, she also hated spirituality. The confusions come from being taught to rely on the so-called five senses and these senses will not show us 'God'. God must be *before* the creation of the mind and therefore can't be found within it. The seer, Ramana Maharshi once said: "Existence or Consciousness is the only reality. Consciousness plus waking we call waking. Consciousness plus sleep we call sleep. Consciousness plus dream, we call dream. Consciousness is the screen on which all the pictures come and go. The screen is real, the pictures are mere shadows on it."[15] We can't change the reflection without changing what is reflecting it. We're given a blank sheet of paper to create our world on and we've scribbled all over it in the most horrible way; now we can't read our own writing. It's been scrawled on by society and we've been bombarded with bogus information from every direction; we can't read this writing either.

We must *be* before the creation of the mind because we're doing the writing, creating, transmitting, receiving and we're doing the dreaming! Who were we when the paper was blank? Where did the piece of paper come from?

Our Cluttered Mind

To find what is concealed, brush away the cobwebs.

W e've all accumulated a great deal of information and beliefs over the years, been constantly corrected and steered in a compliant direction. We've learnt:

- What a circle is, a square, colours and how to mix them,
- History, mathematics and grammar,
- To fight, argue and feel sorry for ourselves,
- How to interact with others through various television programmes,
- Unhappiness, fear, dissatisfaction, insecurity and disappointment,
- How to store stress and anger and how to be in dysfunctional relationships,
- That we can bury it all if we take drugs and drink alcohol.

We've absorbed so much more; now we have an opportunity to get rid of the lot. Can we do it? Do we want to?

When we discover that the mess in our world is coming from our own mind, when we realise it's a *collective* mind, when we see we've been investing our most valuable assets in an external structure and when we're able to discern that the mind is cluttered, what can we *do* about it? An intelligence needing no assistance will guide us, as and when we're ready to take each step; we need only allow it to do so and stay focused on our goals. We've got much more inside us than is visible with just a fleeting glance. Our lives have become what they are because of information overload and if we're not happy, we can stop listening to it.

Instead of watching television try turning it off for one week; shut down all media sources. It's got to be worth trying for a more peaceful life; not a huge sacrifice to make. If you turn it on again in a week it'll seem very different to you, but only if you haven't peeked at it down the pub, in the chip shop or through your neighbour's window while suffering withdrawal symptoms. We seek peace in the world but when we turn off the noise and find it, we become bored and restless. It's like driving at seventy mph on the motorway and then turning off on to a quiet country road at thirty miles per hour; it feels like you're not moving. There's a period of adjustment to wind down from the frenzied activity of a media-fuelled existence. There are many people who say the television is *company* and my mother was one of them; how can a machine be company? How has it become possible to live life - in front of a screen - passively watching other people living theirs? Our lives have become what they are now because of our actions and if we're not happy, we must stop doing what created them. We need to stop waiting for someone else to 'make a difference', or to change our world. The world won't change … *we* have to.

This may seem like an odd statement but in the realm of the abstract, things don't work as they did in the 'concrete' one. A new awareness arises that extends our self-imposed boundaries enabling us to think in an entirely new way. As long as we're reliant on a system to provide us with the security we seek, which it doesn't do, we'll not be able to see the clutter in our minds. There's a transition between the known and the unknown and it's this murky river we fear entering; perhaps because we don't want to leave or perhaps because of the uncertainty of what lies ahead. We don't feel we're good enough or that we deserve better so we stay where we are just in case we find ourselves out on a limb; homeless, starving and alone. These are just a few of the ways we've been taught to live in fear and all these fears live in the river.

There are some ways in which physical work can help us through this transition. Let's see how we can change something with regard to our accumulated clutter. Say for example, we've been storing things in the attic of our home for many years and it's so cluttered we can't get into it or find a particular item we're looking for; we've also forgotten most of the things we put up there. We're terrified of the thought of clearing it out for several reasons; it's a *lot* of work, we don't want to part with things because they might prove useful someday, they might increase in value, they have sentiment attached to them, they're not doing any harm up there, we could make a lot of money at a car boot sale one day and we might want to pass them on to our children. These are just some of our delaying tactics which project into the future and draw from the past; not too different from our minds. So we delay and delay, keep the hatch closed and try to forget there's anything up there. This is exactly what we do with projections into the future and our past experiences; the mind doesn't live in the now.

I know someone whose attic was a full, dark and musty place; he'd been storing things up there for thirty-five years and these included such things as; baby toys and equipment; books, lamps and shades, iron beds, empty cardboard boxes, buckets and spades, old record decks and an old car windscreen for a car he no longer had. An opportunity arose for him to get rid of the lot and it took many weekends, courage, donations and numerous trips to the rubbish dump but on his final descent from the ladder leading up there, he came down with a huge smile on his face and dusted off his hands. In the physical realm, physical work was needed. However, he'd cleared a great deal of historical clutter from his mind at the same time and this hadn't been his intention; he felt freer and never went up there again. It's not necessary to go through a physical process, but it was an added bonus. By realising he could now let go of things he'd been clinging to, he simplified his life and never looked back or missed anything he'd disposed of. More importantly, he recognised how much better he felt inside. A huge bonus was that he never passed this clutter on to his children.

By recognising our minds are cluttered with all its implications, the process of clearing has already begun without us lifting a finger. For example:

- Which memories do you hold on tightly to?
- Do you bear a grudge that you're reluctant to let go of?
- What resentments do you cling to?

Answer these questions honestly and then question the answers to begin the process. There's a need for determination and it's not a soft option; we need to take the plunge and be prepared to get 'wet'. It's no good re-arranging the clutter or dusting it off, because it's still *there* taking up space; it has to go. Things will change for the better if we return to point zero. If we can let go of everything there's no attic to clear. The clutter is not solid; it doesn't exist anymore than the past or future yet we keep it under lock and key. It can't be seen and it's not tangible. It's there because thought created it and we believe it's real - the reason it remains is we aren't willing to let go of it and can't imagine freedom from its weight.

One reason I never completed my autobiography is that my mind kept arguing with me. When I wasn't writing my mind told me I ought to be; when I wrote, it told me I was wasting my time. My mind wouldn't let go of these issues or others and as a consequence I put them to one side for many years; the mind is always contrary. It'll tell you one thing and when you listen to it, it'll tell you another; its contents are all in a muddle. I wanted to show people they could recover from their problems or past traumas if they were strong, but my mind argued and argued and it's still arguing even though I'm writing an entirely different book. I know no matter what I do, it'll still argue with me. The difference now, is that I understand the process better. My mind is increasingly silent.

~~~

Does a baby come from somewhere silent into this world? I've often wondered at what age its *spirit* enters the body, if that's how it works. Something tells me it's at the moment of birth but I'm not certain and I don't think anyone can be. It must be quite a shocking experience when a baby first opens its eyes; I wonder what it thinks, if anything at all, of its world and its inability to communicate in it. In my experiences, with my three children, babies don't feel separate from anything. Their world is full of innocence, excitement and exploration. A baby doesn't know if a person is tall, short, fat, thin, rich or poor; it can't see nationality or race; it observes with no judgement. It has no opinions about religions or politics and it knows no fear. It has no understanding of language and it doesn't care if it's wearing pink or blue. A new-born child doesn't know its name and doesn't know ours either; it doesn't know anything except hunger, pain, comfort and discomfort. It's essential a baby be held, loved and cared for as it can't manage even the most basic of its needs without us; these are imperative for its healthy development.

We project our needs on to a baby and we pass on the corrupt information that has been written on to our own minds; it's passed on through siblings too. As a baby learns it becomes separated and judgemental; it can be badly behaved and spoilt because we want to give it all the things we feel we were deprived of. It grows up resentful because we punish it as our parents punished us. It also becomes confused and develops some of our traits; how can a baby become anything else when we've scrawled our bad experiences over its pure and beautiful blank piece of paper? We may not feel we're *personally* responsible for this but we *do* contribute towards it; a baby also picks these things up from friends, schools, books and entertainment. In fifty or so years' time these babies will be the administrators of our world and all we can expect is continuity of the system we have now; though more extreme because the mind of society is absorbing more and more unimportant information.

This process has been repeated throughout generations and it's so ingrained that we don't know it's there. The collective mind is a filthy place full of hatred, conflict, selfishness and confusion and the events that led us here were less harmful than the damage caused by holding on to the memories of them. We have to make a conscious decision to return to the state of a new-born baby; innocence. It's through innocence we can find peace and clarity and through innocence we can see the world through a baby's eyes. The veil of our experiences must be removed in order that we can see again the beauty of Creation and the discovery of it. A flower doesn't need to be told how to open in the mornings or an acorn how to grow into an oak tree. The baby came into its world with a 'clear mind' and it's us who filled it with nonsense. We can learn a great deal from life from watching a baby and listening to young toddlers. When toddlers ask us 'Why? Why? Why?' they're usually being more reasonable than we are. We reply - irritated - because we know the 'whys' go on forever and we don't like children asking 'too many questions'. We've stopped learning from children and we teach them the way we were taught. We buy books about bringing up babies; this must be innate. Why do we need to learn from a book about when to feed a child, what to feed a child and when to put it to sleep? Why do we need instruction manuals on how to become a human being?

Change is Possible

Changing our life is an uphill struggle ... until we get to the top.

O ur expectations on a path of self-discovery are greater than what happens. Many of us are given a false perspective by the *enlightenment* industry and mistakenly expect a 'Road to Damascus' epiphany; all our problems disappearing in the moment. When this doesn't happen we become discouraged; clarity about 'who we are' isn't going to arrive in an 'abracadabra' fashion. It takes work, courage and commitment; it's not a hat we can take off when it suits us - it's a whole new way of life and it begins with us.

Looking at people without judgement or criticism regardless of who they are takes practise. Our long standing beliefs can't be wiped away like chalk from a blackboard; we have to constantly correct ourselves because these are old habits and the mind holds on to them. This can be frustrating when we put all our efforts into changing; we can't see the results even though we're desperate for them. We want to love everybody but there are still people we trip over. A word of warning: the initial enthusiasm and excitement we felt - when we began our journey - evaporates when we encounter these obstacles and distractions. They become our excuse not to progress. Overcoming these 'hurdles' helps to strengthen us further; keeping us on track.

In theory, I understood that we're all 'One' but in practise, I didn't feel it. I couldn't see how *I* could be part of something so magnificent and not know about it. Consciousness and One were words buzzing around the internet faster than spam. The concept was hard to get to grips with; it meant accepting that people I didn't like were - *shock horror* - part of *me*! With hindsight, this was because I didn't feel I belonged to a 'group' on equal terms; I'd always been an outsider. 'One' felt like an exclusive group and triggered old memories that told me I wasn't welcome; or worthy. The feeling could be likened to turning up at a gala ball with an entrance ticket that says 'No Admission'. Just as with the spiritual group in Brighton the people I encountered were the same; divided, confused and self-centred.

We want to be 'There' but can't because we won't give ourselves time to raise our consciousness level - we want to arrive at our destination without all the hassle of the journey. How easy would it be to understand a story by reading just the first and last pages of a book? We don't want to face our shadows. As

I recognised the patterns of these thoughts and watched them; they occurred less frequently. It isn't necessary to change anything at all; merely to observe rather than take action. When we can see and comprehend this, changes take place without our interference; we don't need to fuel them. We can then walk down the street and instead of seeing stereotypes we see Humanity as a whole; we're all harbouring resentments, all suffering, all searching and all seeking freedom from conflict.

~~~

I don't subscribe to the beliefs - in some modern self-help books - that claim we can do what we want in the world even if it means murder and mayhem. Yes we can do it but, is it intelligent or in our highest interest to do so? It isn't if we wish to access higher levels of consciousness and I don't believe these can be accessed without; grace, good intention, wisdom or a sincere heart. I don't believe these realms can be 'gate-crashed' with the use of drugs. Sure, people can access other realms and there are many of them. Can we be sure where we are when we take drugs? We can't be sure where we are when we don't. We don't know what or where these realms are; how can we trust them? Drugs aren't the key to awareness; we must get there alone.

Are we here just to play? If so, wouldn't the possibility exist for us all? From birth, we're faced with difficulties and struggles that don't belong in a 'playground'. I don't believe we're here to cartwheel our way around the earth visiting its wonderful places. There's so much to see and do that we can't do it all in one lifetime; given the type of society we live in. There are too many borders and barriers in place preventing us doing that freely and more are being put up for the next generation. We're too busy wanting the things our society produces and we want it all now. We're attracted to ownership of cars, homes and the paraphernalia we fill them with and we want them - no matter what the cost. Most of all we're attracted to other people's 'successes' and 'failures'; celebrities and gossip.

If we're here to play - and we do enjoy playing - we seem to have lost the plot. Play is aggressive; we play with an 'opponent'. Humanity forgot how to have fun a long time ago; even young children can't play together for long without conflict arising. We've lost so much sensitivity to the earth and to each other that playing (other than in a prescribed form; parks, toys, playgrounds, sports etc.) has become impossible. This is clear when watching children in groups, men playing football or any social gathering; we're far too competitive.

I watched quite a few children playing football when I used to take my son training. I saw competing parents standing behind the lines pushing and egging their sons on; transferring their own beliefs (information) on to them. It was hard to tell who the real competitors were; the children playing football, or the parents competing for their own superiority. Sometimes I'd see a father's disappointment from his own childhood being projected on to his son, who didn't enjoy the game. This can result in the child feeling insecure and inadequate; seeking the approval of others for the rest of his life. Learning how to change our ingrained habits and not pass them on to our children goes a long way to improving the society we live in. Children need to be allowed to live their lives without making up for *ours*. Should we shape them into someone we consider to be our 'ideal'? Competition is a struggle for supremacy and this must mean we want to *defeat* someone else; does this sound like 'war' to you?

The father mentioned above was looking to his son to fulfil the missed successes of his own past ambitions rather than encouraging the child to find his own talent. The children are keen to receive their parent's approval and are unable to get it. The world has become what it is today because not enough people question their actions or think about the consequences those actions will have on their children and society. We're far too accepting of what society tells us we should *do* and *be*; the comfortable option. This mentality has been passed on from our ancestors and will linger on into future generations, if we allow it to.

~~~

If we take the underground to work every day, beginning our journey at Victoria and terminating at King's Cross and we always go anticlockwise on the Circle Line, we'll never know there are alternative routes that, if nothing else, provide us with a different experience. For a change, we could go in a clockwise direction or we could take the Victoria Line. We'll pass different stations and see new faces and have a different experience; we may even come across an old friend. This new experience sharpens our minds because we have to pay far more attention on an unfamiliar route and this requires the attention of the *conscious* mind rather than the *subconscious* one; this can happen when we're willing to make changes to our 'routines' which in their own way are 'addictions'.

Why are our beliefs stale? We've been subjected to so much repetition that we accept it as 'normal'; we don't question the boredom or ugliness of it. Also, because we've been brought up and educated in order to perpetuate the functioning of a society that encourages violence, immorality, competition and injustice in order to profit financially and egotistically. Financially, because the rich get richer and the poor get poorer; egotistically, because where there's money there's power and where there's power, subservience. There's only so far we can inflate a balloon before it bursts. We're put under a great deal of stress from birth and the build-up of tension results in resentment and conflict. We've given away our power and though we don't trust the people we've given it to, we're afraid (or don't want) to take it back.

Self-help books can't help too much. The way to help ourselves is to seek the truth and to be sincere in our search without making selfish demands like trying to manifest a new car; more money; a boyfriend or anything else. Why not start climbing the mountain instead of walking around its base poking it with a stick in an attempt to move it or check it's strong enough to take our load? Most of us never make the climb. Our intentions must be pure and a greater appreciation of this comes with time and patience. Until I opened my heart and gave up 'control' I couldn't see I was writing the wrong book. I'd never thought about writing a self-help/philosophy book. Instead, for many years I struggled and swam upstream never making any progress. I couldn't accept the autobiography I'd worked so hard on wasn't going to be read.

Self-help books can't do the 'job' for us because they're written by people who've found their *own* way by which ever means they needed and these may not be the same as ours. They can guide us, but our path may lead us on another road altogether. We can't be aware of the writers' intentions either and this is *very* important; I discuss why in the next chapter. It's important to understand our own intentions and I still question my own. Our cluttered minds are incapable of rational thought and the annoying voice in our heads interrupts just when we think we're making progress. Self-help books also serve to provide much needed comfort and security; they tell us just what we want to hear and it's not necessarily in our best interest. I'm not knocking them and I've read quite a few, but what I'm saying is *we* must put into practise these concepts ourselves and for each one of us the process varies. This book is also a self-help book but I'd say it's more about philosophy which, according to one dictionary definition is "an attitude of rationality, patience, composure, and calm in the presence of troubles and annoyances."[16] To debate the matter is not worth the effort and would serve no good purpose.

Another way in which we can make changes is to be honest with ourselves. Recognising our own imperfections and taking responsibility for them is not an easy task. Included in these are our insecurities, self-hatred, prejudices, judgements and our expectations of others. We lie a great deal too but we call these lies, diplomacy, tact, consideration, common sense, light on the truth and even 'necessary'. One example of this is how we lie to someone who asks us whether or not we like their new dress or hairstyle. In general, we'll say it suits them and it's lovely even if we loathe it. We'll also lie if someone asks us if they've lost weight (and they haven't); we tell them what they want to hear. Quite often we search for flattery and *want* to be lied to. For example, if we ask someone if we've lost weight or not, we already know the truth and it's usually 'no' or we wouldn't need to ask. Do we really want an honest answer? But if someone can confirm the lie for us it makes us feel better and we accept it as truth. Lying has become an okay thing to do because we convince ourselves we do it for the benefit of others; to avoid offending them.

When we lie to ourselves, which we do, we then begin to justify it. For example, if we're an alcoholic or want to give up smoking or lose weight we make up excuses, which permit us to procrastinate because we don't really want to do it. I know of people who've told lies so long they end up believing them themselves. Are our lies always for our own benefit or gain? Have you ever telephoned someone and said "I'm calling on behalf of a friend" when it was for yourself? My sister used to ask me to make telephone calls for her. She couldn't understand why I refused; I couldn't understand why she wouldn't do it herself. This is a strange kind of lie because there's no real need for it and it makes no difference to the outcome; the person on the other end of the telephone can't see us. Why do we want to hide and if we can't be seen, what is it we're hiding? Why do we hide behind internet monikers and often have a variety of them for the same social media? We can change this behaviour and though it can make us feel vulnerable, we begin to feel much stronger and more self-confident once we get over the hurdles; we also can't get 'caught out' in the lie at a later date. Vulnerability is strength.

I'm a pretty black and white character and generally get straight to the point cutting out all the middle stuff which I call 'colouring in'. What it means is I can see the point without all the detail and when I'm given detail I often lose track of conversations; I'm always asking for the short version of the longer stories people recount. I do the same with films and watch the end first to see if I like it; it doesn't spoil the film at all for me and nowadays I see most films as formulaic. I've gone off the subject of lying but here's how it connects.

I see a lie as a *lie* which means it's an untruth and there can be no 'grade' or 'scale' of lying. For example we may lie to our children when we cook a blended vegetable soup and not tell them a particular vegetable they dislike is in it; we may even deny we put it in if they ask. To me, either way is lying because both are deceitful and deceit is a lie. But my friends say this isn't a lie because it's for the good of the children who wouldn't eat it otherwise. In another example, one child wanted a particular brand of tomato sauce and the parent substituted the contents of an empty branded bottle with a different brand. The child ate this for years without complaining. Is this lying? How would you feel if you found out someone was doing this to you, like selling you fake designer label clothing?

Any lie, in my opinion, as it's untrue is not a good idea because it's the lie that goes into the Consciousness field and it reflects on each and every one of us. When we add up all the big lies with all the so-called little ones, there's a great many 'lies' out there. So it doesn't matter if it's a 'white lie' or an 'outright lie' or whatever name we wish to give it; it's not the truth. When we start to study our own behaviour we begin to recognise some not very nice traits we acquired over the years and wouldn't have attributed to ourselves. These same traits were at the heart of our criticism of others. Just by recognising these traits we're making changes; change must occur when our consciousness rises to a higher level.

We analyse everything in this world. What are we looking for in this analysis and do we really want to find it? We buy books, but no matter how many of them tell us what we *need* to hear, we pretend we haven't heard it. We're seeking permission to continue doing what we're already doing; but the books won't give it to us. We make every excuse under the sun and convince ourselves we don't need to change. We're avoiding facing ourselves in the mirror of 'nakedness'. Human beings are diligent when it comes to searching for something they don't really want to know or see; we know where not to look. One of the reasons for this behaviour is to delay our need for action and permit us to continue procrastinating; another is that we enjoy our illusions.

Why do we over-analyse these books? We enjoy being the way we are and search half-heartedly for change; we're not really ready to take the plunge? But when we analyse we're really analysing ourselves and not the book; the world exists only inside our heads. Something inside us wants to stay the way we are and avoid making changes. In order to change we must first accept we're not as nice as we pretend to be and that we've a tendency to inertia. Why, isn't important, but recognising that we do it is.

We prefer the familiarity of the comfort zone we've encased ourselves in, rather than dipping our toes in cold water elsewhere; it's a fear of the unknown. We're afraid of losing friends, annoying family, losing our jobs or our partners; it puts distance between us. Changing ourselves will inevitably lead to changes in our lives, of this there is no doubt. It changes the way the world sees us and it changes the way we see the world; we become strangers in it. This path has to be lived; it's not something you do on a rainy day when there's nothing else to pass the time with.

Information

Tune into another channel for more information.

During our lifetimes and after a person dies, our legacy permeates the Consciousness field, just as when we throw a stone into the water and the ripples spread out. The ripples of what we did with our life remain in the field; the memories, actions, emotions, intentions and bitterness; the *information* remains and it's 'clutter'. It's not just your mind - it's *our* mind; there's no real separation. The ripples of past miseries don't just disappear; if they did we couldn't access their information - we couldn't talk about them. If we don't heal and raise our level of consciousness, our fears, frustrations and anxieties remain trapped somewhere in space and time, in a cycle. They become 'immortal'; we don't allow them to die. We still watch war films and documentaries and go to the graveyards of all the dead; the information is still here. Humanity lost a lot of lives in senseless wars and it hasn't learnt from them. We've convinced ourselves we need to remember these wars to prevent them happening again; this is illogical. Taken to another level, it's the same as going through our lives remembering all the horrors of our childhood and re-enacting them whenever we want a reminder of how awful they were so that they won't happen again; it makes no sense whatsoever. The mindset of Humanity won't change while it's trudging around in this cesspit of its past bloody atrocities. These wars have always happened and will always happen as long as we put our energy into them. We choose whether or not to remain in the deep end of this 'cesspit' - there *are* other options.

The world becomes a simpler place to live in when we discern it's made up of everything our senses perceive:

- The taste of an apple,
- The touch of a piece of wood,
- The smell of a peach,
- The sound of a bird,
- The sight of a sunrise,
- Our memories of childhood friends,

Everything is information; a continuous stream of it. If we record a rewritable disk to listen to and we get fed up with listening to 'Learn French the Easy

Way' we have the option to rewrite the information and begin learning 'Spanish', or listen to an audio book. The process of rewriting will erase the French lessons from the past and re-write the disk with something new. We can change our information.

Since our 'birth', information has been written on to our minds by our parents, family, educators, ourselves and the media; its roots are buried deep and we continue to absorb more information, which obscures our inner senses. In an interview with Conscious TV, Bruce Lipton said "When I put in the new programs, all of a sudden I started to find … my life completely turned around. All wonderful things started happening …"[17] We can change without help from anyone just by changing our thoughts and grasping the processes of our minds. It all sounds a little weird and because it's an abstract concept we don't comprehend how we can do it; we don't think we're clever enough. This is not true; anyone can do this. All we have to do is think about it and raise the questions and the changes will take care of themselves. We can get the hang of it quite fast. It's a bit like learning to ride a bicycle; if we struggle, we fall down.

The subconscious mind works rather like an autopilot on a set course which it won't deviate from without outside influence. This influence comes from the pilot who can change course; the pilot is our conscious mind. Many people live on autopilot without realising it. The conscious mind is in the Now, between thoughts, and it's clear of all the clutter and distractions that the subconscious mind won't let go of. It sounds strange but this is because it's so simple and the idea of writing information on to our mind seems ridiculous. We've been taught to re-write information with computers through a keyboard but we can't comprehend the process without inserting a disk or re-coding a computer program; we can't relate this to our mind.

We may buy what we think to be the latest computer or tablet but we still have the same basic programs on it; nothing's actually changed. The social media is already on the computer when we buy it; all we have to do is put our handles and passwords in - it's all done for us, whether we want it to or not. We're like amazing computers ourselves and far more amazing than any computer technology existing in society today. We don't need to know anything about science and we don't need a university education; this gets in the way of our spiritual progress rather than helping it. Science is a wonderful thing but it can't bring us to inner peace.

A strong enough will, brings changes into our lives and it's rather like the 'placebo' effect, in as much as "the effect is due to the power of suggestion."[18] I've changed my life many times in the past and I've always dreaded the future at the turning point. Now when I begin a new adventure the past and this *dread of the future* I used to feel seem so silly; it takes a bit of practise to see it this way and the biggest hurdle to overcome, you've guessed it, is the mind. It interrupts, convinced it'll all go wrong and it doesn't stop hammering this message in. It's robust and by watching it in action, we can gain a great deal of power over the control it has. The mind drags us down if we let it but we can take control so we're not influenced by the 'me' who wants to re-write information and the 'me' that doesn't. The mind will argue with us far less when we watch its reactions closely; it's negative and uncertain because this is the way the world is and has been for a long time. The mind is limited; it draws from the past and it can't see beyond; it is the 'cache' of Humanity. We resist change and only *we* can do something about it. The placebo effect is not very different to self-hypnosis; they're both essentially suggestion.

We've choices but sometimes we can't see them because the clouds are too dense and dark. If we want to break free from the clouds it's necessary to discern the traumas or difficulties of our pasts and recognise that we must come to terms with them; they can make us strong. We can choose to sit in a corner with our heads between our knees feeling glum, helpless, hard-done-by and perhaps take drugs or drink alcohol in an attempt to hide from our problems - or we can choose to help *ourselves*. The power of suggestion can entrap us; it's in our hands and not the hands of a 'specialist' or an outside 'authority'. Suggest we're helpless and we'll be unable to see our own power; suggest we're strong and once the seed is planted sit back and watch it grow, but we can't just leave it in the ground and walk away. Both are suggestions by thought and therefore not from the heart. The seed of the heart is harder to locate and this seed will not flourish on barren land. I've learnt to be grateful for my childhood and the difficulties that arose from it as without them I wouldn't be the person I am today. It took many years to stop believing I'd been given the 'short straw'; I gave it to myself. When we abandon all notions of straws; the load is lighter.

I can't emphasise enough that the only way to change is from within. There's no other way - no-one will come knocking on our door to save us or lead us into 'heaven'. I'm an ex-procrastinator who's struggled with life and always dipped my toes in water that was either too hot or too cold. I made myself fit into someone else's life because I didn't believe I'd the tools to create my own. A higher level of consciousness won't come to us; *we* have to go to it. It's only by altering our perspective and choosing different information that we bring harmony into our lives 'now'; we don't have to wait. We make more effort to explain why we can't do something than it would take to achieve it. We believe we don't have power because we've been told it time and time again. It isn't true. We store what we've been told; memory is information!

If a child's ideas are belittled and rejected, then rejection in adulthood could produce out-of-proportion angry or other emotional responses. The rejections trigger *learnt* mechanistic responses from our memories. So for example, if someone pointed a finger aggressively at us when we were younger and started screaming and shouting; we'll feel the same emotion if someone does it now; they need only point a finger to trigger our reaction. We react to the stimuli, autopilot kicks in and this is how arguments and disagreements occur. These reactions come from memory and they'll remain 'on alert' until we recognise how we submit to them. Triggers sit like landmines in our minds, waiting to be trodden on. By recognising this process, we begin to discern how our emotions can get out of control and in no time at all we're able to stop the inevitable detonation. The ability to do this stays with us and we're able to respond better in our relationships with family members, friends or acquaintances.

As our consciousness level rises so does our ability to react to old problems in new ways. Sometimes it feels as though we're not making progress but this is the mind putting up resistance and this voice, which is insistent, shouldn't be listened to. When a drop of rain falls into a stream it doesn't just disappear; it becomes the stream. From the raindrop to the ocean the process is fully automatic. The raindrop doesn't struggle and we don't need to either; struggle is resistance. If we force questions then the struggle prevents clarity; struggle is also 'information' and the results it gets are frustration and failure. The resistance resulting from our 'struggle program' is like a barrier between us and new information; this is why we don't, or can't, listen to anyone else's views or see the world from their perspective.

We're holding on to what we've been taught and we're clinging to what's familiar because we're comfortable with it. It's part of our programming to accept this safety net. If we decide to let go and I mean *really* let go of our programming, then new information can and will be written. Everything is information; how can it be anything else? If we've any doubts about 'information' then let's think about a baby. It begins as a single cell and information written on its DNA instructs it to divide in the most incredible programming language; the instructions are hard-wired, like the BIOS in a computer that controls basic hardware functions. If we still doubt, then let's think about how a single cell can produce such an incredible and magnificent human being? Where do the instructions come from for the cell to divide into two identical cells and develop into a hair, a bladder, a liver, a vein or a finger? How do identical cells go off and become different things? How do they form an eye? How do they form veins and the blood that flows through them for our entire lifetimes? Where do the instructions come from that start the heart beating, the ears hearing, the eyes seeing and the incredible number of other functions we're blessed with? How many different functions do these cells perform? How do they create our fingerprints; unique to each human being? How does thought occur? How many people have ever given these phenomena any thought at all? To be a 'human being' is something we take for granted, rather than reflect upon the Wonder of it. We're *joy-riding* in these bodies and know nothing about them or how they *actually* work. We use them to play games, dress up, push them to their limits and decorate them with jewels. We're absolutely amazing, yet don't think about the miracle of life while living out our relatively mundane existence. We ignore the miracles that surround us; and then hope that one will drop into our laps. If we wrote down the processes needed to perform these functions we would need more than the biggest library in the world to store all the information in.

Comfort and Security

Break out of your comfort cage.

F rom the moment we're born we're kept in close proximity by our guardians, whether kindly or not; our basic needs were taken care of otherwise we wouldn't be alive today. However, our psychological needs weren't and our questions on this subject were rejected and discouraged. We need *true* psychological security so we can grow up free to question and explore, or at least try to find out about our true purpose in this world - without any fear or obstructions. When we can do this, we'll stop leaving our problems for our children to inherit. We must seek the truth of our existence; it isn't very different to finding our way out of a complicated and ingenious labyrinth - way beyond our technological capabilities. This labyrinth can be likened to a Book of our own creation, entirely written by us, to be read and understood to be the Book of all our experiences.

I can't recall ever having met a human being who was happy or contented. They've been coy, rebellious, aggressive, bullies, cunning, greedy, envious, vain, clingy, false and the characteristic list goes on and on. We all wear a mask to disguise these traits and it isn't until we peel them off that our true nature will be revealed. I can attribute all these traits to myself at various times in the past but I wouldn't have admitted to them at the time. I've yet to meet a happy and secure member of the human race. The result of our upbringing is we're afraid and self-loathing and it's for *these* reasons we seek comfort and security in physical things. Because we were denied these in our youth, we fear the loss of the little we get and crave more, but there are few comforters in the world other than possessions, bank balances, entertainment, the lies we tell ourselves and familiar faces. So we're left searching for but unable to find what we need most in the world. We fear violence, loneliness and the end of our own existence and these fears are born from the society we've created. We're judgemental, competitive, inconsiderate, superior and selfish; I don't paint a pretty picture of Humanity, do I? Success is not measured by how much good we do in our lives or how much joy we bring to others. As mentioned earlier in this book the label 'do-gooder' has a bad name and so does any form of spirituality. How is it possible we reject these? The train called 'society' is a runaway and it's accelerating; it'll take a miracle to stop it. On the other hand, runaway trains must crash or run out of fuel sooner or later.

Success is measured by salaries, savings, weight, class, house size, car, academic achievements, friends on facebook, followers on twitter and what version of technical accessories we walk around with. Our ambitions include being able to pay off our mortgages, get fit, meet our ideal partner, have wonderful holidays and to save enough money for our old age. Consider this; we go to our graves without any of it. What about the people who die before they reach retirement age? What have they worked all their lives for? Is it any wonder we seek comfort and security? Is it any wonder we've found artificial forms of them hiding ourselves inside virtual reality games? We now hide from each other behind the mask of the internet with the ability to keep our status 'invisible'. When we hide from others we're hiding our own shame; why else don't we want to be seen? We can't face ourselves and because of this we can't face the truth about our existence; it sounds too far-fetched.

~~~

Why do we need approval and how did we become so insecure? A baby may be given a comfort blanket, a dummy or a soft toy to comfort it and when they're taken away, because it's considered silly for older children to have them, the baby will suffer from the loss of the emotional comfort they provided. If a baby isn't given these pacifiers they still seek comfort because it's in our nature to need to be held and loved; it's essential for our good health. Without it we become withdrawn and insecure and these thoughts in the mind of a child are unhealthy and long lasting. They manifest themselves in illness and behavioural disturbances such as rebellion, anorexia, violence, depression, aggression, withdrawal, bullying, self-abuse and the seeking of abuse by others; quite a horrible list. A child will misbehave to get attention as it gets older and even a *punishment* gives him the attention he craves; he needs the 'hit'. Every time a baby is denied emotional support it buries the need for it a little deeper. Ideally, a baby should have complete attention from 'at home' parents, day and night but most families can't afford to do this; both need to go out to work, so they employ someone else to guard the baby until their return. When we're tired out or just too busy we put our children in playpens, cots or cribs (cages) … think about this concept a little before rejecting it outright. We do this because society has made it very difficult not to; we have to pay ever increasing and unreasonable bills.

We require comfort when something is missing in our lives; what we get is the consolation prize. What we lack is psychological security and self knowledge; without these we can't experience freedom. The artificial comfort we're given is usually given for the convenience of the parents. Because the need for security is innate we seek it elsewhere; we've not been educated in a way that enables us to provide it for ourselves. If we don't find it we look for the familiar comforts we've become accustomed to. Security blankets and the like pacify a baby; they don't provide security. Our need for psychological security has been replaced by something physical. We need security so much that we accept it wherever we can find it and this is a big problem in society; particularly if we come from abusive backgrounds. Our children play in structured playgrounds enclosed by fences; why aren't they climbing trees anymore? Are we going to keep them so safe and physically secure they'll end up under lock and key? The world is *alive* and we don't notice it.

We've become dependent on physical things and other people. The security we think we get from them is an illusion and it has the opposite effect. For this reason, because of a strong dependency, we continue to seek security and comfort from outside sources; this problem isn't talked about in society. The more we accumulate, the more we want and the more we struggle to let go. We've become dependent on other people to confirm our own existence and we look to them to tell us what our place in the world should be (accountant, dustman, upper class etc.) -anywhere we can fit in. If we can't fit in we turn to alcohol, drugs and other addictive substances or habits because we feel safe hiding behind them. Over-indulgence is the biggest comforter in today's society and manifests itself mostly in food, money, pleasure, exercise and entertainment.

We look to authority figures for what we lack as though they're different to us in some way; they're *not* and they've the same problems and insecurities that we do; they've sought security in material things and ignored their spiritual journey. Because they've the same problems, they can't help us; they can't know the deepest levels of the psyche or their own insecurities. This is because we're always looking outside for comforts and not on the inside, where we don't need any. Comforters are given by our parents when we're babies and the pattern continues when we're old enough to go to school with points systems and gold stars for our work and 'correct' behaviour.

When we make an effort in this society, or excel in something like an exam, a sport, acting, science, a job or anything else, our 'reward' is physical and an illusion; a certificate, a medal, an Oscar, a pay rise or even the Nobel prize. We also get rewards such as 'recognition' and 'compliments'. If we reflect for a moment on how this works we can see it's these comforters that increase the power of our egos. We like rewards because they allow us to feel proud of ourselves and encourage us to 'do better'. They also give us outside approval which allows us to experience the feeling of worthiness; when we get it, we strive to attain more. The rewards are temporary and therefore not worth having; this world is also temporary. We've been taught to strive for artificial excellence, both physically and academically, which is measured by grades or rewards.

We've become accustomed to seeking security, but we're unable to find it. We look for:

- Financial security, in order that we lack for nothing right up to our deaths,
- Personal security through things like self-defence and relationships,
- Electronic security for our homes, cars and other belongings,

- Physical security through fitness, diets and health,
- Psychological security through all the above, the media and the approval of others;

However, all we get are illusory security and comfort. We've created foolish ideas, like 'comfort foods' and 'retail therapy'; is Humanity ready to see that these are not only illusions but ridiculous concepts? They're 'pop therapy'; trendy, misleading and impermanent. We can't find happiness or satisfaction in them and the reason for this is we're wrapped up in poor imitations of true and permanent security; this can't be found on the outside.

Comfort in wars is a particularly difficult subject because we're complacent about them. Their regularity makes them the 'norm' and we accept war as unavoidable and as being a part of life; we accept it as inevitable. Our greatest comfort from wars is our own survival of them and we believe we're protected by governments who are 'looking after our needs' - this is an illusion; war can't bring peace. War brings death and destruction and it's about time we woke up to this. A soldier goes to war prepared to kill or be murdered and that's not a very clever thing to do. Wars serve to create more conflict because they create bitterness and hatred between whatever nations or authorities are fighting it out and also to those observing them; they create further division. More and more the only comfort and security we can depend on is 'survival'.

Absurdities

Picture a disco ball; can one tiny mirror be aware of the others? Are they not all part of the ball? Can the tiny mirror be aware of itself?

Don't you think humans are curious beings? People are bloody-minded, contradictory, cruel, kind, funny, sad, inconsistent and capable of feats of outstanding brilliance and phenomenal stupidity. What drives us to behave in this manner? What drives us to insist we're right when we know we're wrong (as it were)? We like our lives to be difficult and we ensure they stay that way; woe betide anyone who tries to make our life easier. Dissatisfied with our lot in life we spend time creating and perfecting our alter ego; often based on one of society's *role models*. Francois de la Rochefoucauld, a 17th century French author said "We become so accustomed to disguise ourselves to others that at last we are disguised to ourselves."[19] Not much has changed, has it?

Changing our appearance can be likened to replacing the label on a bottle of wine; the contents remain the same. No matter how stylish we are or how long we spend every day on our appearance; we remove our disguises when we go to bed just like everyone else. We're fundamentally the same as each other; we hide behind our masks. When we wake up in the morning after a 'night out' we look ragged and wouldn't leave our houses without *camouflage*. I've a friend who won't open the front door without putting her 'face' on - no matter who's calling. Is it more important that we like our own image or that other people do? Any alteration we make to our external appearance is because of programming. This programming gives importance to fashion, make-up, mimicry, competition, self-judgement and vanity. It comes from images and expectations placed in our minds and most of us aren't aware that we're trying to live up to expectations; we're the most unnatural beings on the *planet*.

Some women walk around in uncomfortable stilettos and no matter how much pain they're in; they still wear them and this can lead to having our feet operated on in later life. In general, a man must keep up a 'macho' image and not do things like 'cry' or 'show pain'. Just how foolish are we:

- We tattoo and pierce our body parts,
- Get drunk, stoned, overeat, starve,

- Humiliate ourselves, just to be on television
- Squeeze ourselves into clothes that are too tight,
- Turn celebrities into gods,
- Fight, cheat, defend and ignore truth,
- Transform our bodies through plastic surgery; to name just a few.

We agree to and enjoy suffering in return for our images. Are we nuts or what?

Outside, and within academic circles few people want to know who they really are. We don't think about this subject and want to make the most of our bodies before they wrinkle and wear out; we're 'clutching at straws'. On the whole, Humanity doesn't care where it came from or where it's going. We change our behaviour according to who we're speaking to such as; our parents, doctors, lawyers, employers or our friends. We rarely behave in the same way when we're alone and the relationship we have with ourselves can't be understood by another - *we* don't understand it. No-one can ever truly know another person. How amazing is this fact? We know *and* don't know we're playing these roles; our chosen persona snaps into place as and when required.

People scan us; as though we're a vulgar piece of art or an object to be desired. We play 'judge' because it's far easier to judge others than it is ourselves. What does judging others confirm and in what way does it comfort us? Are we judging by our own standards or the standards we would like to have? We decide instantly whether or not we like another person on looks alone and the impression we form of them comes from programming; it comes from memory. For example, they may not be wearing fashionable clothing, or we may think they're too fat, too short or 'could do better'. Most of us believe we're better than we actually are; but we don't feel good about ourselves at all. We're frauds and we choose our personalities from the variety that are on offer; we select and combine them.

It's sad that we propagate this culture. We do it because of deep-seated insecurities and the suppression of our psychological needs. You must have noticed the way we behave with mobile phones, particularly when they weren't 'omnipresent'. It's easy to tell when someone isn't *really* talking or texting anybody, but rather pretending to be. We do these things because we don't want people to see our weaknesses or think we're not popular or 'normal'. It's a terrible thing to feel alone in a crowd; the phone becomes our ally. We can be 'loud in a crowd' when we talk on our phones or socialise with friends; we don't care if no-one wants to listen to our conversations; it's our penny masquerade. Why are we dishonest about our behaviour and ignorant of the wishes of others? Why do we want people to notice and like us? Why do we want to think we're 'better' than *we* think we are? Underneath the protective shield we don, we're all vulnerable and we're all insecure.

There's a great expression; 'to be a fly on the wall'. Imagine being a fly on the wall of a friend, relative, or a well-known figure. I'm certain you'd find out things you never knew or could have guessed about them and some of those things would be shocking, particularly if you've known them for a long time. We remove some of our masks when we're alone and some of these changes may be minor, like putting our feet up on the sofa with shoes on or they may be major, such as having deep-seated perversions. But behind closed doors there's a great deal going on we're not willing to share with others, no matter how close we are to them. When we're alone we feel a sense of freedom as we can't be criticised or judged. However, when we're on this path of self-discovery we lose that feeling of *freedom* because we become our own critics and there's nowhere to hide.

We know there are many masks we hide behind that we're reluctant to take off. We fear stripping ourselves naked more than we fear anything else. What would you see if you were a fly on your own wall? What would you change about yourself? Just how many roles do we play simultaneously and how do we choose which persona to put on and for whom? Do we create a new role when we meet a new person? We know how to play a great many parts and we don't need scripts, directors, crews or a producer; we do the lot on our own without even thinking about it. We never take off all our masks - we wear them on many levels - but we know they're not us.

Our behaviour, when we're alone can be complicated. The world becomes more confusing when we realise that we don't understand *ourselves*. Think about the man I mentioned earlier who plays the role of a 'captain' on a fleet of ships in a virtual reality game. Who is he in the game? On the one hand he may be an *all-powerful* head of a fleet with many compliant subjects at his 'beck and call', who must - without complaining - obey his orders. On the other hand, as human beings are all fakes in one way or another there's a good chance he could be lying about the role he's playing online. Perhaps his role is more humble such as scrubbing decks, but he's pretending to have a higher rank?

This gets complicated when we realise he has to play multiple roles at the same time. The 'actor' at his computer terminal is cleverly directing the actor on the screen and supplying him with the script; the captain can't make errors because the character of the player would show through. Other cast members in the game wouldn't suspect the man behind the computer is perhaps of short stature, insecure, has no work and probably never set foot on a ship in his life. The man behind the screen is the puppeteer and he's pulling all the strings. Who is pulling his? It would be disconcerting for a person playing out these simultaneous roles to have someone walk into the room and 'catch them in the act', as it were. The sudden switch to the role they usually play when we're around - not the puppeteer or captain - would leave them somewhat disoriented as they wonder how much we'd seen or heard. We don't appreciate our personal space being invaded and we need to instantly put on a mask; which one would depend on who's walked in on us and what they'd seen. Have you ever had unexpected visitors who walk into a room at the most inopportune times and realise something about you they didn't know before?

Imagine what it would be like to look into a mirror and not see the face we've become accustomed to. Understanding this concept is important because as long as we look outside to change ourselves whether it's 'extreme' through plastic surgery or 'subtle' like putting on a new pair of earrings, we can't change. It's all an act and an illusion. An illusion created by the society we live in; created by us. We don't *want* to look inside ourselves and this is because in some absurd way we're frightened of finding out the truth; we don't want to let go of the illusions and we don't want to see the shadows we cast. We don't want to change what's familiar; we fear non-existence. We prefer to stay with the 'ego' because the alternative is too horrible to contemplate. It's these fears that solidify our belief in our *name* as being who we are. If we give up the image and the name we think there'll be nothing left.

Society tells us what to wear, what to do and what not to do. It tells us from an early age so it becomes ingrained through laws, signs, rules, controls and the media. It tells us what to watch on the television and what to do in our free time through clever manipulation; we don't know it's doing it because we believe we're free. Have you noticed how many people play tennis when Wimbledon's on the television or how there are more joggers leading up to the London Marathon, regardless of whether they're running in it? We feel motivated and inspired by the 'devotees'. We love to do what others are doing and we copy language trends too. Where and when did we first hear the word 'awesome'?

We're told who to judge and who not to so that we'll listen to some people and not to others. We tend to look down on so-called lowly professions such as dustmen or cleaners and respect others such as lawyers and doctors. Is a lawyer a better human being than a dustman? If we think about it we can see we're not at all free and that we submit to dogma without being aware of it. Despite the appearance of choices given to us through advertising; they are illusions of freedom with a thick wall around them. We work mostly until retirement age and therefore, the best years of our lives are lived under pressure and stress, rarely having any free time to think about life; even our holidays can be traumatic. We can't know freedom because we live within the boundaries society has put in place. We think we're free but it's hard to know what true freedom is; we adapt the parts we play according to our surroundings. We must go to school, work, pay taxes, buy or rent houses, we must, we must and we must. When did you last do anything *really* different? If we can't see these restrictions then it's because we've accepted them so well that we don't know they're there. Some people are happy for their lives to be routine and one of those routines is our annual holiday, but this is *not* freedom. I don't wish to go any deeper into restrictions here as it won't serve any good purpose. What matters is discovering our true nature as opposed to the one we've manifested on the *outside*; what matters more, for now, is recognising they're not the same thing.

A baby writes its life on a blank sheet of paper. The mind records everything the baby's senses perceive from the moment it's born until its death.

It could be likened to a baby researching and writing the script of the play he's starring in. We don't remember all these but they're recorded as the baby explores its world and they mould the character the baby will become. If a baby is given too much *attention* rather than *love* when he cries, he will cry even more and much louder when he doesn't get it. How many children have you seen having tantrums in supermarkets or in the streets? The children have recorded old, well-established information and patterns and they know, innately, what to do with them. They can't record new information because the society they live in is 'old'. What appears new to us - fashion or technology - is the same clock with a different face on it. Any attempt by the child to find out more about himself is stifled, one way or another; usually by us not having the time or inclination to listen to his questions. Paradoxically, we think our own children are wonderful little people who've unique characters, but on the other hand, we're training them to fit into a society that'll never allow them to develop their uniqueness. We literally 'spoil' them. Often we can't answer the questions they ask because we don't know the answers, but this doesn't mean we can't encourage the questions. I know of a child (aged eight) who asked his mother: Why am I here? What do I do? The mother replied "You go back to bed, that's what you do." This question couldn't be answered and we don't have the time or curiosity to think about it. Gradually, children stop asking these questions and because they're unanswered the child becomes confused and buries his inquisitiveness. This same child later (aged ten) asked his grandfather 'How will I know what to do when I'm fourteen?' He'd changed from asking a question in the present to one projected into the future. He did this because we're taught from the past (history) and think into the future (school, job, retirement). Most important, is that both questions showed that he didn't understand his place in this world and was thinking about his purpose *here*, even four years after the first question; he probably still does. We're taught that everything will come to us if we do as we're told and work hard - it'll come in the future. We wait until we're well into our fifties or sixties, but we can wait until we're in our graves - it'll not arrive. We don't know what it is we're waiting for.

We begin our lives excitedly and wonder and marvel about everything around us, but this beauty and impulse is soon stifled and even made taboo. We tell children untruths. We tell them about a tooth fairy and place some coins under their pillows when they lose a tooth. We tell them about Father Christmas and lie about who brought the presents under the tree and we know they're lies. We tell them lies and give them rewards for believing them. We don't think about the consequences of lying to them because society tells us it's ok to do so. We then develop their confusion by telling them it's wrong to tell lies and we punish them when they do it.

Because we're so busy with our lives, we allow children the 'remote control' for the television and have no idea what they watch when we're not around; this allows society to shape them further. Children are curious and they will flick channels as soon as we leave the room; they have the remote control and with it, they're being remotely controlled. If we don't break these patterns then our children are just, as Roger Waters put it, "another brick in the wall."[20] In effect, we're shaping them the way we were shaped and we don't allow the wonderful, magnificent and brilliant 'individual' to develop. We allow them to watch television and films and these are 'behavioural instructions' disguised as education or entertainment. The purpose of television is to support the current system of society. Society will *form* children so their only function is the continuity of the world we've created. Society is us and the changes must be made by us. The most arduous task in the world must be to change ourselves.

Another way individuality is stifled is by standardising our worlds. There isn't much for us to do if you think about it. Make a list of things you can do that are *achievable* within the next twelve months that you haven't done before; there won't be much on it because we're too stuck within boundaries, commitments and schedules. The choices we have are limited. What are the actual choices of leisure activities for the average person? What could you go and do tonight? Rather than create beneficial pastimes for ourselves, we're merely kept occupied. Is it significant that entertainment is *provided* for us?

The world is online and we've participated in its creation, even if we've never touched a computer; we're One. Websites are now mostly made from templates and we're encouraged to be creative when using them? How is this possible? We have standardised letters in word processing applications. We're moulded and shaped to continue the growth of a society that's sick, lethargic, burdened and profitable. A child's life is more or less mapped out from the moment it begins; with few variations usually related to a choice of career or future partner. Our lives are templates, moulded and categorised; it's rare to see true creativity. One of the problems with a world like this is that 'thinking' will become obsolete one day.

We live like automatons and we've become blinded by the illusions. What does it mean to be an individual? No-one knows as we've all been fed into the same sausage machine and we cling to what's familiar; for our comfort and security. On one level we've graded ourselves against other members of the human race by birth, wealth and class systems; this is so silly. It's a bit like saying one tulip is better than another - we're all the same; we're each other. On another level, being an individual means behaving differently to the rest. It means following what we believe is the right path for us and staying on it no matter what. The first thing to recognise is that our choices are limited, by society, if we don't change anything. This must take effort and will not come about on its own. An alcoholic can't be helped until they recognise and want to recover from the problem - I know this very well as I've had close and regular contact with several of them. The first thing to do after recognition of the illness is to get rid of the bottles. The same applies to society; believing in the familiar is an addiction. The principle is the same for all problems or insecurities. We need to recognise what's actually happening and we need to *want* to let go.

Once we see what's happening we know it was obvious all along; we'd ignored it all. We heal without too much effort; a drop of water that's returned to the ocean doesn't struggle. The decision to change ourselves must come from within. We think this is impossible because we've been taught we must all stand united in order to make our nation strong; but a strong nation can be likened to an impenetrable wall; it can't be broken in *or* out of. It's freedom within boundaries. If Humanity stands together it can become strong too; but we don't believe we can make a difference so we don't bother trying. We don't believe an individual or a small group can make a difference; we're shown discouraging examples of this like, minority political parties running for government or independent shops unable to compete with the giants. We can do it; it's easy if we do it together. Strength is within us all and true strength is not physical. Choose to change ourselves and really mean it. If we don't place limitations or conditions in front of our decision; there aren't any. Never give up! We tend to believe someone else will do it for us and become dependent on science to find solutions to the world's problems or perhaps we're waiting for the Messiah to come and save us; one of our most absurd ideas. We must save ourselves. If it's *all* an illusion what does it matter? It rather depends on whether or not you're enjoying it or if you believe you've a purpose.

When we choose to change, the mind is furious; it'll fight to maintain security in what's familiar and for its own survival. But the mind has only ever had power over us because we gave it away. When the mind dolls out absurd thoughts, we must look straight at them and ask ourselves 'Who thought it?' This may seem silly at first because we've not been taught to think this way, but we can learn to adjust if we're motivated and determined. The thoughts quickly disappear when we watch them come and go; the more we practise the better the results, but the more we fight, the stronger the cold hard chains of the mind become. The other night I awoke in the middle of the night and my mind was chattering away about an ex and reminding me that he still had some of my belongings. I smiled, because I recognised the pattern and the thought dissolved. But it never used to be this easy and I've spent many a night in the past tossing and turning, trying to silence the conversations my mind insisted on having - it wouldn't leave me alone. The mind is mischievous.

As long as we remain divided, we can't become united; as long as the drop remains out of the ocean, it's separate. It may feel scary to return but once in the ocean there is no more fear and no more loneliness. Governments can't heal this divide; they maintain continuity, because the people who make up the governments are *themselves* divided; they are us. It's all us, at every level, but we've given our power to others and don't know how to get it back again. Do we want it? We wait and think the world will live in peace one day in the future, that governments will not be corrupt, that wars won't exist, that no-one will starve and that there'll be no more homeless people, but this isn't true. If we're honest with ourselves it's clear to see that the world's becoming a harder and more violent place to live in.

We think we're *really* individuals but this could not be further from the truth; we're One. Like the glass square on the disco ball, we don't know we're part of a 'whole'. We're born, parented, schooled, prepared for work, get married, have kids, buy homes and wait for our retirement and grandchildren, who don't always arrive before our deaths. Of course there are variations to this but not many and not enough to make a difference to Humanity or the world we live in, unless we 'choose' to.

Fear of Dying

Some things we can change, but not the inevitable.

There's a great deal more to the 'mystery of life' than I could've imagined ten years ago; it becomes more mysterious as I continue to let go of dogmatic beliefs and attachments. Living is merely an illusion; which means 'death' is an illusion too. Life is a cycle: it has a beginning and an end; we don't. I tried to share this good news with friends; I was puzzled about why no-one would even consider it. One of my dear friends said I was "mad" and another "deluded" and I was asked "What if you're wrong?" I replied "If I'm wrong I go to my grave having lived happily, if I'm right I go to my grave having lived happily; I've nothing to lose." One friend has been working hard so she'd be *comfortable* in her retirement and I told her she's already got enough money to do that with, to which she asked: What if I live till I'm ninety? I replied: What if you *don't*? From the look on her face, I don't think she'd ever considered the possibility. I seek the truth and I can't live in hope of *this or that* so far away in a future that doesn't exist; now is the time to ask the questions. We don't need a reference book and we don't need to be able to understand ancient texts in order to find knowledge.

Death is an end to something but what is it an end to? As mentioned before, we're born and since that moment we've been recording our lives, as though on a CD in the mind. It's the mind / memory that we leave behind when we die, together with all its confusing and contradictory contents. What dies is the image, the personality we've created, the 'scrawled' on piece of paper and all the baggage with it. The ego is what we've been creating, shaping and clinging on to all our lives, rather like throwing a vase on a pottery wheel; the ego is a bolt-on. An artist doesn't die if we destroy his painting; it's merely an expression of him. Death is an end to; illusion, desire, fear, sickness, grudges, worry and stress. We don't have to wait for physical death to lose these labels. When we strive to better ourselves we die a little every day and as we let go of ingrained beliefs, we die a little more. The ego can die before the body; we don't have to hold on to it. We can climb out of the river now if we want to.

Why do we fear death? Is it because we don't know what it means and though there's lots of information available, none of it's verifiable. Do we fear it because it's unknown? Just like everything else we experience, death is information and we all have access to it. Death is frightening to those of us that haven't taken time to really think about it. What exactly is it we want to hold on to; the pain, stress, fear, bank accounts or perhaps our relationships? We're actors who after playing out our roles refuse to be written out of the script; we've played our parts for our lifetime and can't let go of ourselves, or the others in the Cast. We don't want to go to our own funeral. We don't like ourselves but we can't let go of the images or the world we've created.

Death is feared quite early on in life and to such an extent that we count birthdays, wrinkles, grey hairs and after a certain age there are those who begin counting backwards as though it could change the inevitable. We take care of our appearance on the outside, sometimes meticulously, but we don't take care of our minds; our minds are the greatest hoarders and they don't let go of information, without putting up a fight. After someone close to us dies we remember the good in them and while they're alive we remember the bad. What does the mind have to do with this? In what way is death different to any other new experience?

Why are we sad at a funeral? I've spoken to people who've said they can't get upset at funerals but feel guilty because they're expected to do so. Some people get carried away and enjoy the drama; some are genuinely upset at the death of a close friend or relative and some feel they've been cheated and left alone to cope. In the latter case, do we miss the person who died because we depended on them and now feel abandoned? Why do we have funerals? If it's to say 'goodbye' to a loved one then why do we remember the anniversaries of their death years later? Death is a mystery, but, it's the 'living' that cares about it. Dead people aren't at the funeral, only what were their bodies; their essence is not inside; nor has it died. Does a funeral remind us one day we'll die ourselves? We find it easy to talk about someone else's death but not our own. We avoid the recently bereaved because we feel awkward and don't know what to say to comfort them; their sorrow is too great for us to bear. We can't share in their grief for the simple reason that we don't feel it unless, we were close to the person who died. Do we not want to talk about death because we're afraid of our own? Humanity needs to talk about these things sooner or later because they're not going to change.

Children would talk openly about these issues but we *protect* them. A boy who's 'lost' his grandfather may be told to be careful what he says to his grandmother at the funeral. Children accept death far easier than we do. Does the innocence of children intimidate or embarrass us? Perhaps we're ashamed? Wouldn't it be better if we were open about this subject? If we open the dark door of death so it's no longer a taboo subject we have to tiptoe around, our fears would subside. Children don't fear death until we *teach* them to by passing our own fears on to them. We scare them with stories about what happens after death, such as hell, oblivion and the wrath of God. Little wonder a great number of children develop a fear of the dark, create imaginary friends or become withdrawn; we've seeded their nightmares.

All this fear stems from fears passed on to us and from what we've been told or shown. None of it's justifiable; we live in fear of the unknown rather than the known. This rather reminds me of being terrified of vegetables when I was a child, particularly green ones; now there's nothing I love more on my dinner plate. What happens after death is unknown so we're afraid of it. But here's the thing - our bodies are going to expire whether we like it or not. Each and every one of us can be certain of this part of 'destiny' at least. When we know what this entails and accept it, we alleviate irrational fears. We prepare ourselves for all sorts of eventualities:

- Going to school,
- A job interview,
- Going on holiday,
- Going to the dentist,
- Getting married,
- The birth of a child,
- And even our retirement.

We prepare for everything ... except death.

If we think about the thoughts accompanying fear we'll see that they come from memory. It can be argued we love this fear. We've created a climate of fear from our desire for gratuitous violence in films. More and more of these films are made and the demand for them has not slowed. Why do we want to see more graphic images of violence? What information are we writing onto our minds and how do the images we put there affect us? Fear results from this information and the images we see in these films. Can we expect not to feel fear as a result of them? We're writing our own nightmares! Could we watch this violence enacted against a friend or family member with the same emotions? Why is it different watching it on a screen? What about the horrors on the news broadcasts and in the newspapers? If we surround ourselves with horror, bad news or terror, then fear is what we're going to feel. We're disconnected from each other and we can't see the ripples of our actions.

We're afraid of the method by which we'll die, but not by the method by which we live. Why do we fear how we die? Is it because we've been continuously 'entertained' by violent films and fear we'll become victims of the same fate? These violent images and stories have been engraved on to our minds; we don't forget them. Could it be we're afraid of so-called everlasting darkness? Perhaps we want to stay alive because we're afraid of 'heaven and hell' religious stories and we don't think we've lived well enough to deserve heaven.

Is there something beyond fear? Let's imagine there's nothing after this life and we cease existing, entirely and completely. How would we recognise the moment of disappointment? Everything would cease so fast we wouldn't even know about it. I can't see how anyone can believe in non-existence; the subject can't have been adequately thought out. On the other hand, if we die and there's something 'afterwards' there'll be no disappointment and no need whatsoever to fear anything. So where's the problem? Why is the subject, since time began, still debated; there are only two options after all and as I've shown, we'll only ever *know* about one of them?

I know of someone who was dying of cancer and hoped he'd stay alive long enough to get an iPhone5 when it was released. This shows how strongly we've become attached to material things, rather than life itself. We want to make the most of them and can't let go of attachments so we invest in gadgets and toys to amuse ourselves. We write last wills and testaments; we're preparing to die, but only in respect to the living. We're not looking at death properly. In order to prepare to die we need to see what death is and then we'll see that more important than having the latest *toys*, is letting go of the attachment we have to them. It doesn't mean we have to give everything away; it means we can see them for what they are; transient and meaningless. We can't delay death any more than we can our next birthday so, wouldn't it be a good idea if Humanity came to terms with it.

We don't want to let go of our identities, which are the personalities we created for our character's experience; the ego is an identity. We've nurtured, clothed, loved, hated, and protected it since the moment we were born; sounds rather like what we did with a Barbie Doll or Action Man when we were children. We also don't want to let go of the family and friend connections we've built up; we cling on for dear life to everything including our possessions. The living mourn the dead and I've no doubt in my mind that the dead don't mourn the living. They don't care for what they left behind or, the size of the monument we put up for them. As fantastic as it may seem, it's all happening inside our mind.

Death brings release from all illusions and fear. Why do we want to hold on to them so much? All things in this world are illusions and impermanent. Time breaks down every *thing*; it becomes something else, just like a caterpillar to a butterfly. It doesn't take too much reflection to see we can't cease 'existing'. Existence is the only thing that's real. Try closing your eyes one night while lying in bed or relaxing in the bath and imagine non-existence; imagine the 'end' of you. You can't do this because whatever you do, there's always an observer; the observer can't die and neither can the awareness of it. Three important questions here are:

- What is existence?
- What is awareness?
- Who is the observer?

~~~

I've a friend who had a car accident in which he was seriously injured. He had an amazing near death experience. He was outside his body, clinically dead and he says he was everything … Everything. He saw a man in the car suffering and noticed his injuries; he remembers thinking "Oh my God … the poor guy." He didn't recognise it as himself; whilst out of his body he was not suffering at all. My friend saw colours he's unable to describe and told me they don't exist in our visible spectrum. On another occasion the same man's father was dying of cancer and was unconscious in hospital. He was flaying his arms about and hallucinating; he sat up in bed and kept calling out "Daddy! Daddy!" He stared blankly at my friend; who sensed his father wasn't 'in there' and couldn't actually see him - he died the following morning. Dr Peter Fenwick, neuropsychiatrist, has done some interesting studies on near death experiences. He asks the question "How is it that you can have cognition, or, an alert mind, when you're clinically dead? It doesn't make sense."[21] It does if we stop seeing life and death as a linear experience and if we stop believing that we're the ego and the body. Two days before my mother died, she felt something touch her shoulder and heard a voice saying "Come with me now." This was quite disturbing for her and unexpected; she'd never given it much thought before. She told her nurse but the nurse said "Don't worry about it. It's normal and probably the drugs." I don't think so! This nurse had been present for many similar experiences and I've heard other stories about nurses who've seen this behaviour and heard these stories many times. They are common and yet, ignored.

We've been conditioned to believe all sorts of nonsense and we make those beliefs our reality; our minds are all muddled up. There are those who believe that as we die we see what we *expect* to see because we've been programmed to see it; in near death experiences too. They argue that we created the images because we're so afraid of dying that we've given ourselves a crutch. We don't have to go too far on our journey to see this isn't 'entirely' true. It's not worth me spending any more time on it here. We need to begin to think differently about life and death; thinking is not enough on its own. We must change our perspective and raise our vibration in order to see more. Death is release from this life. What, if anything, is the legacy we leave behind? What, if anything, can we take with us?

Letting Go

If we don't let go of illusions, how will we recognise truth?

L et go! Make the decision and just *let* go! You won't get; paid, approval, new friends, facebook likes or followers - your friends will think you've lost the plot. *You* might think you've lost it. On the other hand, you'll get peace of mind, a sense of purpose and a perspective of the world that you've not seen before.

Letting go is like learning to swim; we can all do it but we're frightened of the water and don't want anyone to see us make a fool of ourselves. There'll always be someone waiting to say 'I told you so' if things go wrong. We're far too proud. What does it mean to be proud? Are we not just affirming our own 'excellence' when we wear that mask? Pride makes us dig our heels in; we're not going to budge. Resentment makes us grip harder and we'll scream and shout to hold on to something even if it's cutting into our hand. Have you ever tossed and turned in bed at night grumbling and seething about something somebody said to you, gripping on to it with your teeth; we need the stress more than the sleep. We make ourselves ill holding on to negative emotions because we don't want to let go. Yet no matter how hard we grip, letting go is a simple action that brings immediate relief.

Many people fall out because of some event they refuse to let go of - often carrying their bitterness to the grave. How much joy have they missed out on and how much suffering have they willingly endured by not putting their differences behind them? When *anger*, for example, begins to rise we can let it go - or allow it to grow into something destructive. If we let go of this anger rather than hold on to its tail, we can avoid conflict and pain.

When we find ourselves stuck in unhealthy relationships, professional or personal, we need to think about what's holding us in them. Often, we believe there's no way out but the true reason we stay is fear. There's always a way out but we can't be bothered with all the hassle and the ego tells us it's foolish to leave a place of 'security'; even though it's an illusion. We don't want to leave our belongings, our homes, split financial assets, divide friends and we don't want to start from scratch. We care about what people think and in some circumstances we may fear repercussions. We complain and blame each other, yet we're reluctant to change the things we complain about and content to live with our lot; we're lazy. Help is always available and if we have to go to a shelter initially then, so be it. The first step is tough but if we find the courage to start the process, we regain control of our lives and that's got to be worth something. It's not as hard as we fear and once over the initial hurdle, we begin to feel stronger. It's a bit like pumping dirty water out of the washing machine; only clean water is pumped into it again. Our own limitations are our only obstacles. We can't see them because we're looking into the crowd for someone to help us; we can only help ourselves.

~~~

When we let go of desire and start to look at what we've got rather than what we haven't, our world changes dramatically. We appreciate that we've always had something to eat and drink - if we hadn't we wouldn't still be here. When we continue to crave 'material things' and the 'latest models', selfish desire becomes our reason for living, regardless of whether we want these things for ourselves or for someone else. We can be at our greediest when we divorce or when someone close to us dies. We grab all we can and when a family member dies we expect our *dues*, even if we haven't spoken to them for years. We could walk away and let go of the harmful feelings we harbour, but we let greed get in the way as if it'll compensate us in some way. It never does; it only gives us more negativity to hold on to. Many suffer in the wake of these grievances.

Family conflicts are one of the biggest causes of negative emotions. The home is where conditioning begins and where our psychological needs are first suppressed. Events arise that we hold on to and we start building our defences. We add to these over the years and are reluctant to take them down. These barriers protect us, but they also lock us securely in behind them. We construct our walls one brick at a time and we make them robust. The mind flags up past negative experiences warning us about the *consequences* of removing these barriers; such as, being vulnerable and allowing ourselves to be perceived as weak. When we meet other people we see each other through the invisible walls we've erected; ours and theirs. The communication between us is filtered and we can never discover what lies 'behind the wall' of another. We know this on a subconscious level and it gives rise to suspicion, misunderstanding and disagreement. Between nations this same mindset leads to war. How can Humanity live in harmony under these conditions? Dismantling our defence system is an uphill struggle but until we do; we can't see the beauty that lies within.

~~~

We're not encouraged to think for ourselves. We've help-lines for everything. These include help for abuse, alcoholism, stopping smoking, depression, legal advice, mental health, breast feeding and reporting crimes. We're always calling for 'help' so it's not surprising we're unable to help ourselves. Why does Humanity need so much help? How can we improve society when we rely on an unhealthy system for guidance? Authority is one of the things we fear to let go of because we're not used to being *responsible* for ourselves; the many rules and regulations that govern Humanity make this seem impossible. Take a look at all the road signs when you next go out and about and ask yourself 'how' and 'why' they came into being. It would be difficult for us to do without them; harder than you may imagine as we aren't aware of the number of 'directions' we unwittingly follow daily. Thinking and common sense wither away through lack of use in this 'live by numbers' world. We need to *allow* change to happen; this means letting go of past events and not groping for future ones that we can never reach.

We try to secure our future because we're afraid of the spectres we've been shown of; the elderly, the starving, the sick, the alone, the vulnerable and the forgotten. So we strive to accumulate more things in order that we may not go *without* one day; we hoard our paraphernalia and leave others to clear up after our death. However, we don't think beyond our deaths except through a 'last will and testament'; then we cut ourselves off from anything beyond that point. As long as we place the word 'death' on a 'finish line', we'll fear crossing it.

~~~

It's essential to remove our masks so we can learn how to stop hiding behind them. Do you ever really reveal yourself to anyone? We need to let go of; prejudices, dogma, anger, guilt and everything else from the past as these preoccupations only serve to cloud our 'goal'; the only destination we need pay attention to. These preoccupations are what the mind busies 'itself' with and if you try to suppress them, they become stronger. Who do we harm by holding on to them? Isn't it only ourselves? The mind resists change and it wants to keep busy. It works non-stop without a break; it's the ball and chain we've shackled to our ankles and it's heavy. The mind wants to protect itself and all its contents; like a child clinging to an old tin full of treasured memories. The mind's determination and ability to cling to the past shouldn't be underestimated as it knows every trick in the book; one of the most common being, 'delay today until tomorrow'. It's kept itself under lock and key, loves its relics and doesn't want to be *free* of them.

You can be free if you want to; if you're willing to *come into existence* on your own merit instead of relying on the mind's negativity or authority to control your life. Our path is personal and we can't follow anyone else's; we're unique and so are our journeys. We can go our own way but as long as we pretend we can't, we'll keep looking in the right hand for what the left hand is holding. We don't have to live 'hard-done-by' or 'trapped' in a world we're desperately unhappy in or accept without reason that we're powerless to transform ourselves. We've been looking in all the *known* places outside of ourselves for guidance and meaning to our lives but they're in the past (books etc.) and the future (hope); the key to unveiling our true nature lies in-between, in the Now. We can change when we're *ready* for change; not before.

At one point in my life, trying to like everyone became an uphill battle and it was a blessing when I realised, I didn't have to. I didn't have to be liked and I didn't have to like anyone; I found freedom in that. I was then free to follow my heart. We change our attitude towards other people when we stop criticising them and realise that we're all the same; we all carry the same problems and tribulations on our shoulders and want to be free of them. It's a lovely feeling realising we don't need other people to like us; we don't need their approval and don't care if they don't give it. Let go of thinking we're separate. We're One.

We need to come together again and we can only do this by replacing negative thoughts with positive action. Ironically, coming back together again involves further separation; from the physical. When we're walking a path seeking 'peace of mind' we become disconnected from things that were once important in our daily lives. For example, office politics, going shopping, having the latest gadget or not missing the next episode of our favourite soap opera. A spiritual change or rising of consciousness level reveals the futility and monotony of these relatively mundane activities. If we realise the truth of this we can't help but change - it becomes impossible to behave in the same way or to accept the complacency of the society we created. Once realised, there's no way back to the old thought patterns and we don't look for one; we can't live the lie any more. If we *hear* this truth but *don't* realise it, we don't change; hearing the truth is like hearing a nice tune; we have our ears tickled and tap our feet to the beat. The feeling is warm and fuzzy and we like the comfort it brings; however, comfort and pleasure are *all* it brings and these have nothing to do with change.

~~~

Nothing grows without a seed. The mind tells us not to bother thinking outside the box and whether or not we listen to it, is up to us; as the ancient Greek aphorism goes "Know Thyself" - nothing could be more important or worth knowing. We think we know ourselves but what we know is the ego; it wants to hold us where we are. It wants us to wait for a 'hero' to save us; I don't advise waiting for one. This is a lonely road and few will be prepared to join you on it. If you've read the previous chapters and are still asking yourself questions posed in them or more of your own, then you've already begun letting go of obstacles.

If you can marvel at the sun on the horizon or its rays stretching out from the clouds, if you can see the beauty of creation in them, then you can no longer take the world for granted. There is much magic and beauty all around us. All we have to do is learn to look at it again and to appreciate it; to be grateful and to decide we're through with pain and suffering. We can learn from each new experience and gain a great deal by looking for the lesson it wants to teach us. To see the lessons, open the door that says 'poor me' on it and walk through.

~~~

Changing is for each one of us, alone; it can't be shared. As we change we find resistance to our journey, from friends, colleagues and relatives; they can't see what we can see and they think we're being misled. This was explained in The Matrix film by 'Agent Smith' who said "Billions of people [are] just living out their lives, oblivious."[22] People don't want to think in a different way and they're not interested in spiritual 'truth'. Most people can't 'see' and though a high percentage believes in a god of some form, they're not willing to make any sacrifice to find out if it's true or not. One reason for this is that their world is entirely physical. When we pray, we're asking the universe to come to us. When we change, we make the journey ourselves.

When I watched the glorious sunset I described in the preface I was *everything* and everything was me; I couldn't tell where I began or ended. I've experienced this several times now; these moments are wonderful and can't be explained with words but if I had to give it a go, I'd say it's a disconnection from the mind and body and a reconnection to all that Is. Thought isn't there and neither are our senses. Our universe is complete and lacks nothing at all; we must all return to Love sooner or later.

Who am I?

All stories lie between a front and back cover.

I used to lie in the bath repeatedly asking this question and get frustrated about not receiving an answer. I'd think 'Come on … tell me … isn't asking the question all I've got to do?' but answers never came. The question isn't a token you can feed into a machine and out pops a fortune cookie. Although I can't explain to you how to ask it other than to say 'from your heart'; if you persist, no matter what, the answers will come.

You are the sun that brings the light
The moon and stars that shine at night
You are the day that ebbs and flows
You are the wind and where it blows …
… Is still unknown - a mystery
That will unfold for you and me
You are the waves that rush to shore
You are the birds that love to soar
The sand, the wood, the forest too
The sea, the land, the false and true
You are the clouds, the rain and snow
You're up above - You're down below
You are the seed - You are the tree
Responsible for all you see
The fat, the thin, the colour blue
The brown, the black, the yellow too
The light, the dark, the in-between
The play, the act and every scene
You're Adam and You're also Eve
You're all you can and can't perceive
You're in the air and on the ground
You're everything - you are profound
You are the water and the fire
You're all of these and can't expire
The dog, the cat, the cow, the ewe

The innocence - the conscience too
The Universe and far beyond
Creation and its loving bond
Every wish you could ask for
You're all of this, and so much more
You're inside and you're outside too
You're every single point of view
You are the One who's lost in space
You are the secret hiding place
You're everything that's born from thought
Pre-anything that you've been taught
You are the game of dot to dot
The wonder is ... you are the LOT!
Remove the veil that hides your eyes
Go in and find the greatest prize.

Afterword

"Solitary trees, if they grow at all, grow strong."[23] Winston Churchill

I mentioned at the beginning of this book that my views may change as I progressed with writing it. This has proved to be the case and posed many editing challenges for me. It's been a steep learning curve as 'I faced myself' and I've been humbled by the experience.

As alluded to earlier, this book is not meant to provide answers and neither does it attempt to do so. Perhaps you've been challenged by some of the questions raised and are now asking some of your own. Like me you may have once held strong views about things in the world that you now see in a different light. If this is the case then this book has achieved its objective.

If we look at things in the world through innocent eyes our views change. It's worth thinking about the effect we have on other people and the effect they have on us. I now see the rather overweight girl who was raising and lowering her arms, as an expression of myself. I can't criticise or feel anything but love for her; I am her. The thoughts I'd had about her came from my education and conditioning; these were projected into my memory from other unhealthy minds. We're all connected and this doesn't mean we belong to a particular family like the Taylor's or Joneses living 'next door'; our family name is Love.

If we became conscious of this, the world would show us very different experiences, but it's not that simple. It'll take many generations to change the world - if it can be changed at all. Like it or not, this is the 'human experience' and part of grace is accepting things as they are, along with all the horrors life frequently presents to each and every one of us. The beauty of our world remains evident for those who would but look. When we speak to each other we speak more from the mind than the heart. More often than not we swallow the honest words and speak the 'politically correct' or 'impulsive' ones; often whatever's in our mouth comes out, without thought. How many times have you posted a message on social media and then either regretted or when possible, deleted it? If we don't change ourselves then it won't matter how many cakes we bake for a village fête, how much money or goods we donate to good causes or how many doors we knock on with good intentions, we're just papering over the cracks. Without metamorphosis, it's just more of the same. We all have a journey to make; Humanity *has* a purpose.

Joining a group and listening to whoever is leading the group doesn't bring clarity. Jiddu Krishnamurti said "Truth has no tradition, it can't be handed down"[24] and this means no matter who we listen to, we can't 'inherit' their wisdom. We must follow our own processes to attain wisdom. This doesn't mean we can't learn from spiritual teachers but it does mean we can think about what they say using our intelligence. Recognising our *own* ignorance and how tiny we are relative to the universe brings wisdom, but as long as we remain self-important tending only to our own agenda, we don't find it.

It's a convenient crutch to blame someone else for our predicament. A common belief is "I can't change because my parents messed me up too much". It's an excuse put forward by the mind; it's a delay mechanism and it isn't true. If we believe our parents are responsible for our unhappiness we must have given them our power; no wonder we can't change. If you believe your parents made you unhappy, what is preventing you finding happiness now? If we take back responsibility we empower ourselves; part of wisdom is not abusing that power. Things look different when we replace *insecurity* with *power* and although we'll find this disconcerting and scary at first, we learn fast that we're much stronger than we ever thought possible; we recognise just how much responsibility for our own lives we've given to others. There's an old proverb that says 'When the student is ready, the master appears'. When we take responsibility for ourselves, do we become our own masters?

Bibliography

[1] Petrie, John, *Winston Churchill Quotes*. (http://www.nationalchurchillmuseum.org/wit-wisdom-quotes.html [4 June 2013])

[2] Harris, Kevin. *Collected Quotes from Albert Einstein* (1995) (http://rescomp.stanford.edu/~cheshire/EinsteinQuotes.html [6 May 2013])

[3] Davies, W. H. *Leisure*. (http://www.greenfolder.co.nz/WHD/poetry/Leisure.html. [28th July 2013])

[4] Google. (https://www.google.co.uk/#q=self+help [2 September 2013])

[5] Confucius, *The Great Learning* (translated by James Legge). (Internet Classics Archive of MIT - http://classics.mit.edu/Confucius/learning.html. [15th July 2013])

[6] *The Matrix* film 1999 (Motion Picture, US: Warner Bros)

[7] ushisotry.org. Ancient Civilizations Online Textbook, *Gladiators, Chariots, and the Roman Games* (2013) (http://www.ushistory.org/civ/6e.asp [31st July 2013])

[8] Harris, Kevin, *Collected Quotes from Albert Einstein* (1995) (http://rescomp.stanford.edu/~cheshire/EinsteinQuotes.html [21 May 2013])

[9] Linguistic Society of America. *How Many Languages Are There in the World?* (http://www.linguisticsociety.org/content/how-many-languages-are-there-world [6/09/2013])

[10] Sagan, Carl. Druyan, Ann. Soter, Steven (writers) *Cosmos: A Personal Voyage*, (Episode 9) The Lives of the Stars. (1980)

[11] Gandhi, Mahatma. Gandhi International Institute for Peace, *Essential Quotes of Mahatma Gandhi* (http://www.gandhianpeace.com/quotes.html [28 August 2013])

[12] Chesterton, G. K. *The Scandal of Father Brown*, (Chapter 'The Point of a Pin') (http://gutenberg.net.au/ebooks02/0201031.txt [11 Oct 2013])

[13] Bach, Richard, *Illusions* (P.57 Element, 2003)

[14] The Free Dictionary by Farlex, (http://www.thefreedictionary.com/education [18 June 2013])

[15] Arunachala Ashrama. *The Teachings of Sri Ramana Maharshi*, (http://www.arunachala.org/ramana/teachings/ [17 July 2013])

[16] Dictionary.com, (http://dictionary.reference.com/browse/philosophy [21 August 2013])

[17] Interview with Ian McNay on Conscious television. (http://www.youtube.com/watch?v=VYYXq1Ox4sk [8 August 2013])

[18] Biology Online, (http://www.biology-online.org/dictionary/Placebo_effect [10 Sept 2013])

[19] Francois Duc De La Rochefoucauld. *Reflections or Sentences and Moral Maxims* No. 119. (http://www.gutenberg.org/files/9105/9105-h/9105-h.htm [11 July 2013])

[20] Waters, Roger. (1979). Another Brick in the Wall on *The Wall*. Pink Floyd Music Publishers Ltd.

[21] Interview with Ian McNay on Conscious Television. (http://www.youtube.com/watch?v=-6kDMl6N3C4 [25 September 2013])

[22] *The Matrix film* 1999 (Motion Picture, US: Warner Bros)

[23] Petrie, John, *Winston Churchill Quotes*.
(http://www.nationalchurchillmuseum.org/wit-wisdom-quotes.html [28 June 2013])

[24] Krishnamurti, Jiddu. - Krishnamurti Teachings in Krishnamurti's Journal (para. 169) (http://www.jkrishnamurti.org/krishnamurti-teachings/view-context.php?tid=42&chid=318&w=%22All+those+years+passed+without+leaving+scars&s=Context [18 September 2013])

Just Around The Bend: Más o Menos

Originally published in France by RPG Publishing 2014

Standalone ISBN: 978-2-9546811-4-6

Walk straight ahead
Listen to no-one
Trust not in the walls or doorways
For they will mislead
And close behind you
As you walk through
The forest, not knowing
Where you've come from
Or where you're going …
If anywhere at all.

For every experience that's made me who I am today, I'm grateful. That I've been guided and given the strength to continue on my journey. I'm grateful. That I no longer seek (or need) the approval of others, I'm grateful. That I've been fortunate enough to have been shown so much beauty while I'm still living, I'm grateful. For help getting over the hurdle that prevented me writing my books - for so many years I fought it - I'm grateful.

If we've a purpose in this life, then surely it must be to live with purpose.

Thank you

Godfrey for believing in me
and for all your help and support
~~~~~

Aleena for so much inspiration
Mike
Anne
'little red ball'
Hazel

Preface

Remove yourself from the loop of self-destruction.

If you haven't read *On The Other Hand* you'll be unaware that I've been married six times (four officially). You might be asking yourself why I didn't learn the first time, or even the second or third. Some of you might want to know what went wrong, who was at fault and how things panned out. However, feasting on the bones of my past serves no good purpose and isn't the point of this book. Realising this was paramount to the decision I made not to publish my autobiography. I've looked closely at the repetitive patterns of my life and taken full responsibility for them, refusing to continue laying the blame elsewhere; I'm much happier now.

We can break the cycle of self-imprisonment; enforced only by the walls we constructed *ourselves*; quite often they're made of faux materials as once the mind gets hold of an idea it always decorates it to its own particular style. I can assure you that although I've torn many walls down, I'm not more fortunate than you (far from it) neither am I stronger or luckier; I just made a decision not to live behind them anymore. The strength of these walls is proportional to the strength of our agreement to live our lives behind them. One of the toughest walls for me to remove was the one that prevented me from writing. Writing was an itch I just had to scratch and the greatest difficulty I faced was overcoming the belief that I couldn't reach the spot. Another itch told me I couldn't change and that I wasn't strong enough. I now recognise these as walls put up by my fierce resistance to responsibility and the negative influences of people around me who I allowed to tell me I wasn't good enough.

The *ordeals* that tormented me in my youth became the weapons used in a war against the world. Imagine living in a world where we no longer believe that war can lead to peace. War can't lead to peace any more than ignorance can lead to knowledge. War leads to premature death, pain, suffering, hatred, fear and more separation. The hardest thing to understand in my childhood was why there are such cruelties in the world; I couldn't see why any one person would want to hurt or harm another. I had a feeling of helplessness inside me and felt powerless to change my life without outside help. This was mostly because I was always asking 'why' and was focused on my own misery. We can always call for help but there's really no point, unless we're prepared to work in line with that call.

My war continued until I was ready and willing to bring an end to it; until I was willing to let go of fear. Torment only occurs *inside* us; it occurs because we hold on tightly to the very things we'd be better off letting go of. These things are created by the mind and it's maddened when we want to let go of them. The tools I utilised to find my way out of misery were tenacity, a willingness to let go of all *attachment* and a deep-seated knowledge that there's more to me than a human body. All these removed me from what I was brought up to believe was a *place of safety*.

I explained in *On The Other Hand* why questioning is important and I asked something like four hundred and forty questions in it. I've asked myself many more since and I'm still asking them. Questioning brings about *unlearning* and therefore freedom from what has held us in our prison of conditioned beliefs. I've received several messages saying that the questions 'just kept on coming'. Yes they do and that's why I gave the book a subtitle; *The Little Anthology of Big Questions*. When I told a friend of mine I'd started writing another book, she asked me if it would have the *answers* in it. It won't, but if it did they wouldn't help anyone but me; they'd be my answers which aren't the same as yours and when I get an answer, I question it. We've had all our questions answered (or ignored) from the moment we could ask them; by the media, our parents, and teachers; society has been holding our hand, steering Humanity in the direction it wants it to go in. The answers have built up what we believe we know about the world and challenging those beliefs can be tough because they're deep-seated and driven by fear. Rather than being about finding more confusing answers, the questions are about challenging what we've come to accept as true. When challenging the truths we think we know, it's not necessary to replace them with others.

A lot has changed for me and many mornings I've woken up and wondered where I am, even though I'm still *here*. Most mornings my world feels like a different place to the one I went to sleep in the night before; each day feels fresh and new. You're more than welcome to join me on my journey through this book. I feel like the waters are still flowing and I've not and don't expect to come to a halt. Paradoxically, I'm not going *anywhere* at all. It's not easy to challenge our world and it's certainly not easy to grasp some of these concepts, but it's worthwhile and doable. It's difficult because the majority of the world is racing in one direction and you and I - as you're reading this - have decided to go in another. I don't trust any information now other than what I've thought out and realised for myself. I haven't found answers, neither do I look for any, but I've found something that makes me feel driven and I know it's the only place worth driving to.

Introduction

We got ourselves into this mess - only we can get ourselves out of it.

For those of you who've read my first book *On The Other Hand*, you'll be pleased to hear that there are fewer questions in this book. The reason being that once we start asking questions and observe our mind operating we realise how much control it has over our lives, it quietens. I've also decided to dispense with the need for a bibliography or quotes to support the things I write. With hindsight, I probably felt the need to back up some of my thoughts, but this is no longer the case; I prefer to speak in my own words, rather than the words of others. Anyone can see the things I've written; they're no secret. This is *my* voice and I'm reluctant to use any other now; my first chapter *A Bit of a Rant* covers the subject of quotes a little more.

By observing our thought processes we tune in to a higher vibration; it's inevitable. At first we find it hard to let go of the familiar, because we've so much noise going on in our heads that we can't keep up with the pace. It's rather like listening to or watching two films simultaneously in fast forward; our two conflicting voices.

Before going any further I'd like to make it perfectly clear, for the fluidity of this book, that I use the pronoun *we* a great deal. This is how I see us; we are One. Yes, it's not always 100% appropriate to use the proverbial *we* but I don't intend to continually stop my train of thoughts to explain this. If you feel this 'we' doesn't apply to you then please feel free not to apply it; for the purposes of this book its meaning is general.

When we're on a journey of self-discovery the river flows so fast that it's hard to keep up with. We often have to slow down a bit and take stock while we catch our breath. Consequently we miss much in the Now. Imagine being carried away in a fast-flowing river; you won't be able to see everything going on around you whilst trying to avoid going over the waterfall you're approaching. In the same way we can't see around the bend, or behind a curtain or door but there comes a point when they no longer present obstacles because we're not afraid any more. As explained in *On The Other Hand* there's only the Here and Now; clearly the title of this book is a physical metaphor for somewhere metaphysically, far closer to home. We look to physical solutions for metaphysical puzzles; whatever we do physically won't provide a permanent solution.

For our woes we look to tranquillisers, anti-depressants, sleeping pills, alcohol, chocolate, mind-altering drugs, entertainments, things, someone-to-lean-on and psychotherapy, but we never seem to get well. We need to find solutions to our own problems or our healing won't be permanent. We can't change the hearts of others, not ever, so it really is a waste of time trying. If you doubt this then think about whether or not anyone can change *you*. Doctors are necessary for many illnesses and injuries but there are many other ailments that we can help ourselves with such as; depression or anxiety. One of the issues that would benefit Humanity to examine is why there's so much disease in the world, rather than how can we cure it? There are no medicines that can cure sadness, frustration, despair, loneliness or a broken spirit. We have to face these for ourselves in order to raise our vibration. We can only do it Now by understanding the mind and how it controls us. We've become so used to conflicts and helplessness that challenging them is not something we're very good at. However, like falling off a bike while learning to ride it, we can get back on it again and ride off in any direction we choose. There's nothing keeping us down other than the thought that we can't, or don't want to, get up again.

Think about what self-help is. It's about helping *ourselves* without relying on assistance from any authority other than our own. We read and rave about new self-help books as we may the latest diet. These diets may help us to lose a few pounds and we feel better for it, but when we come off them again we regain the weight and often, more. When this happens we also suffer with disappointment in ourselves, lower self-esteem and higher levels of self-hatred. Any positive effects we feel are temporary and that can't be worth striving for; there has to be a permanent change of lifestyle in order to feel the positive benefits. It's an ongoing process.

There are those who experience an instant conversion from unconsciousness to Consciousness, but they're few and far between and the majority of us take a far longer road to Damascus. Many of us can be discouraged by 'epiphany' stories, particularly when we're told they're so rare; I was one of them. This book is for those of us who take longer to realise what we already know on one level and to keep you company on your 'journey'. Don't give up. It must happen if you want it to. We're never alone and never have been.

The author of a self-help book, more often than not, tells us how they found *their* way and this is not necessarily the right way for us; which is why the effects don't last. It's difficult enough to find out who we really are and even more difficult to walk in someone else's footsteps. For many years I looked outside for help and the more I tried to find it there, the more frustrated I became with the world and the more I withdrew into my shell. It wasn't until I finally understood that I already have all the power I'd ever need, right here and Now, that I took responsibility for myself. The most essential ingredient in that change is the *will* to put an end to our own pain and suffering instead of lackadaisically hoping someone else will change it all for us. When we raise our vibration we're helping ourselves, but as long as our focus and awareness are on our inability to do it, or we're waiting for someone else to administer a magic formula, climbing out of the abyss will seem to be an impossible task. If we're helped by an outside force then it's that force that becomes stronger rather than ourselves.

This book considers some concepts that have come into my field of vision since writing *On The Other Hand*. The more we focus on and become aware of how our mind works, the more insights we get; only we choose which of these we want to listen to or implement in our lives. The more we focus on and are aware of our difficulties, the more those difficulties continue to be a negative influence and therefore, destructive. It's necessary to continually remind ourselves to turn around when our thoughts wander back to our old ways, but all we need to do when this happens is reconnect to the new ways; with practise, as with everything, we get much better at staying in power.

I decided to illustrate this book with a character I designed for no other reason other than I enjoy making them and wanted to share them with you. I call this character Dilly (which means something or someone remarkable). Dilly is a 'thought form' that thinks and he shows off some of our most endearing human traits. At present, he'll only appear in the paperback versions of this book.

A Bit of a Rant

We speak sweet intentions, but our hearts remain silent.

I talked about social media and some of its effects in society today in my last book, but since writing it I've realised a great deal more. Social media isn't sociable; it's a-social. In my experience, these sites are used increasingly to spread inspirational quotes; a sort of pick 'n' mix philosophy that come from a variety of sources from the ancient Greeks to modern day 'life coaches'. We don't spread our own inspiration or speak our own words of wisdom. I don't say these quotes should stop. I'm saying let's discuss them in a meaningful way rather than just clicking on a 'like' button and treating them like a piece of art we hang on our 'walls'. Some of these quotes have thousands of likes but only a handful of comments; in what way are we inspired, or inspiring, when we do this? On the whole, inspirational quotes have become the junk mail of social media and its presence is only exceeded by advertising. So many quotes are distributed that their potency and original beauty are greatly diluted and therefore devoid of meaning and quickly forgotten. I asked a girl, who posts these as though they were confetti, if she can remember what she posted the previous day. Her answer was "No". I've had to unfollow quite a few people simply because there's no other way to stop the spam. As if it weren't enough that we're being spammed by advertisers, businesses and scams ... we're now spamming our family and friends.

～～～

What happens when one of our friends persistently posts things we don't want to see? We've two choices ... delete them or put up with them. If we delete them there are consequences and if we put up with them the same applies. This leads to further separation and mischief in society. I had a friend who introduced me to her new boyfriend and we became good friends; we all knew each other personally. When she decided to end her relationship with him a year later, she said I should follow suit. I refused of course and she was very upset about it, saying that I wasn't a good friend to her. I didn't go further into this drama of hers nor agree to pass messages between the two online. Needless to say she and I aren't friends now. To me we couldn't have been such good friends in the first place. Humanity can be so childish and immature. During my lifetime I've heard more wisdom from children than I have from adults; it's time for Humanity to grow up.

A contact of mine on one of these sites said in a post "smartphones have made this world a lonelier place" and this is partly true. It's not the phones that have made the world into a lonelier place to live in but our agreement to live our lives through them; they're a technical accessory to the human mind. Phones can't bring people together as we must be apart in order to use them. Now we meet in games and chat rooms and mostly we've no idea with whom we're interacting. Instead of friends in real life we've friends on contact lists who we'll probably never meet. The more we frequent social sites the more a-social we become and the more the 'cloud' becomes filled with the phenomenal confusion of our minds; it will never make sense so there's no point in trying to make sense of it. It's important to see that the cloud is a collective reflection of the mind of Humanity - not looking too good right now. Recognising it, goes a long way to finding our own peace of mind because we can walk away without withdrawal symptoms and we don't rely on it for company or approval. That doesn't mean we have to stop using it; it means we don't have to be online every moment in case we miss something we consider to be vital to our lives.

Technology keeps Humanity apart rather than bringing it together. The internet has become our 'cloak of invisibility' and only *we* choose when, or which masks we don when we're online. We can hide or lay low and choose who goes into which type of friend group but it's important to see that for each friend group we put on a different mask; we're never complete when we do that. Another tricky part to this is that we hide the parts we like about ourselves the least, so, just as we don't know who we're really talking to, neither do the people we chat with; our screens are always in-between us. At the very least a need to lay low must mean that we don't trust everyone on our friends list in which case, why do we have them on there? Some of us have multiple accounts that flicker between visible and invisible modes like fairy lights on a Christmas

Mask off   Mask on

tree. To bring this into the light, think about how well we know the people we communicate with online; in most cases we don't know if they smoke, how tall they are or if they live in the country they claim to live in. We don't tend to ask these questions of people online or even converse with them and we can't confirm that the image they put of themselves on their profile is actually them, or recent for that matter. All we actually know about these 'friends' is what we've read on their walls - creating the image they want us to form of them - and that's about it. The internet is a place for a meeting of minds, predominantly unhealthy ones. There are more stealth observers on social media websites than there are active participants. If you want proof of this just look at anyone's page who has a reasonable number of friends and see how many actually post.

Too often we broadcast information but we don't receive it. I've had some 'private' chats with people who keep on typing - message after message - despite my requests that they pause so that I can respond to their original comment. We don't see the person we're talking to as human: people type at us, rather than to us. More often than not we're interested in our own world and don't want to read what anyone else has written. We want to out-do and compete with each other. So social media is a place to broadcast to the masses rather than to an individual and also a place where family members can keep up-to-date with each other. Nothing on these sites is personal or private; yet it's also both. Even if we keep our personal life quiet there's a good chance that someone else may talk about us or post our embarrassing photographs on their page or stealth private groups. Fear of this keeps us from being open and honest because we're always suspicious and *en garde*. We're becoming more and more like the people in E. M. Forster's short story *The Machine Stops* (1909), as we increasingly withdraw from the outside world into our rooms where we spend a great deal of time in front of screens with little to no physical contact. Yes, the internet was *predicted* that far back, before we even had radios let alone televisions. We've become slaves to the servant we created and we're not looking for our freedom.

Ironically, Humanity, long separated, is coming together as One; it's a highly controlled and confused One. It's a depraved One and we created it. It's a One made up entirely of the contents of our minds, which are extremely unhealthy: it's a wireless One. In other words, it removes the need for human physical touch and interaction; it lacks heart. Will future generations be able to read body language at all? The internet can also be used for good. I use it to promote my books in order to raise even just one question in the minds of those who, like me, are curious about their existence or are confused about the world we live in. I say I use it to promote my books but those who know me personally know I don't go too far with that; I'd make a lousy salesperson as I simply don't care enough about it. I trust that those who're meant to read my books will find them; I trust in our Universe and I know that none of us are alone. We're all guided and that means you too.

The internet is a fabulous way to reach out and all conceivable information can be found on it; finding it is just a question of knowing where to look and entering the correct keywords. We can search for violence or pornographic material and millions of results are found. We can also search for something more meaningful like how Humanity could live better lives. Then proceeding with caution through the abundance of misleading and immature information it's possible to find little gems that lead to profound changes in our lives. The problem is not the internet, it's the mental health of the society that uses it. It's particularly confusing when so many of us declare 'I'm Free' from behind a security screen. The internet is the largest library in the world and in it we've got access to everything we've ever known on this earth; it's also the largest hiding place. There's a great deal on the internet that's healthy for us and a great deal that isn't; the problem is choice.

Just Around the Bend

We're waiting for miracles that in our hearts, we know won't arrive; we have to make them happen.

The wonders of the Universe are so far away and beyond our comprehension; the stars, other galaxies or God. We're unable to reach up to touch them but still we're fascinated and frustrated by the skies because we don't really know what's 'out there'. We also hope that whatever we find will be better than what we have here. An individual can't build their own rocket to go into outer space in order to take a closer look; they can only see the images that are publicised - and hope. Closer to home; good health, happiness, peace on earth and a debt free life appear to be unattainable for our generation and this is the case for our children too. Let me try to put this into perspective for you. We're so many billions of people living on a planet that in Universal or cosmic terms is less than the size of a speck of dust. We don't know who we are or what our purpose is yet we're all running around trying to achieve something called 'success' before our exit into oblivion, heaven or the 'hot place' (you may have some other favourite). We're leaving havoc behind us mostly because we're waiting for either a miraculous phenomenon to occur, or the arrival of a saviour to put the world to rights; we ignore the odds against these.

No wonder there's so much anguish in this world and no visible hope for our future; we prefer to hide in the world of films, games and social media; in so many ways they're distractions from our lives and seemingly more interesting. However, they're about as much use to our awareness as a key is without a lock; they're just some of the tools of aberration and procrastination, or to put it another way, they keep us living in ignorance, superstition and fear. The distractions, because we focus so strongly on them, silence the mind as long as we remain engrossed; they're therapy, which is any activity that relieves tension. However, when we stop the mind is noisy again which results in us wanting to go back to the games or whatever distraction is our own particular favourite. We participate in these feel-good-pastimes whether it's by savouring a freshly-brewed cup of coffee, eating chocolate or parading down a high street in a new outfit. Whatever leisure activities we choose, even a noisy rave party, they temporarily release us from our incessant mind chatter. When we find ways to quieten the mind we make them habitual.

When we put all this together with the fact that every human being suffers or has suffered in some way, it's no surprise we don't want to look inside ourselves; each one of us knows what we've buried so deeply. Understanding the mind of Humanity is as complicated and mysterious as understanding the Universe. We agree to wait in hope for the future because we can't see how this world or our lives have any worthwhile purpose with things the way they are: there's nothing to gain other than more money or more bills. In general, we get little to no job satisfaction because there's none to be had. Most of our jobs are mundane, mechanical and meaningless. The only result that can come out of a world like this is that more and more people become ill and depressed; increasingly unable to cope with their lives, yet still we wait for a brighter future that's always, just around the bend. Considering the above, we're waiting for miracles that no-one believes in. We can't even *see* the bend, let alone around it.

What we're actually waiting for can vary such as birthdays, anniversaries, Christmas, appointments, annual bonuses, change or retirement. Sometimes we're so keen for them to arrive that we prepare in advance like shopping for Christmas four months earlier or saving money for our old age; ultimately, we're fine-tuning our deaths before thinking about why we're alive. Instead of living our lives purposefully we're waiting for someone else to improve them for us; like governments or an inspirational speaker / author. If we want to live in a peaceful world we have to work together to raise Consciousness; we're One. Let's consider happiness, instead of misery.

A great deal of Humanity's time is spent waiting for the future to arrive - our whole lives - but it never arrives and it never will. It can't arrive for one good reason; it doesn't exist and therefore, the bend is infinite. We wouldn't queue today to catch a boat arriving next week. We're queuing to live and don't realise that there's only Now. We're queuing up a dead end waiting for someone else to bring this impossible future to us; science, governments, help books, super heroes and the like. For some strange reason we believe they'll succeed in doing it one day, if not for us then for our children. However, what we actually get is another version of something technical like a bigger, wider, flatter or higher resolution screen, a new artificial flavour or a promise of a cure for cancer in the future. It's barely enough to build up hopes and doesn't warrant the trust we put in these authorities. All too often we're 'running on the spot' and one day leads into another that isn't very different from the last. Long term, we're rushing around the clock; in no particular hurry with no idea where we're going and we're allowing ourselves to be entertained while we're doing it.

I once had a dream that took me a few years just to begin to fathom. In it a voice said "We're multi-dimensional time travellers". How is this possible? The future and past exist only in our minds. Only the future can exist on a working clock face as no clock is accurate enough to pinpoint the Now; just like us the clock's hands chase a future they'll never reach - time obscures the Now until the clock stops ticking. The future exists in our imagination; in pictures of a paradise island and in promises of a stress-free existence when we no longer have to work. For the majority of people this couldn't be further from the truth; for some the greatest bonus is the privilege of free transport passes and a secure retirement home. The past also is only a thought; we live in the past when we dwell on it and the longer we dwell on it the deeper its roots go and the more venomous its poison. Sure there are happy memories too, but the mind is only interested in drawing our attention to the less positive ones. The future and past are thought forms; we wait for the future and remember the past so what precisely are we doing *Now*? If this makes any kind of sense to you then you'll understand when I say that the mind can be seen as a 'time machine'. The contents of the mind are thoughts from our pasts and hopes for our future and we spend our lives collecting and remembering these; thought is never in the Now. How did we lose the Now? We learnt to remember the past and to look forward to the future.

I had an experience many years ago that I couldn't understand and it couldn't be explained. It was one afternoon after having had a light general anaesthetic and a laparoscopy; I was taking a nap at home, and painkillers. I dreamt I was in my bed and a large picture with a three-inch picture frame around it fell from its hook onto the floor. I leant over in bed to see the damage and the safety glass had cracked in one corner, but not too badly. The room was exactly the same as the room I was sleeping in. The picture had hung on the wall for four years. Now this is where my experience gets interesting. I was startled by the dream and woke up. As I lifted my head from the pillow I watched a repeat of the whole event - even the crack was the same. I've never repaired the picture. The future is not something we can wait for and incredibly, I watched the same event twice. I don't need it to be analysed. Drugs can cause tricks of the mind but *this* trick can't be explained in any way that would satisfy me. This happened and I was the only witness. I was so excited that I spent over two hours on the phone telling friends all about it. People have doubts when something strange happens to someone else but not when it happens to them; no-one can convince us otherwise. When you know, you *know*, and you can never turn your back on it.

Just around the bend reveals something the vast majority of us can't or won't see even though we complain about our lives so much. We put off self-realisation mostly because we believe we've time on our side, but we can never have time on our side. Time brings wrinkles and infirmity - not revelations. A young lady once ask me "How much time do I have here?" How much easier our lives would be if we knew answers to questions like that; perhaps we might think twice about procrastination. We find and defend every excuse to continue with things the way they are, like 'I want to change, but I was hurt, so I can't'. We put up barriers in order to prevent our 'progress'. I put progress in inverted commas because there really is no such thing when it comes to realising who we are. We've nothing at all to learn. Living this life is rather like wandering around a forest looking for something we haven't lost. We can't understand this until we find it. Yes I know this doesn't make complete sense at the moment, but it does when we realise that what we're looking for is not outside but *inside*. Imagine looking out of your lounge window all your life without ever knowing what was in the lounge.

We're already everything we'll ever be but we pretend otherwise. The same young lady (mentioned above) asked me what advice I could give her, so I suggested she observe her mind and find out how it works. She said "Yes ok, but the observing is hard" and "I keep myself busy so I don't have to think". This is calling for help but sending away the lifeboat. The road to revelation has no bargain basements, no special offers and no group workshops; the work isn't easy for the majority of people and it takes more than just five minutes. A great many people are put off at the first hurdle; this first hurdle is only a deterrent and it can be passed. It exists in time only. We ask 'how can we observe our mind' but in my experience we really don't want to. What we really want is to be given confirmation that we *can't* do it; we're looking for a sick-note so we don't have to be an active participant in raising our Consciousness level; we want our 'advisor' to be responsible for our journey so that *we* don't have to be. In other words, we're skiving. Society is pampered and lazy. It doesn't want change if it has to work for it and it doesn't want to make sacrifices. We want everything delivered to our doorsteps just like our takeaways and shopping. There's no path to realisation if we're dependent on others to show us the way; we can only find it for ourselves.

Why can't we just find it? If we're everything that ever was or ever will be why can't we know this now? In truth, because we don't want it badly enough and put it off for as long as we can; we think we're in control of our lives but this is so far from the truth. We don't even 'play it safe' - well a few do, but mostly we would prefer our place to be reserved while we look elsewhere; we keep our options open. Here are a few excuses we make to prevent ourselves seeing the truth about our world:

- I'll do it tomorrow.
- I've got a full-time job.
- I've lots of mouths to feed.
- I want to but I just don't have the time.
- It's alright for you …

Do any of these sound like familiar excuses? These are all arguments put forward by the mind. We're afraid to look around the bend because we're not sure what's there (if anything at all) and the mind keeps us afraid for as long as we allow it to. Just around the bend can seem too far away and too much effort to reach. Going around the bend is an insecure experience and this is a key reason why we don't do it; for some strange reason we believe we've something to lose, like our sanity. We don't want to take chances that we can't guarantee will pay off and there's no complaints department should things not pan out as we'd like them to - it's a leap of faith (later chapter). So we bide our time hoping someone will keep *our* seat free for us on the next boat. In other words, we let others do the work, such as scientists or politicians as though they were capable of finding a shortcut and we become their silent audience. The mind is like a car - either we're driving or it's freewheeling in which case it'll collide with something sooner or later, unless we take control of it.

Do you really believe you're an irrelevant reject of this universe? Two important questions we can ask ourselves are 'Have I reached the highest height I'm capable of reaching' and 'Do I put my heart and soul into the things I want to achieve'. If you answer 'Yes' to either of these, then why are you reading this book? It can be of no use to you. If you answer 'No' to them - well, recognising this is a great step forward, as it were.

The more we delay what we all know innately we must do sooner or later, the more our shame and guilt build up. The effects on our health and stress levels are horrendous. I declared to my partner that I was going to stop smoking in exchange for a new laptop. He was looking at them online and called me over to look at a particularly interesting one. I said "I'd stop smoking for that" and we went out the same day and he bought it for me. Now I was in a bit of a pickle because I'd made a promise and the present didn't feel like a good time to fulfil it; I quite enjoyed smoking. It took me six months to prepare for the mental marathon and after that time, with only two cigarettes left in my packet I told him I wouldn't buy any more. He doubted me and I don't blame him. He said "you'll want some later this evening so we better buy a packet just in case" but I stood my ground and said "No. These two are the last two". I smoked and enjoyed them and threw the empty packet into the bin; I've not touched another one since. The guilt I felt over the six months grew and grew and more so because he never mentioned it or reminded me of my promise. The relief after stopping was amazing and I was never tempted to start again. When we put our minds to something and we really want to achieve it, we're almost there; the next step is to put the plan into action and then to keep our eye on the goal.

Because of our inertia we can't collectively see beyond this reality, but I can assure you this reality is temporary and transitive. Whatever we do has consequences and whatever decisions we make in this life are our responsibility. We can't always see the results of our actions but that doesn't mean they don't exist. We all have to leave this world empty handed - the same way we arrived. Now is the only time to think about what we're doing here and if we've enough time to do it. Humanity is heading somewhere and we're carrying a tremendous and heavy burden with us. Each one of us can lighten that burden by observing ourselves closely and not passing our grievances and foolishness on for the next generation to sort out. Nothing in this world is worth holding on to nor is it possible to take with us when we die. Those who do decide to look further into their minds and question their own dogmas, are mostly considered to be, just around the bend. Overcoming this criticism may well prove to be the greatest obstacle; it depends on whether you care about the judgement of others.

As long as there is a need for approval and a consensus to live in fear, we can't see the world as it truly is. By abdicating our responsibility and putting our trust in other people, we agree to be controlled by them doing what they think is best for us, or rather for *them*. Society doesn't encourage individuality or the questioning of its rituals, rather, it encourages inertia in these matters. We sponsor and commercialise physical strength, beauty, acting ability and wealth, applauding them with awards of one sort or another. But, if a person wants to change this world into a happier place to live in, we label them a bad influence; *this* is insanity.

Scotty? Beam me up!

Completeness

When we stop looking for help, we realise we never needed any.

I was obsessed with the idea of dying when I was young. I wanted to die before I reached the age of thirty and I wasn't at all afraid of it; I did it so frequently in my dreams. Thirty somehow seemed very *old* to me; it was *grown-up* and being a grown-up was the last thing I wanted to be. Every grown up I'd ever known was unkind, indifferent or hypocritical; sometimes all three. I was fifteen when struck with an insane idea. My family were gathered around the dinner table and as usual, my sister and I were invisible and unheard. I left the room unnoticed, went to the bathroom and gathered all the painkillers I could find - there were plenty. I took them up to my bedroom with a couple of glasses of water and sat down in front of my dressing table. I swallowed and counted them one at a time until I'd taken forty. I felt no fear or emotion but I did feel that this act would bring out some sort of emotion in my father - a change of heart. I left the house and went to the nearest phone booth to call a friend and told him what I'd done. He took me to the hospital. I still felt no fear or emotion. The stomach pump wasn't fun at all; I rather hated the experience but harder to swallow was the reaction of my father. He arrived at the hospital at their request, sat down by my bedside and wrote me a cheque for £50. He handed it to me to buy something to cheer myself up and then he returned home. I decided that didn't work too well at all and I never repeated it; no-one ever mentioned the incident again. At this point in my life - and for many years following - I believed I needed my father's love to make me complete. I never got it so I unconsciously sought it elsewhere.

~~~

Divorce and re-marriage are the acceptable norm and a divorcee is often regarded as being 'back on the market'; what a strange term. Blinded by confusion, I was insecure, naïve and searching for a dream; unaware it was only an illusion. My only purpose was to get married, have children and not to make the same mistakes my parents made - putting my children into an orphanage. I married many times because I was unable to discern then what I see clearly now. Foolishly I believed I could right the wrongs of the past. To believe that something from the outside could make me complete meant I saw myself as *incomplete*. I was searching for a 'normal' family in order to become part of a *whole*, rather than a fragment, but this search is a diversion from what really needs to be done. I wanted to be a better parent to my children than my parents had been to me; this is like looking for a future that can change our past. It's also looking for someone to fulfil our dreams for us and holding up a flag that says 'Rescue Me'.

This is the life we've been encouraged to strive for through 'happily ever after' films and stories. I was searching for my fairy-tale-ending before I'd even begun to live. The fantasy became an obsession and I thought about nothing else. I'd no ambitions other than to live in a doll's house, walk through the door wearing a white wedding dress and to have my own front door key to lock the world out; letting someone else take responsibility for me. What I didn't know then is that I was locking myself in. When things inevitably went wrong, I quickly found a replacement crutch to lean on because I was afraid to be alone. The marital vow 'till death do us part' has lost its importance for most of us and perhaps should be replaced by 'until I wake up' and realise there are no knights in shining armour, no princesses to save, no short-cuts to self-knowledge and no-one who can carry us to our *Self*.

Never think more of someone than you think of yourself. When we fall for someone, we tend to ignore their shortfalls (or view them as endearing) so that in the rush of romance they appear to be our ideal partner. I now see this as insanity driven by irrational need. We need someone else to be solid for us, to hold our hand, give meaning to our life and give us what we think we lack. In order to live with our *flaws* rather than our *strengths* we look up to someone; creating a symbiotic relationship, but we're not aware we're doing it; it's a survival instinct. What we're really trying to do is *join* ourself to someone else, but two people can't make each other complete or fill the void in each other's lives. We do it because if we didn't put our hope in others, we'd have to face ourselves.

By looking up to someone else, we place ourselves beneath them. This gives us an excuse to stay exactly where we want to be and they become our *prop*; we surrender to them. The pedestal we've stood them on is constructed from need and desire. In much the same way we look to society to be this 'prop' and get comfort from being a part of something bigger than ourselves; we play a passive role. Deep in our hearts we know that the key to our freedom lies 'within' and the reason we don't admit to it, is because we're not ready to be self-contained.

By finding people we believe need our help or can help us, we somehow feel worthwhile and it avoids us taking a long hard look at ourselves for the more esoteric questions that may give meaning to our lives. What we're really looking for is a distraction from the stresses in our everyday life. If fairy tales are to be believed then in order to live happily ever after, we must find our prince or princess; this only gives us an excuse to believe that our happiness hasn't arrived yet because of some misfortune. The reality is that these relationships are deep in work, dirty dishes, children, nappies, paying bills, stress, frustration and being able to fluently converse on cultural and 'soap opera' current affairs. Problems arise because just as we want to continue with the status quo, so do the people we find. In other words, they don't want to change any more than we do. Initially the relationship feels energised because we've 'balanced' ourselves, but it's only a matter of time before the batteries run down and we realise the truth; we're still incomplete and our companion doesn't have our missing pieces.

We want to be with a new partner twenty four hours a day and if the relationship is based on symbiotic need, sooner or later we'll want to be as far away from each other as possible. This is one of the reasons relationships can become stale; nothing actually changes because we're relying on someone else to make those changes for us. Think of it as two people sitting either end of a see-saw; they're dependent on each other and if one gets off, then the other comes crashing down. However, if a couple find completeness in themselves, rather than each other, they'll stand a good chance of having a healthy and progressive relationship. A relationship in which two roses can bloom side-by-side.

Why do we need to look up to someone else to make us complete? This is a question of faith, but it's a false faith. What we actually look for is our shadow; that which we're afraid to claim as ourself, which is why we externalise our search. The person we find is doing the same thing; they also feel incomplete. A shadow is not necessarily dark; it's the parts of us that we deny existence to. Someone content to live a wicked life has a light shadow; he knows he's not living in his highest interest, but he never listens to that inner voice. However, we're only window shopping and the shop front will always keep us separated. Let me explain this a little more. We're on one side of the glass looking into the shop for what we think we need. What we believe we need is looking straight back at us. So why isn't it a perfect match? Because it's not really us. It's part of somebody else. We already have what we're looking for to make us complete but we're (1) in denial of that and (2) unwilling to confirm it by taking a look. This is an insecurity. We think so little of ourselves that it seems impossible that we're all we ever need. Just as in our high streets it's in these shop windows that desire is born and this desire can never bear fruit that won't one day rot. One tree can't bear the fruit of another. We see what we want to see, listen for the words we want to hear and only accept that which suits our agenda.

It's also for these reasons that we choose to ignore the mischief of governments. There isn't a soul who doesn't know that governments are corrupt, dysfunctional and never stick to their manifesto promises. They bring poverty, misery, illness, war and neglect to the people they govern. Despite this knowledge we choose to mechanically re-elect them to govern our world. We do this for several reasons including fear, laziness and insecurity - yet few will admit to that. We look to them to do what we believe we can't, yet we know full well they can't either.

~~~

Often we turn our attention to celebrities and see what we want to see via the various forms of media and social interaction outlets. We ignore any notion that the images we have of these icons have been created by others; they're faux. The characters Clint Eastwood plays in the spaghetti westerns are good examples of this; we're led to believe they're tough, indestructible and in complete control of their lives. However, this image is an on-screen image and not the character of the actor off-screen. As a small child I turned my attention to David Cassidy though I'd no idea who he was. I listened to his songs, *I Think I Love You* and *Daydreamer* again and again, imagining I was good enough to be the girl he was singing to; getting lost in the illusion. But it wasn't because I wanted his life; it was because I didn't like my own and because according to the lyrics, he understood me. Listening to his songs gave me temporary relief from what was then, an incredibly noisy mind. It's also about energy; he had it and I didn't and by mimicking him, I felt some of that energy. This is one of the reasons there are so many copycat and lookalike artists in the world; they haven't found their own purpose / skill. The same principle applies when we copy fashion and other trends shown to us through celebrities or advertising campaigns.

When we look closer at what's happening here we see that we only see snapshots of successful people's lives and then wear their names on T-Shirts or model ourselves on them. We become the character's 'fan' because we feel a void in our own lives and in some odd way they fill it, by proxy. This is an illusion and if the actor so much as trips over a pebble in real life the illusion is either destroyed or ignored. If ignored we continue to believe and make excuses for their momentary lapse and if destroyed, we seek someone else to take their place. Characters on-screen are powerful and influential in our lives, regardless of whether they're villains or heroes and this is true in blockbuster films or the more minor, but no less influential, soap operas. We can't see that the actors are just like us; we see what we want to see, hear what we want to hear and make them into our gods. Like in dreams we must one day wake up and realise that what we believe to be real, isn't. The word 'fan' is derived from 'fanatic'; that's got to be worth pondering. Following someone else's habits and behaviours is rather like reading someone's book and then writing our name over theirs; plagiarising someone's life. We've our own book to write. We all have the ability to be creative but we don't believe we can do it even though we do it every moment of our lives.

If someone tries to tell us the truth about the person we glorify, we don't want to know and put up a huge amount of resistance in order to reinforce our beloved delusions. This is true even if the person we're glorifying tells it to us and refuses to accept our irrational inflated opinions of them. Placing someone on a pedestal they're unable to stand on causes problems in relationships; the relationship is based on a false notion and the pedestal will crack under the pressure. Because of this it can never bring peace or happiness, other than of a temporary nature. The situation will always require a victim and someone to be their saviour, who is also incomplete; they need someone to *save* and believe they can do it.

The delusion is more wide-angled than it seems at first glance. On its lowest level it's where a person may choose to remain in an abusive relationship. We often believe we can't survive without the person involved and keep going under the delusion that things will change one day. In a lot of cases we're convinced we're responsible for our partner's behaviour. Why? Because they convinced us of it. By claiming responsibility for someone else's behaviour we're making excuses for them; it's a small price to pay and it serves both parties. This is an evasive tactic we make in order not to take responsibility for ourselves; it's our albatross. On its highest level the delusion requires the worship of an outside and invisible force, such as any one of the variety of gods we worship (metaphysical or physical). Somewhere in-between lay our relationships with our employers, friends and other family members.

There are people who choose to remain where they are in life and to continue making the same mistakes and there are those who seek them out in order to play out what they enjoy most; control. There are also people who feel an irresistible urge to break the glass and walk away from the destructive and repetitive patterns in their lives. You're one of those, because you're reading this now. More often than not the root causes of this behaviour are irrational fear and apathy. Deep down we already know all we need to know about ourselves and those we come into contact with. If we look closely at our own thoughts we see that we push aside the wise ones in favour of the reckless. Because we don't believe we can survive by ourselves, trust we put in outside forces must, by definition, be misplaced. We put trust in other people to do what we feel unable to do ourselves. A strong character attracts a weaker one but if we look carefully it's easy to see that the weaker character is in complete control; without the consent of a 'weaker' character to dominate, a strong character has no power. Generally speaking, 'weaker' characters are only weak because they've *forgotten* their own strengths, preferring not to remember them because then, they'd have to take responsibility for themselves. It's this way with society too.

We're dissatisfied with ourselves and hope that someone stronger will save us by whisking us away to a place of safety; anyone will do, as long as it's not us. We've also been taught to think that solutions to problems in our lives lie in things like large bank accounts; measurements of our success. Not true? How many people buy lottery tickets every day / week and how many people buy more than one? By looking up to people who've apparently cracked the problem we can make more excuses about why we can't, by putting their good fortune down to luck or talent. We look up to people who have or can achieve what *we* can't and we set them up as our role models; but it's twisted because we can never become them. We set ourselves up to fail and we rely on outside forces to stimulate us. It's a way of living our lives through something or somebody else and its root is apathy.

When we look outside for help or completeness, we also look outside for someone to blame when things go wrong in our lives: we want someone to be responsible and someone who can alleviate our pain and suffering. The most obvious example of this is that we leave the world in the hands of the politicians and corporations - then blame *them* because we're not living in a Garden of Eden - conveniently forgetting that we vote them into power and buy the carrots they dangle in front of us. However, when we're in the driving seat - instead of the 'mind' or a government - there's no need for any adjustment or remedy. There's no need for gender categorisation labels either; weak, strong, housewife or hero and there's no need to try to become something we're not. The only thing we need to *become* is who we already are. We're not fragments but over time we've become 'fragmented'; we're already complete and we only need to realise this. We started believing we're incomplete because we allowed ourselves to be convinced of it, by society. Through vigilance and the observance of our own mind and behaviour we realise that we're not incomplete at all.

Mind Dramas

Yesterday has already happened - we don't have to re-master, splice, edit or re-live it.

E very moment we process information picked up from a variety of sources. On a physical level the sources include teachers, media outlets, books, friends, acquaintances and family. This information is then processed through our filters according to our conditioning. It's not until we step back and think about what's happening that the process becomes apparent. The actions of others pull triggers that appeal to, upset or offend us; they also create fear. Whatever our reaction, its roots lie in our past experiences and we allow them to create what becomes a smash-hit drama, in which we're starring. The root of these dramas is often that we don't feel good enough; we feel unworthy and therefore, insecure. The dramas become *real* and set in motion a chain of events producing emotions and reactions that validate them. Our dreams have the same effects on us. I remember once waking with my partner in the morning and he felt annoyed that I'd smoked a cigarette - I'd recently given them up - but this was just the residual thoughts and feelings from his dream. Nevertheless, the emotions were real for him and though he *knew* I hadn't smoked he found it hard to ignore his dream. Our dreams can seem so real that when we wake up from them we react as though we were really *there* and participating in the storyline. Nightmares from my childhood were exactly like that and in one I woke up just as I was about to be shot. I awoke in a cold sweat and felt a tight pain in my chest; symptoms of fear or dread; as though it were really happening.

We've been creating the dramas for so long now that we don't realise we're doing it; we absorb the effects like emotional sponges. Take for example watching a film in the cinema. Our reactions to scenes in the film depend on the genre and include, but aren't limited to sadness, remorse, anger, fear, disgust, revelation, shock, horror, compassion and hope. Yet, all we did to bring about these reactions was buy a ticket and take our seat. Nothing happened to us personally and we haven't interacted with anyone off-screen. The drama isn't real; it's information from sounds and images perceived by our senses. It's happening in our mind; a hard concept to grasp initially but when it falls into place we wonder how we never noticed it before. We literally, during some scenes, sit on the edge of our seats in fear or anticipation (sometimes both) as the action grips our senses dragging us into the reality of the film as though we were participating in it.

One of the most famous scenes that terrified audiences worldwide was the shower scene in the film *Psycho* where the character played by Janet Leigh met her end. Auditory and visual memories from this scene remain in our minds. Proof that this happens is that I still remember them now and if you know the film, so do you; they're embedded. There were reports that some people apparently feared getting into their showers after watching *Psycho* (1960). Sound and vision were used to produce the same effect in the film *Jaws* (1975) but instead of dreading a shower, many people feared swimming in the sea after watching it. Our reactions to scenes like these are far stronger when we watch the evolving three-dimensional films because they're more realistic. Sometimes our reactions are so strong that we double check we've locked all the windows and doors when we get back home again.

Why do we like these self-induced fear experiences? Perhaps it's because we survive them and walk out of the cinema unscathed. Perhaps it's because our mind errs on the negative side of life. We enjoy the terror and fear which is why these films and others like them are produced more and more; demand equals supply. Humanity has become disconnected from what they see in such films; our minds don't see the long-term effects that permeate so deeply into society; ignorance, apathy and complacency.

The more we watch such films, the more our reactions to the violence or sex in them are neutralised. Many children watch these films with no *apparent* ill effects and without this content they'd find them boring and passive. They watch these films from a younger and younger age and when they're not watching them they get the same *information* from books and games they download onto their iEquipment. Imagine showing a child an episode of the 1950s / 1970s *Dixon of Dock Green* series today. Its slow and comparatively mild-mannered pace wouldn't hold their attention; it isn't scary or exciting enough. We crave the fast-paced action-packed content for entertainment which matches the increasingly fast-paced and limited perspective of our lives. Consequently, the dramas playing in our minds are just as fearful and fast-paced off-screen as on. We end up not being able to understand the mess and confusion in our minds as much as we can't understand it in the world; we live in fear and perhaps the biggest fear of all is to be in *silence*; we don't know how to be silent. For most people silence means loneliness but this loneliness is really a fear of being left alone with only our mind for company. I know now that loneliness is an inability to live with our shadow. It's the noise inside that knows us so well; when we're alone we can't hide from it. The mind forces us to focus on things we'd rather not focus on (ourselves) and it's for this reason we like to keep busy with work, leisure, play, social media, televisions and music. The louder the noise we can make around us, the less we can hear our mind and the less we can hear ourselves.

We love extreme drama. We live in fear ... but we also love the experience of it, which is why we love roller-coaster rides and other 'scaries'. There's a ride at the Stratosphere Tower in Las Vegas called *Insanity* that spins people round a mechanical arm at a height of 900 feet, generating 3 'G's. Scarier still is a ride called *Big Shot* at the same tower that generates an experience of 4 'G's and as if that wasn't enough you can now be thrust 30 feet over the building at 30mph, if you so choose. There's plenty of people who want to go on these rides. These so called 'thrill' rides have become more and more terrifying and there's a great demand for them. But we don't enjoy these things just because of an adrenaline hit. What we love most of all is that while we're being terrified, in that moment, we're not thinking about our daily worries. While we're being thrust off a building we're not thinking about relationships, bills, work, mowing the lawn or anything else. We're living carefree right inside that moment: the Now.

Less extreme, are dramas like finding the courage to chat up someone at a club or other social venue - though some people may well prefer to be launched off the Stratosphere Tower at 30mph. Somewhere in between there's going for an interview, going to the dentist or standing in a queue at a supermarket checkout getting irate because the cashier is idly chatting while our frozen produce melts. Many other dramas pass through our minds while we're waiting in queues; the mind loves the opportunity to get our full attention. This is particularly true in traffic jams and some of these have miles of tailbacks. Why do queues affect us? Because we temporarily have no choice but to be still and think while we wait; we've no control and our mind seizes the opportunity to create dramas that occupy us. The word *queue* (15th century) means *tail of a beast* and who could argue with that definition? I found this definition in June 2014 on 'dictionary.reference.com'.

Interpersonal relationships are also affected by abstract dramas; mostly imagined. The longer we interact with a person, the more complicated the dramas of our minds regarding them can become. Each interaction reinforces our deep-seated beliefs and prejudices and when you put that alongside our natural tendency to lean towards the *negative* it's easy to see how resentment builds up; without provocation. For example, let's say that a friend borrowed a book from you six months ago and hasn't returned it. How many times would you run the conversation of you asking for it back and enact possible outcomes in your mind, including ending your friendship? Perhaps you want to forget about it but your mind won't let you; even in bed as you're trying to sleep. Each time you remember it, more resentment builds up. You may feel angry, bitter, rejected or used. Whatever the feelings, they get out of proportion and even permeate your dreams. It's important to realise that you've written a drama and that you're playing and continually rehearsing every part in it; including that of the audience and critics. The chances are your friend is completely unaware of your turmoil and forgotten altogether about the book. A gentle reminder may be all that's needed and your mind will quieten, at least where this subject is concerned. It's far better to have peace of mind than to hold onto a grudge based on an imagined scenario. I remember hearing a joke about a man who wanted to borrow his neighbour's lawnmower and he ran an incredible script through his mind predicting the negative outcome of his request. By the time he knocked on the door and the man answered he said "You know what ... you can stuff your lawnmower". This may be a joke but we do this sort of thing all the time; the mind encourages it. We create the drama out of nothing at all.

There's another drama that plays a part in our lives and that's the long-term random repetitive reminders of past pains and suffering. I call these random because they pop up unexpectedly while we're doing or thinking about something unconnected. The mind doesn't want us to forget the past and it's constantly reminding us of things; it replays not only the story, but variations of it, even twenty or thirty years after the event. I was haunted for many years by memories about my father, wondering how or what I could do or say that would make him feel differently about me. The more I focused on the situation, the bigger its influence became in my life. As far back as I can remember these painful and damaging thoughts plagued my days and nights; my father was mostly my waking thought and the last one before I went to sleep, which is why he appeared so often in my dreams. This continued until I was around thirty-five when a psychotherapist explained that I'd given my father my power; it came as quite a shock because I'd believed myself to be powerless. I began to take back my power and to see that there were some things in the world I could never change and first and foremost on the list was *other* people. I realised it was possible to change the self-pity, self-hatred, grudges and bitterness that took up so much space in my mind - by taking responsibility. I saw that the source of my unhappiness was not my father, but me. I'd discovered that the 'me' I thought myself to be, was in fact a clever and highly manipulative fraud. We too often focus on how other people have hurt us and don't realise that we hurt and judge ourselves far more harshly than anyone else could. These dramas hang in frames on the walls of our mind and they'll remain there until we decide to take them down. The walls we've constructed are reinforced and patrolled by the mind; they're an illusion. We don't have to remain behind them.

~~~

We don't just create *our* own dramas but we also jump into other people's productions; regardless of whether we know them or not. One way we do this is to listen to and spread gossip. Why do we do it? Often because we've nothing better to do and nothing more interesting to say or if we do, no-one who wants to listen to it. Often we want to fit in with the person we're talking to and gossip is what's expected in order to rank highly on someone's popularity list. So we spread the latest *newscast* or fabricate another one and marvel at our ingenuity, despite the mini-drama at the back of our minds that knows we don't feel good about it. I bumped into a neighbour of mine a few months ago and she asked if I'd found my dog. I told her I hadn't lost him and she didn't believe me. "Oh well," she puzzled "I suppose it was someone else's dog" before getting into her car and driving off. So I knew I'd been the subject of gossip and it wasn't long before how it started got back to me. We've become expert at gossip and social media has become an unpleasant extension of it. One of the biggest reasons to gossip about other people is that we're dissatisfied with our own lives and another, that we've nothing better to do; we find their lives more interesting than our own.

Another way we enjoy other people's dramas is by being an audience. We love soap operas, slowing down to look at accidents on the motorway (rubber-necking), standing around watching an ambulance crew and being kept up-to-date with scandals; we have a morbid curiosity and love to make a drama out of a crisis. Our mind also loves to imagine what people might think about us, even though we haven't done anything wrong; a form of insecurity. One example is how we behave when we're leaving a shop with our purchases and the alarm bells ring. Every one stares as though we've stolen something and though this is not the case, feelings of shame and embarrassment arise as though we'd *actually* committed the act and these feelings arise because we believe other people think we're guilty. We love to think the worst of people and often what we imagine people think about us isn't true; some of the people staring may simply be feeling relief that it wasn't them that set off the alarms. Why do we care about what people think? It's because we seek approval from outside sources and in this scenario at least, what we get is more like condemnation.

~~~

There are many of us who have a need to bring other people into our drama and this is often at the cost of friendship. This situation arises when someone is so engrossed in their own problems - relationship, health, work or family -

that they can't see anything outside their own story. Even a good listener tires of listening to the same boyfriend / girlfriend problems again and again and struggles to hide the fact. The *victim* will use this lack of interest to deepen their 'unworthy' or 'nobody cares' beliefs. I'd suggest that we don't actually *want* anyone to listen or even to give us advice; what we seek is a sounding-board and validation of our right to feel miserable because we believe the severity of our problem warrants it. If we're given this validation, it confirms the belief that we can't change; this is the pay off.

~~~

Our minds and bodies respond to the information they receive and for this reason it's a good idea to choose what information we 'upload' into them; the information becomes who we think we are and influences how we react to the world around us. The mind recalls memories and therefore, the past. We create our dramas from our memories and only we know the script - no-one else has access to it. One way to stop the noise in our heads is to recognise and watch the thoughts coming and going. Initially this isn't easy as our mind wanders off without us realising it, we daydream or even fall asleep. The thoughts come and go like waves on an ocean but we can choose to surf on them or let them roll to the shore; either way they're still part of the ocean - memories. All too often we catch another wave before the one we're riding on breaks. Sometimes my mind catches me out and I ponder some pointless thoughts for longer than necessary. As soon as I recognise this the thoughts dissolve and I can't find them again; a bit like going upstairs to get something and then forgetting what it was I went up there for. However, the mind quickly replaces the thought with another and at first, we need to repeat the process often. The mind is *wild* and arguing with it will prove fruitless; it holds all information about you and knows all your strengths and weaknesses. It can be recognised and observed and with that comes a greater understanding of who we are and why we dwell on so much negativity. With this understanding the mind quietens and we create fewer, if any, dramas in our lives.

It's possible to stop these dramas once we've set our *intention* to end our pain and suffering. However, in order to work with that intention, vigilance is needed to recognise our 'unhealthy' thought patterns as soon as they manifest. For example, contacting an estranged friend or family member can be a tough beast to conquer. More often than not we can't remember what caused the dispute in the first place or why it's gone on for so long. Pride and foolishness raise their ugly heads *insisting* we hold on to the grudges but by working in line with our 'intention' we can overcome these when we recognise their familiar faces. Mind dramas are the ego's self-defence mechanisms and its armour is strong, particularly when it senses danger. Stubbornness is nothing more than an impenetrable force-field constructed of fears and it's us who are locked behind it. The only obstacle that prevents us from finding peace is *us*. Our ego controls each one of our masks and it's under the protective custody of the mind. The ego loves role-playing games and it's a Master of Disguise.

Independence

We can depend on not becoming independent.

Independence is something we strive for without really comprehending what it is. Amongst other things, the act of seeking independence is seeking separation from the rest of Humanity. Countries fight to become independent, children leave home to become independent and we seek well paid employment in order that one day we may achieve this *independence*. These are somewhat illusory goals for no matter what, we live in dependence of *something*. If we didn't, we wouldn't be where we are now. Humanity is separated but it's also dependent on that separation to keep itself going in the direction it believes it has no choice but to follow; it no longer requires *free will*. If we decide to change course and create a peaceful beautiful world to live in we'll be dependent on each other to do it. Humanity is a team, despite its cells pretending to be individuals and this frame of mind has come about through the coordinated efforts of every one of us. However, whether we like it or not we work together; a nail can't drive itself into the wood and a football can't kick itself into the goal. Even air is dependent on the space it occupies and we're dependent on that air for our next breath. It's only man, in his audacity, who believes otherwise; on some level we all know this is pointless.

We're dependent on the society we've created and it's dependent on us. Each thing in it exists because of another and they can't be separated; everything and everyone is connected and inter-dependent. You exist because your parents brought you into the world.

- Shops exist because of desires.
- Police exist because of crime.
- Beauty parlours exist because of vanity.
- The poor exist because of the rich.
- Starvation exists because of the greedy.
- Doctors exist because of illness.
- Bullies exist because of victims.

Even excuses exist because of a lack of responsibility. Increasingly, foundations and charities exist because we care only for our needs; this leaves others to go without. We live by the right of *entitlement* whether it be to claim unemployment or to leave elderly relatives in homes because we need to be alone with our spouses and children; we can't cope with the elderly or infirm as well as the other responsibilities society places on us. We claim our rights to things we're entitled to but we've become so self-centred that we care not for those who are unable to claim theirs; instead of supporting them we judge and condemn them. Misery and loneliness exist because of separation; the separation of each and every one of us. Anyone who denies that Humanity is separated has forgotten that he's connected to the tramp in the street, the poor, the pitiful and the sorrowful; he's forgotten also that we charge them to live on their own planet. We are One and dependent on each other; the actions of one of us effects the life or lives of others. Some of these effects are minor and some major - like in wars.

We care about ourselves and not about those who pay the price for our vanity and we'll continue to do this while we're dependent on charity to bridge the gap between us. How come you may ask? Because we're excused from responsibility when we do our bit by dropping our pennies in to charity boxes; it doesn't make it any better if you drop pounds in. If we look at this objectively it's easy to see that as long as charities exist between us and those in need, people will continue to go without. We're *all* connected; no-one can be outcast from Consciousness.

Humanity is being willingly driven at high speed to an unknown destination - refusing to consider where it might be going and neither knowing nor caring who the driver is - regardless of the consequences. Humanity blunders on complaining about the driver's intentions and huffing and puffing at - or blaming - the other passengers for the unfortunate casualties along the way. With nothing more to go on than a tacit agreement between the driver and his passengers to drive where he sees fit - he's been given carte blanche to drive off the edge of a cliff if he chooses to. Yet, despite opportunities to disembark at every stop Humanity chooses to remain on board. The twist in the above analogy is that, long term, the driver doesn't know where he's going either; the driver needs us and we think we need the driver.

Scotty! Do you read me?

~~~

One argument I've heard against the non-existence of independence is 'I'm independent. I go to work, support my family, own my own house, take care of my children and depend on no-one'. This is a specious argument and so easy to dismantle. For one thing, we're dependent on our employers for our salaries, pensions and the continuity of our contract. This argument also shows that you care only for your own agenda and therefore, ignore the needs of the rest of Humanity who belong to this world as equally as you do; it's an 'I'm alright' mentality. Another argument is 'I run my own business'; then you're dependent on your clients, materials, paper, pens, banks and many other things. We're as dependent on society as a child is dependent on its parents; dependence is inescapable for everyone.

A multi-millionaire may seem to be independent but he isn't - far from it; he's less independent than the poverty stricken people in third world countries. Money needs maintenance and he'll need trustworthy staff to manage his life and guard his wealth. Like us he still needs to eat and drink and more than anything he's dependent on the silence of the majority to keep him in his privileged position. One of the most difficult things about having money is that we can't let go of it and we always want more which in the long run, means more people go without. No matter how much money we've got we still live in pain, uncertainty and a restlessness that's occurred because of our separation.

Look to nature for proof; everything is inter-dependent and that's one of the things that makes it so wonderful - everything needs everything. We too are part of nature and couldn't exist without it. Yet we've allowed ourselves to become divided in the most insane ways. We'd all like to be *independent* and we all strive for it. We seek independence because we believe that with it will come this thing called security, but we don't really know what that means. Sure, we can become financially secure but that won't heal what's hurting inside us and more importantly it won't remove the real sicknesses of our society - fear and apathy being just two of them. Mostly we fear death and in particular, a painful death. Death to each of us is as natural as apples falling from a tree - it will happen.

Even if it were possible to achieve independence, it would be pointless. It would be like the left leg seeking independence from the right. We're connected; each one of us is an essential component in the design of the world that we've created, yet we choose to view it through a tiny opening of closed curtains and we choose to blame others for its creation. We can only function as One despite our attempts to pretend otherwise. We could achieve what we think of as *freedom*, objectively, by working together - all of us; this planet is rich in food and has enough to sustain us all. The only difference between the majority and financially secure multi-millionaires is the size and quality of the cages we live in. The only thing we all really need in this world is each other, but for now we have to walk alone because the *crowd* aren't ready to see that.

~~~

From a young age we've been subjected to common thoughts and influences. The toys we play with are limiting and designed to help us to fit in with and perpetuate an established society; we need to learn our ABC's and 123's together with dexterity, physical fitness and hand-eye coordination. We learn all the skills needed to work in either blue or white collar fields. Never are we taught that we can think freely or imaginatively about who we are, where we came from or what we're doing here; more importantly, where we may be going. Questioning our existence is strongly discouraged and philosophy is rarely part of any curriculum before we're old enough to attend university, by which time we struggle with metaphysical concepts because for so many years we've been trained to function in our physical world.

We can break free from the influences of others, but we have to be prepared not to care about what anyone else thinks. It's absolutely necessary if we intend to break away from the crowd and think for ourselves, rather than in the limited and subjective way we've been taught. Limited according to our culture and / or conditioning and subjectively because we think of our own position in the world rather than that of others - we're selfish. Without these limiting influences the world becomes objective and our thoughts take the *whole* into consideration before we carry out actions - we become responsible. In this sense we can reclaim our mind and live according to what we believe is the best way, as far as is possible in this world. This involves a good deal of consideration before we speak or act and it's not an easy process; most people abstain from it as we've become lazy and disillusioned. We believe, without a shred of evidence, what we've been told on one level but see the dishonest nature of it on the other; our preference though, is to follow the majority because of peer pressure or fear. When we spend all our time absorbing information from media sources and those who have been conditioned in the same way it's not possible to think for ourselves and thinking for ourselves is the only way to give birth to new thoughts.

What If and Other Worries

Look to the light and the shadows will stretch out behind you.

'What if' is that bucket of water used to quench the fire of joy, inspiration and hope; which we pour over ourselves or somebody else does it for us. 'What if' also gives us permission to worry about something that may or may not happen in the future; it's a pre-order for something that doesn't exist. When we give this some thought we can see that it's a self-limiting activity that saps our valuable energy and fills us with inertia.

'What if' is close to 'but' in as much as it's a clause or condition that cancels out rational thought. For example 'I want to get out more, but what if I get hit by a bus' or 'I want to leave my job but what if I can't find another one'. It gives us an excuse not to change a destructive habit and also a false sense of protection, from the future. In other words, by worrying about something we believe that in some way we'll prevent it from happening. 'Worry', 'what if', 'but' and 'fretting' are all symptoms of fear. We look for things to worry about, like whether it's going to rain tomorrow or even further into the future. A problem is something that requires a solution but rather than seek solutions to our current ones, we choose to find others to worry about that haven't happened and may never happen. By doing this we create a great deal of stress in our bodies, often as though the hypothetical event had actually happened - muscles tighten up, we get chest pains, suffer dread, rely on old familiar comforts and make ourselves ill.

Many people don't *want* solutions to their problems because in a perverse way their problems define who they are; paradoxically, we know what the solutions are but prefer to ignore them, pretending they don't exist or are unattainable. We create problems to worry about by continually putting ourselves in problematic situations; like getting drunk then living in fear of being found out - by our parents for example. However, at the same time, we're proud of and even brag about our behaviour to our peers. I remember my sister used to go to school in her uniform but take more *suitable* clothing with her to change into for when she truanted and went out on the town with her friends - worrying yet revelling in the fear of being caught. The only reason to live in fear of being found out is that we're ashamed of our own behaviour and if we're ashamed of it, why do it? We see the danger signs and walk straight past them

145

choosing images for ourselves that make us an *acceptable* part of the 'in crowd'; it's all about peer pressure and this comes initially from films, advertising and other forms of media, like magazines.

We don't have our best interests at heart but expect others to - how strange we are. The mind keeps us in fear of danger regardless of whether that danger exists or not and it's always on guard against attack. The ego wants to survive and is at its happiest when it's not questioned, so to speak. It's having great fun doing whatever it wants to do and when we want to stop its fun it reacts rather like a child that doesn't want to leave a playground - it has a tantrum. Worry is a way for the mind to maintain control and it's through fear-invoking control that we've been dominated for so long. When we begin to think for ourselves, the mind puts up a fight with 'worry warnings'; it creates hypothetical situations that ward off any attempt to reclaim our power. Like the mind, we want to be heard; our personal worries are greater than anyone else's and when we hear someone's story that's more tragic than ours we tend to tune out, waiting for a pause so we can start to tell our own. When we worry so much about our problems, whether hypothetical or not, we're not interested in the dilemmas of others; the ego loves to be in the limelight and it's not a good listener.

Worry is a tool of self-confinement. For example, by worrying that we may get attacked while out shopping, we can get ourselves into such a state that we stop going out altogether - barricading ourselves into a believed place of 'safety'. I know of a lady who taped up her letterbox out of fear someone would set her house on fire during the London riots; she doesn't even live in London but was gripped by the broadcasts and therefore, the worry. My mother never left her house for years except for hospital appointments and on Christmas day when my brother picked her up to take to his house for dinner. Her only interest in the outside world came from the television which reinforced her beliefs that the outside world was unsafe - confirming that her decision not to go out of the house was the correct one, even just to sit in the garden. My mother *hated* the sun and spirituality and was never afraid to make that perfectly clear. Despite my mother never wanting to leave the house she'd still complain about the weather, even though it made no difference to her world. The more we worry about something the more extreme its effect on us. Worry is a mechanism for withdrawing from society and the outside world; it's living in a padded cell that's locked, from the inside. My mother and I were unable to converse much on the telephone because she wanted to discuss world and local scandals and to share her abhorrence of them for hours on end, but I didn't. We can never find light when we search for it in a darkened room so it's a bit of a waste of time trying, especially when someone is perfectly happy living in the dark.

'What if' is a journey that never ends; we explore every possible negative scenario and each time we do that we inflate the burden that we voluntarily carry. Worry increases our personal torment and the last thing we want to hear is that our worries are unfounded. What, after all, would we do without them?

Worry is a distraction from other things we're avoiding. We use it to make excuses about why we can't help ourselves right now because if we did, the results *could be* catastrophic. We create the monster we want to worry about and then flog ourselves with its whip - we flog other people with it as well, like friends or family. The monster wants to live and we continuously feed it. More than anything it wants an ally - someone to listen to its story.

Society doesn't help at all. The media provides us with a huge range of things to worry about; war, terrorism, sickness, poverty, eviction and violence are just a few examples of these. Closer to home are things like divorce, loneliness and family security, which is why we give our children mobile phones so we can remain in constant contact with them. Children are also given great worries to contend with. They're put under enormous pressure to 'perform' well in school and they're constantly pushed and examined; now they're given SATs tests at the age of seven. For what? To prove they have good memories? What exactly are we grooming them for? The parents worry and so do the children. Later in life these children are put under greater stresses to prepare for more exams, wait months for their exam results and worry continuously about whether they've failed them. The stress is too much for some children who will always worry about 'what if I fail' and they can spend the rest of their lives feeling inadequate. I recently heard about a young boy who committed suicide because he didn't do well in his exams. A healthy society would not do this to its children and we're always too quick to blame the system; *we* created this system - we *are* the system.

Worry is always negative. Who in their right mind worries about 'what if

I pass my exams'. We don't worry about *success* or whether we'll enjoy the next episode of a favourite soap opera but we *do* worry about failure and how we'd fill the 'slot' if our favourite series came to an end. So what is this worry? Quite simply it's a fear of something negative; we fear it because we exclude the positives that match. For example, we talk ourselves into worrying about 'what if' the world comes to an end but we don't want to consider 'what if it doesn't'. Worry is a low vibrational sickness of society and it's deeply embedded. We can however, choose not to live in fear and make a decision to raise our level of Consciousness. This involves a decision not to submit to the will of our mind but to take back control of it; the mind, when it's in control, is negative. When I tried to talk to my mother about going out into the garden or even walking to the gate she became aggressive and insisted that she couldn't. But she *could* and didn't even want to try and strongly resented any suggestion that might lead her away from her self-imprisonment. When we confine ourselves, we keep the doors closed and don't welcome any suggestion that they can be re-opened.

Just as we've locked ourselves inside our homes we lock ourselves behind our screens and through them we contact the world. Even if we've been talking to someone for years online, when push comes to shove, we're mostly afraid to give out our addresses or phone numbers; our online relationships generally depend on our continued anonymity and we now have 'contacts' instead of 'friendships'. Generally speaking, we don't want to meet up with our contacts online and one of the reasons for this is that they would see us as we really are - without our masks. We worry about what's on the outside of our 'security' because we 'what if' about someone is violent or a con-man. We worry about meeting face-to-face someone that we met *online* as we would a stranger knocking on our front door. I've known a few people to shy away when I've offered to send them a copy of my book - they didn't want to give out their address. We've been taught so well to fear strangers and people that we meet online. When we worry continuously about anything at all we're living in fear and as long as we agree to live in fear we'll remain prisoners of our mind and of the society we created.

~~~

Sometimes, we feel a more extreme form of fear - dread! The best way I can describe what I mean by dread is to say that it feels as though something dark and ominous has passed right through us. The emotions that go with this feeling are terror, apprehension and an overwhelming feeling of imminent danger. We learn early on to be afraid, from listening to various types of bedtime stories such as *Peter Pan, The Three Little Pigs* or perhaps *Jack and the Beanstalk*. They're hardly friendly foundations for young, innocent and highly impressionable children. Some of us also picked up these fears from our parents or guardians and some are inherited from other sources. We learnt to be afraid of pirates, giants, tyrants, ogres, burglars under the bed and bogeymen - the list goes on and on. Thought is memory. If you can think it, it's from memory. We've built up all these memories of fears and added to them from sources such as films and other media. More than the memories themselves we remember the emotions related to them - the actual feeling of fear - and it's important to note here that our fears are nothing more than thoughts. We've all learnt something about history and what stands out more than anything is that we've always been at war and that those wars were brutal and heartless. Our minds are awash with horrific images so it's no wonder we know so well how to feel afraid. There's no greater fear than dread so what can we do about it. When it happens, just allow it to pass through; be aware of it and don't resist; it can't harm you in any way. As you become more aware it will occur less frequently and less intensely. This process is faster if we don't subject ourselves to further conditioning from violent films, newscasts or other media terrors. We can choose to watch it all and suffer further or to focus on our awareness and the beauty of the Now. Here are a few more 'what if' scenarios for you to ponder over:

- What if you're truly amazing?
- What if we're missing the point?
- What if we're here to experience?
- What if we stopped fighting?
- What if there's no such thing as death?
- What if our purpose is to raise our Consciousness level?

Imagine dying and then being offered the opportunity to return *here* for a week. The world would be exactly as it is right now but you couldn't be harmed in any way. What would you choose to do with that week that you haven't done before? I've asked a few friends this and not one could come up with an answer.

You're everything! You're a conduit through which the divine speaks and there's no 'what if' about it. No-one can see through your eyes; your perspective belongs to you alone. We know so much more than we've been led to believe and deep down we've no doubts; no academic institution can teach us this. Our energy has been suppressed and *misused* but I can assure you it's still there and no-one can take it away from us, come what may. It's not born and it doesn't die. The only reason we can't feel it is because we haven't been encouraged to ask relevant questions about our lives and our focus has been directed towards the transient rather than the infinite; it's based on desire. We listen with our ears and see with our eyes but these are so limited in Universal terms; more important than what we see and hear, are what we *don't* and this information is available to anyone; no exclusions and no prejudices. Consciousness can be perceived only through the heart. You're the world ... Now ... not in the future.

Emotions and Energy

Emotions are a highly volatile energetic state.

Our emotions are one of the most powerful energetic forces in the Universe. Unchecked, mishandled or manipulated, negative emotions can cause enormous harm to ourselves and those around us; the reverberations of which can be felt for many years to come. Conversely, positive emotions can be a force for much good - no-one ever went to war because they were joyful and happy. How we greet each day and move through it depends on our emotions, but not only that, other people's emotions can have an effect on us too. It isn't until we *sit down* and think about this that the connections between emotions and energy become apparent.

We've all experienced walking down the road and felt the mood of other people coming towards us. Often we can sense if they're angry, afraid, depressed, happy, sad, guilty, ashamed or hostile. What we're actually picking up on is their energy (emotional state) and we adjust our actions accordingly; for example, if we perceive that an approaching group of people is hostile we may choose to cross the road, thus avoiding potential conflict. There are many visible signs that we can read in people's body language such as if they're looking downcast, suspicious or walking with confidence. These emotions might have come from pent up feelings from many years ago or an event they experienced just moments earlier, like meeting up with an old friend. We read each other all the time without realising we're doing it and have no idea how we pick up this energetic information; the process is automatic and acts rather like an early warning system enabling us to react appropriately. This is how we read our world. For the purposes of this chapter I'm interested in how emotions are energy, exude energy and get picked up as energy by us.

Most of us have felt the energy in a room when we unsuspectingly walk in on an argument, or the tension between two people who aren't speaking to each other. Perhaps you've been present when an employee is being humiliated by their boss? I'm sure we can all relate to one of these 'cut the atmosphere with a knife' situations. In most cases differences aren't put aside when we arrive because the need to continue with being *right* is greater than any need to be polite for the sake of someone else; neither party will give in even for a moment. The energy is bouncing around and because it's low vibration we feel tense, awkward and 'dragged down' with an urgent need to leave the room as soon as possible. These situations are difficult enough to cope with but they're in the 'physical world' and we can be sure of the mood and personality of the company we're in. However, the internet has removed vital parts of our 'communication skills' and now we can't rely on gestures or other physical cues like intonation or eye-contact. We act purely on the words, images and emoticons we see on the screen which can so easily be misconstrued.

In this world of the web, we transmit and receive energetic information - instantly - when communicating with each other. This makes it hard to accurately judge what the person we're talking to is *really* feeling, or what their true intentions are; feelings can't be replaced or translated by digital expressions of our faces. We can't hide our feelings when we're standing face-to-face, but online we've the option of telling a different story. For example the acronym for 'rolling on the floor laughing' - *rofl*. Often this is not what we're feeling and we know no-one actually does it. Depending on the conversation we could be crying and at the same time typing *rofl* in order to hide our emotions; for example, hurt feelings. *Rofl* can be a mask to cover our emotions or intentions; we portray ourselves as invulnerable. We can hide our intentions when we talk face-to-face as well, but this is much harder to do and sometimes our true feelings stand out a mile. Imagine a face-to-face conversation where you take the time to choose which facial expression you're going to display. This idea is ridiculous but this is exactly what we do online and it gets awkward if we accidentally click on the wrong emoticon and press send; we can't do that when we're talking face-to-face but we *can* get away with it online. We live in a world of choreographed feelings and emotions manifested as emoticons. The emoticons are a representation of our 'virtual ego' and more often than not this is vastly different from the physical.

Politicians and actors (among others) are trained in all aspects of body language so that they know how to stand, position their hands and how to make eye-contact for best effect. There's a great deal more to this language and we're pretty expert at it - even without training. In the case of politicians, they *learn* it in order to convince the public to believe in them and feign personal strength and ability. The fact that they have to learn it means they don't have the right character for the job, which is why they need a fake persona. If we need to learn how to be convincing then we don't believe in what we're saying and for the well trained eye, the deception is obvious. Humanity is genius when it comes to creating characters which is how we can become such good actors and create things like caricatures or puppets so well. In order to become a good actor or politician we have to be able to hide our true self and in particular, our true emotions. Body language is a tool that can make or break a politician, actor or perhaps a salesman; if their energy isn't tuned in correctly, we're unconvinced by them.
ion

~~~

If we look at online videos that allow comments we often see capitalisation (SHOUTING), which makes these remarks antagonistic and therefore awaiting a response from anyone who'll pick up on the energy - it's a trap. Shouting is an emotional outburst that states what we're saying doesn't hold enough weight on its own, which is why it needs to be reinforced. It also tells the reader, quite clearly, that whoever is shouting isn't going to listen to anyone's responses. If the comments don't get responded to, they end right there, but if we reply to the comment then a string of further and more heated abuse follows; just about everyone is aware of how nasty these threads can become. This is because whoever wrote the comment loves the reactions that help him to express himself with the rest of Humanity in the way that he chooses; he feeds off their energy. Those who continuously respond also like the way the aggressor's hostile comments make them feel. The aggressors love the power it gives them because they can't get this in their *real* life; likewise, others must enjoy being caught in their net. I doubt anyone has ever given someone a 'telling off' online and successfully changed their attitude - quite the contrary. These threads act as magnets for those looking to vent their spleen on the world; whoever is shouting on these threads is really expressing his pent up feelings and the louder he shouts, the more emotional he becomes and the more energy he leaves on the threads to be picked up by other viewers - should they choose to pick it up. These threads are powerful emotional outlets and people feel safe venting on them. More often than not a thread is attacked because something in it resonated with the aggressor; he doesn't feel good and neither do the respondents.

This pattern is similar to our relationship with governments or other authorities - they call the shots and we respond - but we don't change them and they're not listening to us. If we walk away (say *No*), they have no power. Their power comes from our willingness to respond in the expected way to the energy they've chosen to transmit. Next time you walk past a newsagent look at the headlines in the papers; they're either capitalised or in bold (both are shouting). This powerful energy affects us and our response is as negative as the headline. When we observe how we feel when reading these headlines and understand the effects they have on us, they no longer have the same power; we don't feel obliged to pick up the energy they emit.

What's happening between us all is an energetic exchange.

Emotion = e-motion = energy in motion

People who pick up on this energy can still feel it even months or years after it was written. The same applies to re-reading a much-treasured stack of love letters or a sad film we watch again and again. We feel and react with the same emotions as if we're seeing them for the first time; whoever sees them feels the emotion. Energy flows out of us, and it flows back in. We're constantly sending out and absorbing energy to and from a variety of sources and it's important to become aware of this. We may leave our house one morning feeling buoyant, in which case this is the energy we're emitting. However, seeing sensational headlines or meeting a friend who's always full of 'doom and gloom' can drain that energy and replace it with energy of a lower vibration; suddenly that buoyant feeling evaporates and is replaced with a feeling of imminent doom. Somebody who's always gloomy and depressed feels a great need to get rid of - or share - their energy and this is partly why they love to talk to people who're more positive in their outlook. We don't know we're doing it but what we're doing is trying to shed or share our negative energy. When we can't vent our emotions they build up and get stored inside us.

Here's something that happened to me not so long ago. I was driving with my partner to a builder's merchant. A police car appeared behind me and flagged us over. When we stopped two policemen got out. One looked rather *normal* and the other had an aggressive strut and was 'on a mission'. He wore large dark sunglasses; it wasn't a sunny day. I smiled and it was not returned. I asked the officer why I'd been stopped. He said that I'd been talking on a mobile phone whilst I was driving and he looked really pleased that he'd caught me. From that point on he couldn't express the energy he wanted to because I got out, offered him my handbag and gestured that he could search it and my car too. I informed him that he was mistaken because neither I nor my partner have a mobile phone. He insisted that we did and his partner *smiled* knowing full well his colleague was stuck in a hole of his own digging. He never admitted his error or apologised and went off frustrated. This unexpressed energy is always re-absorbed and will probably get expressed all the stronger on the next person he pulls over or perhaps in some other situation. All our pent up emotions must get expressed and vented sooner or later. In this situation I didn't agree to be the wall he could bounce his energy off.

Think of a kettle about to boil. The gas or electricity is the life force and the water our emotions. If we block the vent that allows the steam to escape there's a build-up of pressure inside. Sooner or later the kettle will explode and then there'll be a sudden outburst of steam (emotion). When we let off *steam* it hurts us or hurts others; often both. However, when we allow the steam to escape freely no harm is done and the system works harmoniously. Allowing emotions to control us prevents us living happily. This is because we're always trying to be something other than who we really are; who we're trying to be is based on our past experiences and conditioning. It's unwise to allow ourselves to be led by our emotions - they're highly unstable.

Moods are also emotions and they can last for weeks or years. We often don't know why we're in a particular mood because we can't remember when we started feeling it. However, moods come from suppressed emotions and manifest themselves in things like irritation or anger. We've all met people who are always irritated or angry. My entire teens and twenties were spent in these moods but occasionally I could vent, often by grabbing something and hurling it across the room; I wasn't too selective about what or where I threw objects either. Once when I threw a brick, I missed a man's head by an inch. When pent up emotions erupt, we don't think about what we're going to break or the consequences - rational thought ceases. This is because the need to get these pent up feelings out of our system is far greater than the value of any object we might break in the process. We don't think in these situations; we're in the Now. Sometimes we feel much better after our outburst and sometimes the effects aren't so visible, but they're still there. When we become aware of what's actually going on we're able to regain control of our lives.

~~~

Energy is a collective and powerful experience when we're gathered in groups. The energy bounces between us and increases - like at music festivals. Freddie Mercury for example, could really stir up an audience. The bigger the crowd the more powerful the energy. Supporters at a football match emit an enormous amount of energy because of their sheer numbers. Have you ever heard one end of a stadium when a goal is scored? The energy from the crowd can spur on a team to perform well. If the supporters of *Team A* are more encouraging and active than the supporters in *Team B* the chances are *Team A* will win the match; they're spurred on because of the energy emitted by the crowd. We can feel this energy even if we're not there by watching it on the television. Those who gather en masse in a pub to watch a match also feel the energy and consequently, roar out with their own. Similarly a person sitting at home alone watching a match (I know one of these) will lift off his seat when his team scores a goal; distance is no object for this energy.

Emotions need to be expressed and we'd struggle to interact without them. How could we understand each other if we didn't cry, laugh, sulk, shout or get angry for example? These are our ways of relating to each other and also to ourselves. Like with the steam in the kettle, our emotions need to escape from inside us. Because emotions are energy and we pick up on them, some amusing situations can occur. If for example a person is laughing uncontrollably, it's almost impossible not to join in even if we don't know what they're laughing at - it's contagious and can result in a painful *stitch*; this type of laughter is physically exhausting. Similarly, we can pick up on energy from yawning or crying by another person and involuntarily do the same - mirroring their emotions.

Emotions are an energetic way of expressing what we're feeling. Too often we don't recognise why we're feeling them and this is because the cause can go back many years. Way into my thirties I'd react in the same way to events as I reacted to them in my childhood. If I saw events on television that were similar to things that happened to me, I'd feel the same emotions, such as sadness, fear, dread and frustration; what I saw acted as a trigger to re-awaken older memories. It would often feel as though I were re-living the experience through somebody else. Unlike online with emoticons, these emotions aren't always controllable - particularly when what caused them is deep-seated. How we cope with emotion is different for everybody. Some people can cry over minor events and others can't cry at all. These emotions, however, belong to all of us and like with my example of a kettle, too often we suppress them.

Peace of mind can only be found within; the process is hard work and a full time job on top of whatever else we have to do. However, the more we get to grips with being honest about our own behaviour and character the more peaceful we become. We can think about how we react in conversations. If we concentrate on our own energy rather than the energy of others - we self-moderate - and our world becomes a calmer place to live in. But if we speak aggressively and constantly complain about other people we're putting out a lot of negativity; which comes back and adds to the burden we already carry - we become negativity generators. Another way to look at this is to ask 'If you met yourself, would you want to be your own friend?' or when you're talking to someone, online or off, ask yourself whether you'd like to receive the energy you're emitting. It doesn't matter if we slip every now and then, what matters is persevering and with practice we slip less and less. A most important point about energy is to avoid or say goodbye to those who continually want to drain ours. Because we pick up on energy it's not a good idea to remain in the company of those who want to pass theirs onto us - unless it's positive. Our own energy is precious and when we become aware of that we're no longer willing to part with it or take on the negative energy of others; it's not even an option.

Observation

To observe effectively we need to zoom out, not in.

When we think about observation it tends to fall into one of three categories: something we do, like looking through a telescope; something we have, like the ability to be observant and something we're under, like the ubiquitous security camera. When I first heard the term 'observation' with regard to my thoughts and looking for truth *inside*, I couldn't for the life of me see how that could be possible. All I could think of was that my veins, lungs, kidneys and other internal bodily parts are just that - on the inside - and my eyes look outward. There was also a bigger problem - I'd no idea what I was supposed to be observing or what this so-called *Now* was about. Before even *starting* this observation, my mind stuck out its big foot, tripped me up and I fell before reaching the first hurdle. I'd barely picked myself up when my mind pushed me back down again. It told me I wasn't qualified to do the job and that I'm not an 'expert'. Can anyone be more of an expert on who I really am than *me*? We're generally conditioned to believe that we need professional help for such matters; we most certainly don't for this. Experience is a good teacher but it's no substitute for observation and no-one else can observe for us. It doesn't matter how good the teacher is if the student is inattentive or unwilling to learn. When we observe our mad world it becomes clear that we're all students, no matter what our age, who still have a great deal to learn. No one person can observe or change the chaos of the world; but we can, without a shadow of a doubt, change ourselves and only this will produce the results that most people refuse to give credence to.

Observing ourselves can be tough because our mind interferes all the time - it's insistent and keeps us blinkered within a limited physical perspective. It wants information, evidence, debate, paperwork, action, analysis, cross-referencing and above all, it wants to maintain control; it doesn't want our interference. The mind compares our previous failures with our lack of successes and tells us there's not much point in wasting our precious time as based on past evidence, the project is *doomed*. The mind wants to keep us in our place; it doesn't want to change and it doesn't want a 'co-director'. When we decide to observe our thoughts the mind interrupts and before we know it, often before we've even begun we check for email messages, phone a friend, make a drink, water the garden, awaken an ancient grudge or clean out a kitchen cupboard. We may find that we're just staring at a blank wall, a crack on the ceiling and eerily, sometimes we're staring at nothing at all dreamily unaware of our thoughts; in the latter case we're 'out of mind'. The mind knows a lot of pressing postponement techniques to occupy us with if we become distracted from what it thinks we should be doing. More often than not it bombards us with thoughts that keep us in 'take no action' mode. On the whole we're unaware of the process but it's possible, if we pay attention, to observe the insane stream of unimportant data coming and going.

It does all this so fast that often we quite forget what it was we wanted to consider; by the time we've finished our chores, the thought has dispersed and been replaced by a multitude of others that are more to the mind's liking. Whenever we want freedom from the chatter of our mind it presents us with meaningless hypnotic distractions. It's only a matter of time before questions like 'Who Am I' for example, shout out our name again and the cycle recommences.

~~~

There's something that drives us to question the meaning of our existence, at some point in our lives. It's always there - at the back of our minds - but we tend to ignore it in favour of more 'important' pastimes. Initially the concepts are unfathomable and this is because our minds have been trained to be rigid and negative. The only generally acceptable *knowledge* is from education and other equally ritualised conditioning processes. Sifting for information in books and on the internet about the mystery schools, hidden secrets or this thing called 'enlightenment' is like wallpapering over the existing paper in a room. We need to strip off the old embedded ideas, prejudices and beliefs etc., first. There are so many layers to get through and a great deal of elbow grease is necessary.

This metaphorical room is our responsibility alone and no one else can do the work for us; it's unpaid and arduous. The room is a part of each and every one of us and it's 'Private Property'; we own it outright and always will. It's our *observatory* and we've let it get into a dreadful mess; sooner or later, we need to clear it out. I'd like to point out here that we don't need books or the internet in order to enquire about our true nature; this is accessible to everyone on the planet and with observation, if we truly want to, we'll find what we're looking for. So never give up because you already know all of this - you're remembering it. Don't trust in the mind that will tell you there's 'no proof' and that you're 'wasting your time' because everybody else needs to see and think about this too; don't trust in anything other than your rational voice. *You* are your world and only *you* can change it.

Initially, when we observe ourselves; for example, by challenging the mind, things seem rather strange. Imagine you're driving along a motorway and you're almost out of petrol. You're about to pass a service station and the sign tells you there's another station in forty miles. The mind tells us we'll make it to the second station but the other voice in our heads says 'be wise and fill up here'. However, we tend to listen to the mind as this is our familiar habit, but, this habit gets us into familiar situations - the mind lives on the edge of danger. If we're serious about observing and changing our destructive habits we begin to listen to the more rational voice. When we challenge the negativity of our mind we're moving 'mountains' and the more we do it, the more it becomes second nature, as it were. The first step is to accept that we have destructive habits and the second, to decide that we're through with suffering; yes, it's a decision we have to make. When we make a decision to listen to the rational voice something in us changes; the more we listen to it, the more we change and the less we pollute our world with negative energy and thought. This is because we're no longer allowing the insane mind to control our thoughts; we break the pattern and change direction. In other words, we become responsible for our thoughts and choose which ones to listen to. When we change direction a great deal about human behaviour becomes clear.

Let's take the newspapers and television broadcasts for example, and think about why we pay so much attention to them. We never get good news except maybe when someone has grown a giant pumpkin exceeding any previously seen at garden shows or a politician kisses a baby on the cheek; other than that we may get the occasional good news but it's not *our* good news and it doesn't benefit Humanity. Some people say they *have* to keep up with the news (why?) but these papers get read, the stories get spread in concentrated horror via other media (we call it *social*) and then before we've fully digested yesterday's bad news another helping is offered up to tempt our hungry minds. Reading and absorbing this bad news every day can never be beneficial; it's nothing more than absorbing anxiety and depression which for a lot of people is an unspoken about 'regular meal'. Because we consume this daily it takes hold, like any other habit; it becomes commonplace and no longer startles us, even though we proclaim 'horror'. If we don't read it people think we don't care or that we're closing our eyes to *reality* and if we do then at best we can only join in the spreading of bad news; we can't, practically, do anything about any of it. This doesn't make sense to me at all and if that's 'reality' why do we want to hold onto it so badly? When we pull away from the *River of Disaster* we observe it from a distance and therefore, from a wider perspective. We observe that Humanity, on the whole, really doesn't want to change the world it's living in - otherwise, why is there so much resistance to dispense with the things that drag us down so much? Removing this negative force from our lives has many benefits for our health and mental well-being - life slows down and with it the chaos in our mind.

Everyday things begin to fall into unfamiliar places and things we thought were solid, like our world, aren't any more. All lies get revealed and the hardest lies of all to accept are those we've been telling ourselves for so long; yes, we all tell them at some point in our lives. One of the reasons this is hard to cope with is that in the past we've projected our abhorrence of lies onto others and to realise that *we* do it too is a hard-hitting experience; applying the social labels 'liar' or 'hypocrite' to ourselves is like catching sight of ourself in a mirror and being appalled by our own reflection. It quickly becomes apparent that we are no better than anyone else in this world; it's a humbling experience.

At this point we've two choices; ignore what we've seen, as we've done for many years, or continue to observe these ever-evolving revelations. Each time we recognise a shortcoming in ourself is like stripping off one of our masks; these have become so adhered to our faces that we don't realise we're wearing them. On a deeper level of this observation is the revelation that what we've criticised in others was a projection from deep within ourselves. We're so deeply conditioned against being duped by scams, con-artists or dodgy-builders for example, that we don't recognise we're conning ourselves.

The biggest lie we tell is that our life is an *accident* of nature and that there's nothing after it. We one hundred percent physicalise our existence and kid ourselves that there's nothing after our deaths. But this is a cop out; it's an excuse to justify our temporary enjoyment of the *pleasures* we cherish so much. We justify this enjoyment in order that we don't have to make an effort to change our habitual behaviour; like abstaining from wild parties, playing non-stop games or drinking alcohol and eating to excess - anyone who tries to tell us otherwise is labelled as a 'party pooper'. We're just a bit too quick to stick critical labels on anyone who disagrees with our conditioned beliefs, even though we don't believe them ourselves. However, these things make our lives more bearable because we can forget or at least ignore our problems, albeit temporarily. The mind is more than able to continue this unproductive cycle and plays 'devil's advocate' when it comes to the welfare of Humanity. It does this by ignoring our connection to Consciousness and putting our thoughts and insights down to something physical; in other words, it makes Consciousness, or Spirit, into something 'biodegradable' and therefore 'disposable'. We trample down our conscience always looking to people who'll provide *proofs* to confirm what we want to believe. When we hear what we don't want to hear (like perhaps from this book) although we can see that it makes sense, we convince ourselves that it doesn't. We excuse ourselves and continually seek new reasons not to think about what our lives are really about. Whereas we spend a lot of time complaining about them, they're preferable to nothing at all. Perhaps we do this just in case what we find out confirms our cherished belief that death is *The End*; perhaps we do it because deep down, we know for certain that it isn't.

We can observe our behaviour in many situations and this is necessary if we want to end our suffering. One way to do this is to watch our reactions to others for example by comparing what we're thinking when we talk to them, with what we're actually saying. More often than not they don't match. We can also compare what we really think about someone when we tell them they 'look good', when we don't mean it. By observing in these ways we begin to realise that we're far from honest and then as that realisation sinks in and becomes palatable, we change our behaviour accordingly. My life changed for the better when I took responsibility for my thoughts and how I felt about other people changed a great deal too. Without being prepared to go through a process of self-observation this wouldn't have been possible. When we make an excuse about why we can't do something or change an obsessive habit we're, in fact, confirming our will to remain just as we are. All these things are observable and tell us a great deal about ourselves if we're prepared to examine them honestly and closely enough. Mostly we're not prepared to be honest about our own behaviour because, let's face it, we're all headstrong and determined to do what we want regardless of whether it's in our best interest or not; none of us like being judged by anyone else. Even if we ask the advice of others we generally have no intention of listening to it. Paramount to self-reflection is a willingness to criticise our own motives, actions and intentions, rather than those of others. This book and everything in it are me doing the same; how can it be anything else? This book and *On The Other Hand* have come into being because I made an active decision to follow the 'white rabbit'; I've no choice but to continue following it and this is where it has led me, so far.

By stripping off our masks, usually one at a time, we make ourselves vulnerable to outside criticism - something nobody really likes. Ironically, when this happens we no longer care what anyone thinks or need their approval. This process can take time but I can assure you it's worth the effort and self-reflection. When we dispense with the need for masks, barriers or approval we find that our fears subside very quickly. We wear so many of these masks and only realise we're wearing them after a certain amount of self-reflection *without* allowing our pride or ego to interfere. There are many ways to know ourselves and once we start enquiring one thing leads to another; it's a continuous process. The masks represent a sort of defence system; they act as a shield to hide anything that may make us vulnerable to attack. Have you ever noticed your thoughts during an argument or how you try to stop yourself revealing your true feelings to the person you're arguing with? Have you noticed your thoughts when arguing and you know you're being obstinate, but won't admit to it? Try to catch your thoughts during these moments and recognise how ingenious we can be when it comes to defending 'our corner' regardless of rights or wrongs; I've done quite a lot of this and now, each time I end up laughing at the genius of it all. Try also to notice your thoughts when you're going to sleep. At first when I did this I always fell asleep before I got the chance to notice patterns but now, after persevering, I watch my own 'demons' coming and going and find it rather fun to do. Catch yourself out at the supermarket when you're paying for shopping; watch the thoughts about the cashier or the people in front of or behind you. I used to find some people rather intimidating and others I felt I had power over. What are you thinking now, about me or yourself, after reading this paragraph? Perhaps you're judging me and that's okay but more important than judging me is to recognise and accept that you're doing it, rather than getting caught up in the critical net. The point of observation is not to watch me but to watch *you*; this is the tricky part. The more we observe, the more we see and the more we change; provided we resist the urge to be 'hurt' or 'offended'. Through this type of observation it becomes obvious that there's an observer that's neither the ego nor the mind.

The ego dominates and is defended by the mind that created it. As long as we believe that we're the ego we can't observe ourself and the reason for this is that we filter out the *Observer*. By this subterfuge we've become accustomed to seeing the world through *conditioned* eyes as others would have us see it, rather than as it is. Consequently we can't *observe* the world we've created and close examination of something 'magnificent' - like a flower or the gathering of its pollen by a bee - become just a scientific and logical exercise, as opposed to *miraculous*; the mind filters out true beauty. Close observation of our mind is impossible without the awareness of our two contradictory voices. Once we become aware of their differences it becomes difficult, if not impossible, not to listen to the voice that's in our highest interest.

Attachment

We place a noose around our necks and tell ourselves it'll keep us from falling.

Teaching is mostly done by rote and one of the problems with this is that it presents only one *right* answer. We neither know nor think about these answers - we remember them. This system is useful for things like multiple choice examinations where filling in the blanks is all that's required. We become as attached to these answers as we do any other habit. We're reluctant or afraid (perhaps both) to look at other possibilities revealed only by radical and nonpartisan thought - possibilities that confirm without a doubt that things in this world are never quite what they seem to be. When we learn by rote there's no room for imagination and therefore, nothing new; we're riding on a meme and have closed the door to further knowledge having already reached our conclusions. Being set in our ideas and beliefs we live like an idling engine; ticking over but not getting anywhere.

Sometimes discerning what's happening is just a question of changing our perspective. If for example there's a 1 in 100 chance of winning the lottery, we get more of an idea about what that means when we discern there's a 99 in 100 chance of losing. If the lottery were advertised this way we wouldn't buy tickets. When we turn things around they'll look very different. However, we're taught to think about the odds of *winning* and the word sticks. We're attached to hope and getting lucky - we choose these even though we know it's futile.

We can't see the truth about our world whilst arguing against it. For example, as in the above paragraph, we choose to use the word 'winning' as opposed to 'losing' because no one wants to hear about losing despite it being the more likely outcome. Another problem with learning by rote is that there'll always be those who go against the grain, turning upside down our 'comfortable' world. Because of this, we're in disagreement and fiercely defending our own position with 'No Trespassing' signs written all over us; we defend our memories, our beliefs, our right to be unhappy and our property. There's nothing wrong with having 'things' but problems occur in our lives when those things have *us*. No flag can bestow possession as everything is transitory and changes moment by moment.

Think about a bonfire piled high with wood and twigs, before it's been lit.

Once the fire burns because fuel, air and heat are combined, these pieces of wood turn into hot embers and once the fire burns out, there remains nothing but ashes; the ashes too will eventually compost down. But, there are by-products from this fire - carbon dioxide, light, heat and steam. These get released back into the atmosphere. No doubt they break down in to other components but further information on this subject doesn't belong in this book; I'm not a scientist. The point is that *nothing* is wasted. Among other things, the earth is a giant recycling plant.

- Our bodies recycle the food we eat.
- The paperwork that causes Humanity so much strife disintegrates.
- Buildings crumble.
- Bodies decompose.
- Iron rusts and
- Plant life withers.

The oxidation or corrosion process applies to *every* thing in this world; nothing lasts forever but some things take a short time to change and others much longer. Everything mentioned above was once something else and it continuously changes according to its environment; some things get help from Humanity, like when we combine copper and zinc and turn it into brass.

~~~

We want to hold onto the things that can't last rather than what can. Humanity is seriously missing something when it spends its life chasing a wind it can't catch. The only thing worth striving for in this world is That which is eternal. Have you ever seen greyhound dogs racing? They chase a lure (dummy rabbit or hare) around a track; this gets them running. They do this race after race so they clearly don't learn from past experience and haven't lost hope, but they'll never catch it. We're also offered things we can't have and it's no different to dangling a carrot in front of a donkey - it can never reach it and can get pretty frustrated trying. Sure, someone will win the lottery, get a top job or meet an ideal partner, but that won't change society for the vast majority, which means it won't change society at all. The majority coming together as One - our natural state - is the only way to change this world.

Back to my chapter *Independence* for a moment; whatever we're dependent on is also an attachment. Attachment is a prison we don't want to break free from; it brings a false sense of security and identity with it which is why we struggle to let go. As soon as we're attached to something we become responsible for it. If we attach ourselves to a rope we become responsible for its maintenance; if we don't maintain it then one day it will fray and we'll fall. Attach ourselves to a wave and when it breaks, as it must, we find another one. When we attach ourselves proudly to a particular nation we believe ourselves to be separate from the rest of Humanity. These attachments are our prison walls; whatever we're attached to prevents us from moving on. We've attached ourselves to the inside of a prison that contains all we've been taught and all our memories, emotions, reactions, gadgets, trinkets, beliefs and triggers are in there with us. As with our homes, we go to great lengths to make sure that no one can break in and also to make sure that *we* can't break out! If we're prepared to let go of our belongings or beliefs we achieve a higher level of freedom and this is not as difficult as it first seems to be.

Many years ago I was attached to a particular vegetarian snack from a local shop. I ate them for years and then one day I couldn't find them; the store had decided not to stock them anymore which left me at a bit of a loss for what to replace them with. I'd become dependent on that store for the supply assuming quite wrongly that these would always be available. After that I developed a recipe for my own similar alternative snacks, which tasted even better. Sometimes, what seems to be in our best interest, isn't. When we depend on something we always run the risk of losing it - we also stifle our own creativity. For example, when we follow - to the letter - the recipe 'instructions' on the back of a packet, we forget that we can work things out and adapt them for ourselves.

~~~

I've a friend who keeps all her clothes. She's in her mid-fifties and still has some of her clothes from when she was fifteen. How she finds the room to store them all is beyond me but her wardrobes are packed from top to bottom including in her spare room. Each room has two double wardrobes and depending on the season, these clothes get moved into and out of her attic. When asked why she does this her reply was "I don't like waste". Surely it's more of a waste to cram them into cupboards and not use them. Anyway, I don't believe this excuse and I'd suggest, it's more about a fear of loss or going without one day. It's also about attachment to the memories of when she wore them and her *lost youth*. She won't like me writing about her lost youth but then I'll remind her of a request for me to make her younger than her *mid-fifties*.

Just as we hold onto belongings we hold onto memories of them - in photograph frames or diaries. For example, I remember many years ago being unable to delete a friend's phone number from my address book and he'd died six months earlier. For the first few months I used to dial the number hoping he'd answer. Realising that we must let go is difficult but we all have to do it sooner or later. I couldn't comprehend how someone could leave and never come back. Humanity coming together only to suffer and then separate again made no sense to me then and it still doesn't. We shed tears year after year for the same pains - digging up past memories and reliving the misery of them again and again. The tears expressed our loss years ago but they won't help now. Observing our actions enables us to question them. For example, we can examine whether a process we hold onto is good for us by asking:

- Is this in my highest interest?

- Have I reached my fullest potential?
- Am I doing myself more harm than good?
- Do I want these nightmares to end?
- Do I want peace of mind?
- Do my tears serve any purpose at all?
- Can I turn back time?

When we ask the above questions the answer can only be "Yes" or "No". However, too often we reply "Yes, but" or "No, but". 'But', in this sense, is a weasel word; an escape route that *qualifies* our answer. It's a limitation we place on ourselves and it's nothing more than resistance to letting go of our self-directed dramas. We can, if we choose to, resist that resistance. 'But' is attachment; 'yes' and 'but' can't exist together harmoniously and neither can 'no' and 'but'. 'But' is the excuse we use to disagree with the 'yes' or 'no'. 'But' is a clause, a condition and a doubt. 'yes, but' or 'no, but' are formulas that can't be solved. 'But' is a self-imposed mitigation. 'But' is the small print; it's our terms and conditions before signing.

Sorrow is difficult to live with; it's devastating and it can take a long time to recover from. However, the above questions still apply. There's no need to forget our friends who die but it's possible to re-frame how we look at death. This is so important for Humanity because we all die sooner or later. We have to stop looking at death as though it were unnatural; it's as natural as our births. Yes, we can die from terrible illnesses but death itself is *not* an illness and there's no need to treat it as such. Death from illness is simply death brought about sooner than we would die naturally. Illness is a dreadful thing but if we look at it objectively then surely it would be prudent to ask 'Why is there so much illness in this world', which we can do something about, rather than 'why is there so much death', which we can't. Death is something we invest in - think about war. Let's invest in good health instead.

~~~

So many of us remain angry with relatives, ex-friends or even people we've never met. Often not because they've done anything to harm us but because we expected something from them that they were unable to give us. We try to change other people because it seems easier than changing ourselves. The immovable wall between children and their parents is becoming a bigger and bigger problem. Society insists on separating families now and social media has a great deal to do with this. I've heard so many stories about family (and business) arguments on social pages and let's face it, in anger we do and say the most foolish things. The longer it takes us to come to our senses the deeper the anger becomes rooted and it requires a great effort to remove it. How much anger do we need to store and ferment rather than remove the cause that separates Humanity from itself? The pain of Humanity is self-inflicted and we do more damage to ourself by holding onto it than we do to the people we're angry with. Pride is a big wall to knock down and we're attached to that wall.

The greatest attachment of all is to our ego - who we think we really are - and *that* depends a great deal on our cultural upbringing. The ego is born from the mind; it's a manifestation of it and the mind also creates our 'virtual egos'. The mind wants to hold on to its control and we don't care who's in charge - as long as it's not us. We've absorbed our environment through religion, society, family, culture and education; now we project selective parts of it as our *self* - our ego.

Ego = Energy Going Out.

What we project and put on display as 'who we are' is our ego but it's not who we truly are. Ego is the force that hides our true nature - it's our disguise. When this is what we project and think of ourselves, it becomes impossible to believe in a peaceful and beautiful world. Energy in … Energy out, energy out … energy in. Whatever we project produces a reaction in our lives; if we look sincerely for peace we must one day find it and if we look for aggression then this is what we'll attract. We're multi-faceted, not just a body, and we don't realise it. We cling onto the ego and feed it when it so desires; we allow it to remain under the control of our minds. When we can reconcile who we are so that we wear not even one mask, we'll find peace and no longer need our attachment to the ego.

Why is the ego like this? The confusion comes from choices. From a very young age we've made decisions and choices that we mould into who we think we are or who we want to be. So say for example we choose to be 'good', we suppress our potential to be 'bad'. The *good* is the ego we project, but the *bad* becomes our shadow. We can never lose this shadow as it's firmly attached to us whether we like to believe it or not. Without choices we become complete. If we choose neither the 'good' or 'bad' labels we become observers of the world, without judgement. Think of choices as a game of *One for You*. We choose and give certain characteristics to our ego and our shadow: one for you, one for me, one for you, one for me. The ego we've created is made up of the choices we've given preference to. The shadow is made up of the characteristics we've chosen to reject and hide from general view; we also deny that they belong to us. This leads to confusion and when, for example, we think we're 'good' yet have 'bad' feelings towards others, inner conflict arises.

Have you ever had a bad argument with someone and been really angry with them? We say things we don't mean and then feel shame when we reflect on it later on. We feel this shame because on another level we know that the hurtful things we said were said by our shadow and it *does* mean them. We want to stop ourselves but we're unable to. Why is this? In anger we let go of our restraint; it's like letting an angry dog off its lead. We're just angry and anger is in the Now - it's without thought. So it's natural that in an argument our shadow makes a guest appearance - it leaks out. Our opponent faces the full force of our ego *and* its shadow, which is why things can turn rather nasty. When we're shouting in an argument the ugliest parts of us are exposed. We get back what we cast out *energy out ... energy in*; the energy comes from both sides of the argument and it's out of our control. After a quarrel the energy from it bounces around and it takes a while for it to settle down again. Often it's best that the parties involved go in separate directions and 'cool off' for a while. How long depends on our ability to reason; some people can resolve their disputes very quickly and others can take years - some never get resolved at all.

Equally as important as attachment is detachment. We're attached to people, things, relationships and beliefs and we're also selectively detached from them. I think just about everyone has heard of the nineties popularised phrase and supportive gesture, *talk to the hand*; it couldn't be more dismissive or closed-minded. When we close our minds because we don't want to hear what another person has to say we don't just lock people out of our world, we lock ourselves in. The world will always look subjective to people who do that because they can never learn about or see the point of view of another human being or another nation; they exclude the possibility of something better that can only be seen when we look at the world objectively. Because so many of us take the subjective route, we're separated from each other and therefore, limited as far as finding peace is concerned. Until the *face* listens, it shuts out the new and it shuts out the world.

~~~

I've never met anyone who likes what they see in the mirror. The mirror tells all sorts of horrible tales even when we pretend not to listen to the voice that's unhappy with our hair, eyes, nose, age lines or whatever else we choose to reject. It's not just our physical appearance that we're discontent with; it's also things like unpopularity, caring about what other people think, looking for security or looking for approval. There are many more but I can't list them all. The mirror tells our history and we're reminded of that when we look into it. There's nothing actually wrong with any of us; it's only society that tells us we need to tweak our body and attitude in order to become socially acceptable. For example, we need to be politically correct, trendy, slim, perfectly made up with glossy lipstick, have bigger breasts, be a macho man and be at the very least the *average* height in order not to be considered too short. These are just a few of the ways in which we're made to feel inadequate and there are so many more.

When we're told we don't like ourselves our natural reaction is to deny it, but this is just a defence mechanism. The whole world is insecure and if we can start to see this it reveals something very important. It reveals that nobody likes theirself and that goes for film stars, models on the cat walk or anyone else we'd like to become. Why would they do those jobs if they liked themselves? We're always striving to be someone better than who we think we are but there's little point in making that wish. Instead of trying to like ourselves perhaps it would be beneficial to realise that we don't have to. What we really don't like is based on the opinions of other people and we've let these opinions seed. Our self-dislike comes from a build-up of conditioning - from the expectations of others. The good news about this revelation is that we can stop beating ourselves up. Whatever caused us initially to dislike parts of ourselves has been reinforced over the years. When we keep hitting a nail into a piece of wood with a hammer it gets driven in deeper and deeper which over time changes our self-disapproval into self-hatred. When we can let go of our attachment to becoming something we're not supposed to be, for the approval of others, the world will become a better place to live in.

It's only by reflecting on our character and observing how we react in certain situations that we become aware of our separation from the rest of the world. This separation is the door we've closed and hidden behind. Separation leads us to believe we're better or worse than the rest of Humanity and it looks at the world subjectively. We hold this door tightly shut and allow no predators - not even to peep through the keyhole. It's only in anger or other highly emotional moments that we call on our shadow for support; only when our backs are up against a wall. Why do we need it? It's a part of us and without it we're incomplete. By locking our shadow away we're unable to cope with everything put in front of us. We need both the ego and the shadow to function *smoothly*. When they do there's no need to wear masks; thus enabling us to relax our grip and let go of the fear that our 'dark side' might be exposed. No longer afraid of the 'vulnerability', we then appear to the outside world as we really are.

When we realise we can't open the 'door' because we're pulling it shut rather than pushing it open the world quickly becomes a very different place. In general, we're afraid of the Universe and Consciousness because they represent great power and we've been conditioned to be afraid of powers /

authorities, since we were very young. We're used to feeling 'powerless' and 'inadequate' in the world and the idea that we've power of our own is incomprehensible at this level of consciousness. More than anything we need to let go of our attachments to these beliefs. When we can work in harmony with the ego *and* our shadow, we take back control of our mind.

Faith

Faith is a beautiful thing that can't be known through the clumsiness of language - it resides within.

I'd just finished writing my chapter *Observation* when a lady, with what she called a "burning question", asked her friends online "What keeps you faithful?" My reply was "Faithful to what?" It was then that I realised that up until that moment I hadn't given any thought to what faith is. Faith is a multi-faceted word that generally gets people's backs up because of its strong religious connotations. I told a friend that I was writing a chapter about *faith* and before telling him anything about it I asked what his initial reaction was to the word. He replied "My first thought on the word faith is that all the miseries of the world have been ignored because of it." Faith and religion are words that have become so tightly entwined that they're practically indistinguishable; the meaning of both words can be confusing. A great deal of pain and poisoned memories are associated with these words. In order to think about the word 'faith' we first need to untangle it so that it stands separate from religion, or any other interpretation or influence.

In my opinion, faith is often confused with belief and hope and all three are taken to mean the same thing - to me, that's an error. To believe, is not to *know* that something is true but rather it's a personal preference. We choose to believe something not because it's false or true but because it's convenient or suits our circumstances or culture to believe it; belief doesn't make something true. Hope, on the other hand, is waiting for a future event that may never arrive; rather like hoping that a bus we're waiting for *will* arrive but not knowing for certain that it's coming. Faith is far harder to define and for this reason, hard to have. Faith is more like waiting for the bus but knowing it will arrive - there's no duality and therefore, no doubt. Faith is a combination of 'knowing' and 'trusting', without seeing, and with those comes a realisation that there's so much more we don't know about our world and can't know under our present circumstances. Faith is felt by our very essence and as our faith increases, it can't be shaken as it isn't based on anything we've been taught. Hope is a calculated risk and 'belief' requires no evidence; both however, are roads that can lead to faith - it's embedded in our hearts. To try to explain the meaning of faith and how we can feel it is difficult because mere words just can't do it;

we have to look *between* the lines where words don't exist. Trying to describe faith, is rather like trying to describe what vanilla tastes like; we have to taste it for ourselves. Faith is something that grows and the process begins when we decide to look for truth - it grows alone, inside us. What keeps me faithful on my road and gives meaning to my life is knowing that in this physical world there's absolutely nothing (physical) worth striving for. One way to see this is to think about what *changes* in the world and then to find what doesn't. We were babies, grew taller, our features changed, our walk, the way we talk, what we know and what we don't know, but there's a part of us that doesn't change at all; it's been there since we were born and when we realise this our faith increases. This is the 'observer'.

~~~

The uncovering of truth begins with the disposal of our illusions - by questioning. This is a materialistic world where commercialism thrives at the expense of human welfare and we all know it. It's not always the *things* we create that do the damage but that we create them without regard or thought for the good of our world or Humanity. We do this because we don't see ourselves as *connected*; we're One but we've become separated, greedy and afraid. As long as we've desires and separation in the world or see life as one continuous effort, nothing will change. My faith began to develop when I saw there was nothing in this world that could make me complete; I'd reached an impasse. In other words, my faith grew when I let go of the struggle to become something or someone I wasn't. That left me rather in limbo; I didn't 'fit in' anywhere but was still 'here' and knew I still had something to discover. It was only when I stopped trying to fit in that I realised I could only find completeness in myself; it's only when we're prepared to stop swimming upstream that the struggle ends.

In the past I'd sometimes go to a shopping centre or high street just to look around but rarely found anything to buy because there was nothing I needed or wanted. Nothing could fill the space I felt between me and the rest of the world. I felt utterly bored and unchallenged in these vacuous environments. I found these shopping centres soulless, despite the presence of the heaving crowd and was amazed at the rush they were in to buy things, particularly at Christmas time. I'd sit in a café watching everyone coming and going, queuing to pay for things they probably didn't need, telling off their children (or not), while security guards strutted around keeping an eagle eye on all *potential* criminals. The noise, from the chatter of consumers and each shop playing a different beat on its sound system was hypnotic and deafening. I could never concentrate on my reading or writing - things I loved to do in cafés. No matter where I went, I was invisible to people; so much so that I felt like an alien from a different dimension, unable to communicate and at times that was a lonely experience. Now I see this loneliness as having been my greatest *gift*; it enabled me to think long and hard about everything and that's been paramount on my journey to find out who I am. Because of this feeling of being an *outsider* I was able to look at the world from a distance - from a different perspective. Among other things I saw clearly that even with their new purchases, the people wandering around were unhappy; there were no smiling faces - they were as lost in this world as I was. I didn't like what I saw and despite childhood longings, I no longer wanted to be a part of the crowd. What I needed to find out before anything else, was who I'm *not* and the above experiences helped me to do just that; the process of developing faith at this point, was one of negation.

We have an innate drive to know or to discover something and we're reminded of it *if* we choose to think about the inane rituals of our lives; we perform them but can't always see the emptiness they fill us with. When I realised that everything we could want in this world was pointless I became down-hearted. However, this changed how I saw the world and I very soon lost all my fear of it; the root of fear must ultimately be a *fear of dying* and I pulled that root right out of the ground. Someone asked me recently what the last line of my autobiography would be and I said "I came to this world with nothing and I'm leaving empty-handed - so it goes." I'd come to the realisation that there's a purpose to our lives but it's not to be found in the pursuit of meaningless activities or the accumulation of possessions that we can't take with us when we die.

When we raise our consciousness levels there comes a time when possessions, gadgets and empty pursuits, although they have their place and can be great fun for some people, lose their novelty appeal. What once served as a distraction from the knowledge that we have a higher purpose becomes empty and fatuous - it did for me at least.

This is true for all of us no matter how successful we are in the system of living that we've created for ourselves. Thinking about these things and the insanity of believing that the magnificent human body with all its non-physical accessories (thought, hope, love, laughter etc.) and the capability we have for carrying out such atrocities has led me to know that there's far more to us than *composting* material and that this isn't apparent until we pay it attention. Thinking about life and death and how little we do in between them is a valuable activity; we're born, educated, taught fear, work, retire and then die. There's a great deal more to us than we generally see and considering that last list, it's no wonder that in our suffering we occupy ourselves with trivial entertainments that just pass the time, ignoring the inevitable finale.

The pieces fall into place when we eliminate regulatory, conditioned and limiting beliefs. In doing so, new levels of Consciousness open up to us. However, if we continue to fill our lives with horror stories, how can we reasonably expect to find *peace* or *happiness*; all we can find are nightmares. When we're content to allow others to find solutions to the problems of our world, which we're all a part of, we know in our hearts that it can never happen. For one thing, if our chosen saviours found a solution, the rest of Humanity would remain exactly as they are now - unchanged. Wherever we go we take ourselves with us; no matter how much we want to escape the drudgery of our lives we can't do it without first freeing ourselves from our prisons. So for example, if we hear a new song that inspires us, as they do, we revel in the greatness of the artist or writer; but not in our own. We put our faith in others rather than ourselves. Words in songs, films or books can invite us to become inspired but they can't free us from ourselves no matter how many times we listen to them. In my chapter *Just Around the Bend* I mentioned an experience I once had when a picture fell from my bedroom wall. Inexplicable events like these build faith but only if we resist the urge to dismiss them as coincidence or listen to the unconsidered explanations of others who think we've 'lost the plot'. As long as we don't use the voice we've been given, allowing others to represent us, we remain in our shells of hope and belief.

Faith, in my opinion, is the assurance that I'm doing what's right for me; to write what I feel passionate about and to put my heart and soul into it. As long as we live with a need to fit in with things the world wants us to do we'll never find fulfillment. I know I'm best suited to writing from my heart and I've an enormous amount of faith in that. I fought it for many years and used to feel pretty inadequate when someone would say 'find what you love in the world and do it' and all I could think was 'I don't *love* anything'. But that was a lie and one of the reasons I couldn't write when I was younger was that I didn't have faith in my own ability, which meant no one else believed in me either. In other words, I already knew what I loved but didn't feel competent enough to do it or believe I could make a living at it. So I buried what was true for me and pursued some of the things society encourages us to pursue; romance, family, fitness, arts and crafts and being a 'good citizen' but I never found fulfillment in any of it. This attitude was further moulded by my father who insisted that I find a profession that pays well; my father put income before anything else. However, I never found anything that made me feel at home in the world; something was still missing and when everyone was having a good time at parties and social venues, I was unable to enjoy them. I'd a huge void in my life that no one or nothing could fill; still I continued the struggle to do things I deep down knew were not in my best interest. Once the ways of the world became pointless to me, I was free to find my own way but as long as I tried to fit in somewhere I didn't belong, I was stuck. One change that occurs when faith develops is that this nagging feeling of not belonging ends; there's a deep and inexplicable knowing that we *do* belong. Accepting that I have a purpose and that I'm not 'just around the bend' has made my life meaningful and worthwhile.

One deep and poisonous root in our lives is that it doesn't feel too worthwhile and that's because the things we do don't make a positive difference to the world. We don't see the fruits of our efforts; it's as exhausting as running on the spot and equally frustrating as we know that tomorrow will only bring more of the same. We can be sure of the same depressive news in the newspapers, political arguments and sad faces worldwide. With faith comes a knowing that what we're pursuing *is* worthy of our attention and this is because the faith we have is in *ourselves* and no longer in, or dependent on others.

Each one of us is unique and special and we all have a talent we can fine tune; life is not pointless and it doesn't have to be full of turmoil and pain. It's this way because we choose to enjoy the things that our system produces, even though we know full well the consequences of producing them and we demand more and more because, quite frankly, we don't know what else to do with our time. We choose to let others be responsible for the world and aren't wise about who we choose to do that; we don't want, or know how, to do it ourselves. We've put all our belief and hope in a system that destroys all things beautiful and all that has achieved as a result of that is worldwide misery, guilt and shame. Some things we can't understand, particularly at this level of Consciousness. There's no point in waiting for the world to change; it isn't going to get any better. On the contrary, things are heading in the direction of more madness.

We need to change the only thing we *can* change - ourselves - and have faith that everything else will work out just as it's meant to do. If we don't change, neither will our world. So whereas my friend's first thought was that "all the miseries of the world had been ignored because of" *faith*, in fact, they have been ignored because of the lack of it.

Intention

Intention is a powerful energetic force that creates our world.

What do I mean by intention? Intention is the result we want to achieve from any kind of action we take; our purpose or goal, but it's not the action itself. Intention is what motivates us to do things and if we're not motivated, we become lethargic, bored and mischievous. The intention behind our actions is not necessarily good; quite often we seek results that aren't good for us at all, like if we take revenge or act with menace in mind. For example, when we're driving along a motorway and feel a need to overtake the car in front because the driver is progressing too slowly for our liking; perhaps he's driving an 'old banger' that we feel is less impressive than our own car. Our intention may be to show our ability to drive faster, to show off our car, or we may genuinely want to pass by without any mal-thoughts for the other driver. From my experiences in this situation, people mostly want to get 'in front' as though there were a stigma associated with driving behind another car, or to be more precise, another person; yes, I've done it too. I feel that one of the reasons we do these things is to try to prove to ourselves that we're in some way superior to the person in front of us; the ego loves to show off and it's also looking for security or at least recognition. Most people who needlessly overtake tend to slow down once they're in front which confirms that they just wanted to 'be there'. We're not generally honest with ourselves about our intentions; the excuses we make are the *permission* for our actions. In the example above, the driver may not like driving behind another car, but convinces himself that the car in front is driving too slowly, thereby justifying his own manoeuvres.

Another important part of our intentions is that they're not always clear, which is why we can get into a bit of a muddle at times. When I didn't know what to do with my life the struggle was there because my intention wasn't clear; I didn't know what I really wanted, or so I kept telling myself. As a child I wanted a guitar but I know now that it wasn't so that I could become a brilliant guitarist, it was to write songs; I've always loved writing. Having unclear intentions is often a refusal to follow our heart, mostly because of a lack of faith in ourselves rather than in others. We push our dreams aside, not because of inability, but because if we set the intention we'd have to get on with it;

we're procrastinators. It's for this reason that we become stuck in jobs that don't motivate us as we're doing them purely to pay the bills, buy new toys and prepare ourselves for retirement rather than to fulfil our dreams. It's possible to love our work and when we love what we're doing it isn't hard work at all. Okay, so maybe we can't make a good living at it but as long as we have enough to live on, it's more fulfilling than the drudgery of working at something that doesn't inspire us or feel worthwhile doing. There's not much that's more depressing than spending our days doing things we don't want to and don't like doing. When we get out of our own way and put aside our fears and insecurities they become our strengths rather than our weaknesses, though admittedly we can feel rather unsteady at first.

We don't always do the *right* things for the *right* reasons and not many of us consider the importance of our motives before carrying out our actions. If we did, we'd be horrified by our own connivance, manipulative and often spiteful intentions. Take for example, Christmas time when we give gifts to family members, including those we give out of *obligation* to those we don't like. We spend a lot of time choosing gifts for people we care for but precious little on those we don't. I think we've all done that 'unwanted gift' thing from the previous year - we give it to someone else. I've known people deliberately buy someone a gift in the full knowledge that they wouldn't like it and others who like to 'balance' the scales, choosing gifts of equal value to the ones they expect to receive - this is not the same as a prior arrangement to spend a fixed amount on each other. Either way, this type of gift giving is more perfunctory than a well-intentioned thought out gift.

Our gift giving lacks consideration or good intentions and we too often buy a 'that'll do' present just to get it out of the way. Perhaps we do this out of obligation, because we're pressured, there's too much choice, not enough time or we may just not like the person we're giving it to. There's another way we like to give gifts and that's in order to gain the approval or love of others; this intention never gets the desired results and that's because money can't buy love or approval - nothing can.

I 'over-gave' gifts for many years for the wrong reasons; to gain approval. All I gained were people around me who were no good for me. I attracted people who waited around in my life for the next gift or others who took offence at them. One of my sisters took offence. If she came to my house and admired something I had, I'd give it to her, but she took this to be an act of superiority on my part rather than a loving and generous one. In the end she stopped admiring anything and I stopped giving things to her. We know why we give things to people but we can't understand the mind or trigger that we pull when we give a gift to someone else. Although I gave things for what I considered to be the right reasons - I was never materialistic - there was an underlying intention on my part to gain their approval. From my sister's point of view she thought I was suggesting that she couldn't afford to buy these things on her own.

We're One; we really are. If we take the time to reflect on this, we see it's not just our intentions that count but the collective intentions of everyone else as well. Intention is energy and when the energy we put out isn't good, neither is what comes back. In the case of our intentionally giving someone a gift they won't want, along with the *gift* we're giving negative energy and this comes back to us; usually in the form of a lack of gratitude from a disappointed and underwhelmed recipient and maybe a gift *we* don't like in the future - repercussions and revenge ensuring the continuity of the cycle. Multiply that by everyone who gives just for the sake of it and there's a great deal of negative energy bouncing around. If you don't believe all this, observe how the feel-good level of the lights on the trees, the tinsel and the carols at Christmas time is lowered by the chaos and frenetic activity of the shoppers. Also, observe yourself when you're giving gifts or receiving them, being aware of your heartfelt intentions. How would you feel if you gave a gift to someone who didn't give one back to you? We've lost the art of *giving* and expecting nothing in return and now it's more like exchanging *like for like*.

I remember once being in a hurry to cross a road that wasn't very busy and I didn't feel like walking the distance to the zebra crossing. So I crossed where I was because I consider myself to be intelligent enough to know it's safe to do so. The only vehicle that passed me was a lone motorcyclist and though I wasn't in his way at all he tooted his horn, shook his fist at me and yelled that there was a crossing further along the road. His intention here was not for my well-being but to throw *rules* at me that he valued a bit too highly, for not obeying them in the same way as he would, or wouldn't as the case may be. When we tell others how to behave correctly too often we don't live by our own convictions; listening to what others say and how they say it is a good guide to knowing their intentions. When we act in the way the motorcyclist did, our motives are wrong and therefore, our intentions aren't in line with our best interest; our intention is to complain about something someone else is doing. People like the motorcyclist go out searching for other people to criticise but they don't take the time to look at themselves - the only true way to learn about ourself. This man was more interested in what I was doing which was far less dangerous than him riding his motorbike, angrily shaking his fist whilst yelling at me - his mind was certainly not on the road. Too often our intention is to get people around us to behave the way we think they should, rather than considering how we behave ourselves.

When we analyse these things we begin to think about our intentions, but only if we don't get too caught up in the analysis itself. When we do this we no longer have to ask for the opinions or approval of others - intention alone will get us what we want. The problem here is that we don't always know what we want and this is why so many people are unhappy. When I decided to finally write my book *On The Other Hand*, my intention was that the book would be found by and help anyone that was ready to hear what I wrote on its pages; it was also to remove the block that told me I couldn't do it. Despite the initial *discouragement* from some people, my intention was already set and therefore, productive. I didn't need approval or want any advice and because my intention was set I didn't need any motivation either. Writing became my life, day and night, as with this book; I'm doing what I love to do the most and trusting that the Universe will guide me in it. When our intention is set, it will bear fruit; what kind of fruit depends on whether our intention is good or bad.

The most important aspect of our intentions is that as far as possible we have to live in a way that's in line with them, rather than in opposition. If we intend to become an author for example, we have to get on with the writing - the book won't write itself. After deciding that we've a skill in writing it's important to know what we want to write about and in what genre. It doesn't matter if it isn't popular or even liked; if we feel a need to express ourselves in a particular way then never be put off by anyone else's negativity. Most people offer discouragement rather than encouragement - follow your own heart and don't listen to them. If we spend all our spare time watching television or socialising rather than getting down to the business of writing, then we're not living in line with our intentions and shouldn't be surprised or disappointed that no book is produced.

Gaining confidence and tuning into our talents requires a lot of sacrifices, particularly in our spare time. We all have a talent that we can hone - at least one - and deep down we know what it is. Only fear prevents us from living in a way that's in our best interest - passionately. A life without passion is never rewarding but a life with passion gets us up in the mornings full of motivation for the day ahead. However, waiting for our purpose or passion to come knocking on our door is both pointless and disappointing; we *have* to find them for ourselves. The next important thing to do with our talent or passion is to complete whatever it is we intend to do.

Intention, will bring our dreams to life if we dare to start the ball rolling, as it were; too often we lie to ourselves about our true intention. It's easy to become distracted or disillusioned along the way by the negativity of others because we're in the habit of not taking chances - even if we're bored stiff. We like to stay with what we believe to be *secure* and don't tend to need much discouragement. The biggest discouragements, as always, come from our own mind particularly with regard to things like fitness, diet or any attempt to change from our familiar way of life.

Suppose we consider taking up a sport because we want, or have been encouraged by our doctor for example, to get 'fit'. We might put it off because we 'can't afford' the right kit. They aren't necessary for our project, but we convince ourselves that they are and so put off starting whatever it is we claim we want to do. If we do buy the 'kit', it all too often gets left in the cupboard after one or two seasonal attempts to learn our chosen sport and it's never used again. Often we can repeat this procedure of buying different kits as we try out and test other sports or hobbies in an attempt to find something we *can* excel in. On a similar vein, how many kitchens contain 'must have' good intentioned health gadgets consigned to the back of cupboards; juicers for example. This occurs because we don't know what we want and therefore, can't set our intention; our initial enthusiasm soon dwindles. Changing our familiar habits is always disorientating, particularly when our intention isn't set. The same applies to stopping smoking or any other addictive habit; we claim we want to stop it and that we *will*, but our intention is not true which is why it steers us *not* to succeed. When we begin to think about what intention is, we then start to notice what our intentions really are.

It sounded ridiculous to me when it was suggested that I find what I love and do it; I didn't love anything. It's surprising that few people actually know what they love or what they want to do with their lives, given a choice. One of the reasons we struggle to set our intention is information overload; instead of getting on with what we want to do we ask others whether or not we should do it. The result is inertia, as we're constantly pushed in this or that direction and our passion becomes stifled as we seek approval and 'correctness' - instead of what we really want. However, this process can be reversed and it's really not too difficult to do. Remember the things you love doing and even if you don't get too much free time, return to them at every opportunity.

Humanity is One

We're the only obstacle we need to overcome.

W e're Humanity. Complex, wonderfully made and capable of amazing feats; our creativity knows no bounds. Sadly, this creativity is being used to destroy ourselves rather than to unite us. We can create things of great beauty but then ascribe to them a *value* leading to a need to protect them behind iron bars, security cameras, guards and electric fences. We give things of value more admiration, protection and care than we do the people who created them. It can be alarming to see people pushing and shoving fellow human beings out of the way in their rush to acquire these *possessions* - some of us are even prepared to kill for them. What's the matter with us?

There's so much we've forgotten about that's common to every human being. We want to live forever in a peaceful world where we can live without fear and come and go as we please. However, our history is at *best* 'disturbing' and prevents this sort of freedom. We live so close together but we can never *really* know each other as we don't allow anyone near to that part of us we guard so closely. Unable to show vulnerability because we fear it would leave us prey to those who'd perceive it as weakness, we're reluctant to take that first step to freedom - no one wants to go first. Because of this division we're on the offensive like a coiled snake ready to strike anyone who encroaches our space. At the heart of this posturing there's a sense of loss and confusion about our origin and destination. This hostility is manifested as an 'it's none of your business' attitude, which means we don't like anyone prying past our personal wall that we call *private* - we're walking 'Keep Out' signs. The confusion causes us so much pain that we bury the emotions deeply in order to function in our world where we're encouraged to be attractive, mindless, afraid and tough - paradoxically to be their opposites as well. We're also encouraged to fend for ourselves and compete with each other for *status*, larger homes and faster cars. Because we're encouraged to behave in so many conflicting ways, by people we don't know, it's hardly surprising we don't have a clue who we are.

We live in a world where we don't appreciate each other, neither do we feel appreciated, loved or wanted. A world in which there's so much hatred that we kill, injure or hurt each other with no good reason and leave others homeless and starving; it's Humanity who's responsible and Humanity that remains silent. Until we can see this it'll remain difficult for us to change this world into a better place to live in. Some of you may argue that there are those who *are* loved; I'd have to disagree with you, as I'm talking about a Love that isn't conditional or ephemeral. I'm also speaking about the majority and not the few who realise that this Love is true. A Love that we miss and long to return to - a Love that has no need of money, masks or possessions, isn't selective or conditional and is literally, priceless. We don't have faith or see that a Love like this exists because we're too focused on our separation; nations, countries, towns, families, cultures - just some of the causes of the many problems of our world. These levels of separation are increasing as parents become separated from their children, teachers from their pupils and employers from their employees; of course vice versa too. The concept of our separation and what we may have become separated from are things worth thinking about; essential if we want to close the gap between us.

Humanity is losing its ability to communicate with itself having become dependent on the mass media and a plethora of electronic devices that are crude in Universal terms. We've one language for parents and another for children, thus separating them. For these reasons we're selfish and alert only to the ways we can survive along with those closest to us. Close or not we generally get into arguments and debates where no one person gives way to another and each tries to push their own point forward. Humanity turns its attention outward for solutions to the problems it doesn't fully admit to and we search for 'home sweet homes' that we can't hold onto forever, no matter how much we want, insure, decorate or tweak them. These homes become somewhere we *claim* as our very own and from that we get a sense of *belonging* to both the property and our families. However, I'd suggest that homes built for our security are actually prisons; outside them we don't feel safe and inside, we lock ourselves securely in - we think. Instead of being One Humanity, we've become *one* nation or some other group; One, behind a barrier which is constructed upon the conditions laid down by others. We're physically One, rather than spiritually and the result of this is that we're suspicious of each other to the point of exclusion and prior judgement, even of those we've never met. By contrast, we allow those we don't trust to take charge of the society we created - we're quite mad!

~~~

We repeat the same activities day after day and apart from a few variations, depending on whether it's the weekend or we're on holiday, not much changes. A quick calculation reveals that I've brushed my teeth approximately 40,000 times in my lifetime and that's just one of the many daily repetitive rituals we perform. This is why we like things to celebrate such as birthdays, Christmas or some sporting event and mark these dates on a calendar, erasing each day that leads up to them with an 'X'; rather than living it; we *kiss* our lives goodbye. It's a paradox; we're excited about *waiting* for future events yet frustrated by having to wait for them; we want to be *there* rather than *here*. We wouldn't want to celebrate going to work, shopping, a new television program or the onset of war, but these are a real part of our daily lives. No wonder we get excited about the latest gadgets as they break monotony and give us something to hope for. That we never celebrate the monotonous nature of our lives has got to be worth thinking about, considering most of us suffer with the incessant boredom of them; why else do we look forward to future events. Life itself should be a celebration. The sister of a friend of mine was asked what she'd do if she knew she was going to die in her sleep and her reply was "I'd go to bed early". That's how low the spirit of humanity is right now. Something's very wrong when we celebrate things that don't matter or understand the true meanings of; ignoring the things that do, like Life and each other.

As mentioned earlier, we've so much in common including wonderful bodies that are perfectly suited to perform so many varied tasks. We just have to recognise our conditioning and then we unlock our magnificent potential - we all have it. We can create the most intricate devices such as the clockwork components for a watch, we can study the stars, dance on ice, sing in choirs, imagine unknown life forms and we can *think* about how we came into being. We can compose beautiful music, write poetry and paint masterpieces that transport us to other worlds and / or invoke tears and emotions; inspiring generations to come - we can do so much good. Thinking is a wonderful ability and everyone is able to do it. Sadly, due to the pressures of life we're just chasing our tails and consequently our abilities are seldom realised. We marvel at people on talent shows who are *discovered* quite by chance, but rarely get the opportunity to find out what we're capable of ourselves. When we do find our talent it's often shelved until we've more time or we retire, if we've got enough energy. One of the things we've all got in common is our uniqueness; we're all special in our own unique way.

I'm wonderfully made!

Generally, people don't question how we came to have so many abilities. There are those who believe in the human being as a Universal *accident* of evolution; things and people do evolve but there's a big difference between the metaphysical and physical sides of our lives. Today, we're focused on the physical and our desires but tend to ignore our superior metaphysical qualities. People who think otherwise haven't given the matter any serious thought as our exceptional qualities are crystal clear. Have you ever taken the time to wonder about how we see, touch, taste, smell or hear anything? How many other creatures can claim to be so brilliant or versatile?

It's about time Humanity realised how magnificent it really is and stopped behaving as though each one of us doesn't matter. Life doesn't have to be full of monotony or fear; it's this way because we agree to it and choose to be afraid rather than say 'No' to the things that aren't good for us. The world has many problems and many unhappy people living in it, but we don't have to be that way too. No matter how miserable we feel we ought to become or how guilty we feel about being happy whilst others are suffering, we won't make the world into a better place to live in. We can only make the world happier by being happier in it; every move counts and the more people that make them, the better.

This is what free will is really all about - we can stay in the gloom and unhappy crowd or leave and *reconnect* to our point of Origin. We're infinite beings; we can choose to persevere with our pain and suffering or leave the field. There are those who claim that not keeping up with the disastrous affairs of our planet means that we don't care, but I'll say to them what good does playing 'oh no … how awful' do for the suffering of others? It never *has* done any good and it never will or it would have done so by now. Only coming together again will help the suffering of others and to do this we need to look at the world objectively rather than in the subjective and selfish way that's become a habit. People are suffering, not because they were born in the wrong country, but because suffering is inflicted on them.

We can raise our consciousness but first we *have* to be prepared to find out why it's so low. It's no good just dabbing our wounds with *cotton wool philosophy* or sticking *I love me* notes all over the place; they only work temporarily - if at all - because we're not looking at the root causes of our states of mind. If anything, when we read these notes we reinforce self-hatred because we're lying and we know it. As we read them the stronger feeling is *I don't love myself at all*. For me, it's nothing more than spraying an air freshener into a stale room - it soon smells stale again. When we question the way we've come to know this world and realise that like a stagnant pond it won't change without our intervention, we can begin to put things right. Until the dirty water is cleaned of the *litter of ages*, we'll remain exactly as we are - wallowing in our own filth and blaming each other for our condition. We can't change Jenny Jones next door but we can change how we think about her and see that she suffers just like everyone else. We all have different mechanisms to cope with living in this world and that can be expressed as aggression, illness, self-deprecation, depression, judgement of others and much more. However, the root of the problem is the same - our separation.

~~~

How is it possible to see ourselves as One again? By observing all around us. When we pay attention to our world it becomes apparent that despite each one of us having a unique character and point of view, we share a great deal more in common. By recognising this we can bring together again parts that have been separated for far too long. After all,

- We want to be heard.
- We've been hurt.
- We're unaware of what other people are feeling.
- We've a talent.
- We share this home.
- We're searching for love.
- We want recognition.

- We're afraid.
- We want an easier life.
- We're imperfect.
- We *must* die.
- We're killing time and don't know why.

I could easily fill up two pages with this list. There's so much more that we share but we've forgotten this because of our separation from each other. Regarding the last point I made, the reason we don't know why we're killing time is that we don't take time to consider these things; we're very good at procrastinating. When we pay attention to our similarities, rather than our differences, we reconnect to the whole. When we connect to the whole and realise that we're a part of it, selfishness becomes a thing of the past; it's our selfish and pompous acts that bring about and enforce our separation. When we criticise someone else because they're not like us we alienate ourselves from them. It's not so difficult to focus on what we have in common and it's much more satisfying than focusing on what we don't. When we do this our intention, rather than being competitive, judgemental or derogatory, is noble.

On a practical level, when those nasty old thoughts peep through the cracks, we can watch them closely. So for example, we see coming towards us an unkempt person wearing old worn clothing. We can look at them in one of two ways; with a critical or a compassionate eye. Mostly our first thoughts are critical; that's our conditioning and it's deep-seated. We can take charge of our thoughts and recognise that this is a person just like us - perhaps less fortunate. They may be suffering in ways we can't comprehend; we can't see the world through their eyes and we can't be aware of their pain or suffering; it's possible they're entirely alone in this world. By challenging our original critical thought and replacing it with a non-judgemental one, we then see the person in a totally different light. If we take it several steps further it becomes clear that their predicament isn't their own fault but one brought about by the society created by each and every one of us. As well as considering why a person may be wearing old worn out clothing it's interesting to ask ourselves why we're so bothered by it; what is it about us that needs to criticise others and in what way are we more 'deserving' than they are? If we keep observing ourselves and others like this then the space that separates us gets smaller and we begin to look at people compassionately rather than critically. When we keep catching those thoughts it becomes apparent that we're not so different; we're One. However, if we're determined to think that we're better than others all we really do is increase the space that separates us - isolating ourselves - psychologically and physically, from the rest of Humanity. By paying the same close attention to the thoughts that turn in our heads unrelentingly when we're trying to get to sleep, we'll find that these can be attenuated too.

In this chapter I've attempted to explain my thoughts on how we're all One. Putting into words this abstract concept is not an easy task. However, once we grasp the concept, our separation from each other becomes obvious and our lives take on a more meaningful direction; life is no longer pointless or passé. This is because we realise that we're not and never have been alone; we cease the struggle to try to become something we're not. Have you ever seen a shoal of fish swimming together or a flock of starlings in flight? They move as one for the common good and none of them fight with each other for space or *first place*, yet each one plays their part in the dance. If you haven't seen these you can find videos online; they're worth the effort. Whenever we gather together en masse we're all powerful and intentional, just like the fish and starlings, but as individuals our power and beauty are greatly reduced. When we've One mind we can achieve so many marvellous things in this world. Sadly we use this collective power for the wrong things, particularly war. Imagine a world where we gather together for the good of the planet and mankind; a world where we allow each other to develop the talents we innately have rather than to be educated in a way that suits others. I don't know about you but I for one would love to experience it. We're Humanity and no matter how individual or superior we think we are, we're part of a greater whole. We can't find completeness somewhere *else* any more than an individual part of a one-thousand-piece jigsaw puzzle can. We all belong together and we always will. When we hurt each other what we're really doing is hurting ourself and damaging the world in which we all must live.

We're One

We fear the darkness, yet choose to reside within it.

One day soon we'll re-gather
And wonder from where this madness stemmed
And how we thought we'd never mend
The gaping space that spanned between
Our unadulterated Love for each other
And turned it into war and corruption
As we ran riot
Destroying not only ourselves but others
With our faces devoid of empathy.
You,
My neighbour who I've loved forever
Looked at me with hatred in your eyes
Because you didn't recognise me and
Because I recognised you and said
"Bonjour" with a smile
That you could not return.
You,
My neighbour who obeys without question
Those who do not bless you
Or value your divinity because
They prefer that you live in fear of
The power you once gave them.
You,
My neighbour who has forgotten
On what sacred ground your feet walk upon
And the humble people you trample
Beneath your vanity and pride
Without ever knowing they're there.
One day soon we'll re-gather
And know from where this madness grows
And know we always knew we'd close
The gaping space that spanned between
Our unadulterated Love for each other.

191

Who am I?

Just around the bend the music is still playing but it's at a higher frequency.

It's great to have gotten this far. I've reached the end of my second book and so much has changed for me. Let me correct that statement; I've changed so much in me. If you made it through *On The Other Hand* and we've come together again, just around the bend … thank you for your company and for sharing my journey; it has been life changing for me and I hope it has been for you too. When I see a photograph of myself I don't recognise it as me; I can't ever remember being the image of the person in it and it feels as though it's all happened so very far away, in another land. When I see a copy of my first book I don't recognise that I wrote it; the words seem to never have left my fingers. The past doesn't exist for me and it doesn't exist for you either; changing our perspective makes this perfectly clear. When we realise that neither the past nor future exist it's inevitable that even if only in just small glimpses, we begin, with increasing frequency, to experience the Now. The future doesn't exist either. Everything is connected, here and Now. I'm entirely responsible for my life; I never once imagined I'd ever say a thing like that.

It's all me
Everywhere I go
Left and up
Down and right
Turning myself inside out
And back to front
And in so many other directions
That I have no words for, because -
I
Am the mother of my child
I
Gave birth to it
I
Fed and nurtured it
I
Made my child
What she is today
And created her each and every way
She became an obsession
An un-treasured possession
That I valued, not, in any graceful way
Abandoned and rejected -
She'd
Been left to decay
Then
I
Rose
From her ashes
Dazed and confused
Deconstructed the parts
I'd cruelly abused
I reached and climbed
Every hill I could find
Then in Awe I relished
The Silence of my mind
No-thing at all
Had obviously changed
But
Somehow
Something
Had been rearranged.

Louder Than a Whisper: Clearer Than a Bell

Originally Published in France by RPG Publishing 2015

Standalone ISBN: 978-2-9546811-8-4

Before going any further I'd like to point out that, for the fluidity of this book, I use the pronoun *we* a great deal. This is how I see us; we're One. Yes, it's not always 100% appropriate to use the proverbial *we*. For the purposes of this book its meaning is general.

Thank you

Godfrey for believing in me
and for all your help and support

~~~~~

Mike
Susan
'little red ball'.
Hazel.

Darkness holds the unknown;
which can only be revealed when we venture into it.

Introduction

We can't see the truth about our world with closed minds.

T hreads about a transformational journey through life (pilgrimages, paths, quests, purpose, etc.) are woven through music, poetry, symbols, paintings, films, documentaries and all literature; I just couldn't see the connections for a long time. They're in fantasy, games, hobbies, metaphors; they're in myths, theme parks, theatres, sports and legends too. There's so much information out there whether metaphorical or not; it's 'louder than a whisper; clearer than a bell', which is how this book got its title. We can't see it until we're ready to. We can't see it until we question our way of life and are willing to change it; until the way we live becomes more absurd than the idea that a legend may be trying to tell us something important. When we do see it, the absurdity of the way we live our lives becomes manifest and loses its appeal. This book isn't about those connections; it would take thousands of pages to write a book like that and involve a great deal of research which would be counter-productive, adding dubious knowledge rather than removing it. This book is about my journey, my quest, my change of mind and my determination to question *everything* - to destroy the assumptions that I once accepted as my reality, regardless of where it leads.

~~~

It was many decades ago that I struggled to write my first book - my autobiography. Struggling, because I was trying to write what didn't need to be written (my story of pain) instead of what did (my story of recovery); I was swimming upstream instead of down. It seems incredible that I'm now writing my third book and I've had a lot of time to think about why these books are coming out as they are; they're reflections of my ongoing journey and therefore, also semi-autobiographical.

I don't plan the chapters in any of my books but rather, I allow them to be written as a stream of consciousness. What *didn't* need to be written about was my life story and what *did* was how I learnt to 'let it go' - not allowing myself to be controlled by *things* from the past that can't be located, by us at least. What I'm really writing about is my psychological journey from helplessness, confusion and self-pity to inner strength; a journey of negation and a determination to find what's always been missing from my life; my purpose - *a* purpose - something to make waking up each morning feel worthwhile rather than mundane and repetitive. When I get stuck I sit in front of my computer and hold various questions in mind that are *answered* through my fingers onto a screen or, I move away from my desk and do something entirely different until what I'm going to write about becomes clear - it never takes very long. What's guiding me? I know that whatever it is, it's far greater than 'me'.

I used the term "brutally honest" in the blurb for *On The Other Hand*. One reviewer wrote that the book is "fiercely honest" and when I thought about that I questioned (as is my wont) what is it to be 'brutally' or 'fiercely' honest anyway? We're fractured to such an extent that we have *levels* of honesty and dishonesty which strikes me as rather ridiculous; either something's honest or it isn't; anything else comes from confusion and division. If 'brutal' honesty hits hard then it must be face-to-face with brutal *dishonesty* in order to have that impact. Honest was what I needed to be in order to free my mind and it's by no means an easy trip. To see our reflection in the world *outside* can be a terrifying experience - far more so than the physical reflection we see when looking into a mirror. However, to see *truth* and the *new*, as veils of dishonesty are removed is a priceless experience that can't be equalled and everyone can see these; we only have to question the undeniable pernicious chaos in our world. Many who question the reality of this world and *philosophise* about it are labelled 'insane' but regardless of whatever label anyone wishes to tag me with, my messages are written with love. For me to be told that I'm 'nuts' by others is one thing and it doesn't bother me at all, but when I initially began to question my *own* take on reality, it was another matter altogether.

If this book is about anything, then it's about changing weakness and fear into strength through a process of observation and self-examination; it's about turning the known world up-side-down and it's about walking blindfolded, without fear, along a gossamer thread knowing it can take the strain. It's clear to me now that it was my state-of-mind that prevented me from seeing what I'd *known* all along; here ... now ... *this* is it. So much is revealed to us when we're willing to examine our thoughts, actions and intentions - *all* of them. With this realisation I felt the almost 'evangelical' need to share it and much to my surprise I discovered just how difficult it is, if not impossible, to spread this message. What is it about Humanity that causes it to reject good news and treat it more like a repellent? When we're prepared to look at the world with new eyes from a wider perspective (non-subjective) it becomes a far more beautiful place to live in.

When covering so many simple topics that have become complicated by society certain repetition of thought is necessary and unavoidable. I do however, endeavour to keep this to a minimum. For this reason I may re-visit some points in more than one chapter; this is unavoidable and very much a part of the process of unlearning - some of our conditioning is harder to remove. If I repeat anything to you then I'm also repeating it to myself. It's not enough to ask the question 'Who am I' just once, as though it were a magic curative. It's part of a process that we need to be *fully* absorbed in rather than a hobby. We learnt what we know by rigid rules and strict repetition and we have to unlearn it in the same way with a new pilot at the helm - ourself. When we reduce complexity to simplicity, we arrive at our point of origin, in *this* world at least.

Sensation, Desire & Relevant Reflections

We need so little, but desire so much.

Whilst walking past my local bakery I was stopped in my tracks by a tantalising smell. I was unable to make out if it was sweet or savoury but felt odd sensations that resembled 'cravings'. Regardless, the event was full of flavours, urges, feelings of pleasure and the irresistible 'come and get me' invitation that at one time would've had me walking through the door in an instant, carrying out further 'investigation'. It was while I was lost in these pleasant evocations that it occurred to me what a wonderful and interesting thing had happened; it was all from sensual memory. How is it, I wondered, that I've vastly different aromatic experiences when passing a fishmonger's shop; evoking less appealing memories? It was at that moment I decided to write about the abstract human trait that we call, desire.

Desire is a 'loaded' word *generally* associated with having sexual, gastronomical, financial or religious overtones:

- Sexual - to be desirable to or by another.
- Gastronomical - to desire food; for pleasure (excess?). Desire is not a word we use to describe the needs of people who are starving; food is essential.
- Financial - to bring us *security*; to eliminate personal lack of anything *we* want in this world for the duration of our lifetimes - but not beyond. Need is an entirely different thing; clothing, food and shelter.
- Religious - to bring us the greatest and most elusive prize of all; Heaven - *if* we manage to conquer our desires for anything other than God - but not until we die.

Little wonder our focus is on the first three of these; they're *attainable* within our lifetime. We've heard the word 'desire' or seen images being used in the above contexts more than any other - through subliminal messages and a great deal of early (often religious) conditioning. I told a few friends that I'm writing a chapter called 'Desire' (original chapter title) and asked what their initial reaction was to that word. To one it meant an expensive new car and to others it was an exciting new partner, improved personal appearance, happiness or an increase in wealth; the things we're conditioned to set our sights on. Interestingly, the desire for answers to fundamental questions about the 'meaning of life' were not mentioned. Are we so lost in ourselves that these questions have become undesirable? One person did say they desire 'world peace' but hadn't thought about what that means or how it might be attained; 'world peace' has no more meaning to most people than any other throwaway cliché. In order to understand what desire is we first need to erase our conditioning through a process of enquiry - then look at it afresh. Without questioning the disorder in the world, we can't expect to create order.

~~~

'Want' can be interpreted as 'must have'. We always want more; such as money, a bigger house, car, television or better 'quality' gadgets and when - or if - we get them, we're not satisfied once the novelty wears off. Sometimes we can't fulfil our desires and in particular those we're *encouraged* to strive for. This leaves us feeling a great void in our lives; for example, when we can't find 'romance', good friends or when we desire to be popular, have a 'top job' and at the very least, to be valuable. Those of us who *do* have 'enough' material things are no happier than those who don't; we all have drawers full of discarded past desires. This is because the 'sensation' of desire is far more thrilling than the fulfilment of it and more importantly it breaks the intense monotony of our limited daily lives.

Desire and temptation are closely connected and one can't exist without the other. In order to desire something we must be able to be tempted by it. In the same manner, in order for temptation to exist it must know desire. It's for these reasons that advertising is so powerful. Advertising companies have a great deal of experience and know exactly how to appeal to our senses; we provide them with the information. They also know that our desire for these sensual experiences override our need to be kind to ourselves or each other; they know that we prefer to say 'Yes' to any 'pleasure call' and they know us better than we know ourselves. I can't remember how many times I've bought packets of biscuits or cakes after having been tempted by the packaging and, on opening them, being disappointed by the stark difference between the image and the contents. We know this to be the case yet *still* buy these goods and accept the disappointments as 'one of those things'. In time, we don't expect the contents to match the image on the packet; we accept the anomaly when we should be *outraged* by it and demand a refund. Just how far will we allow this situation to progress? Apathy leads to an insidious undervaluing of ourselves that lowers our expectations until one day, we'll be unperturbed if the packet is empty.

There's a tendency to desire what isn't good for us rather than what is and I'd suggest that this can be put down to a lack of self-worth; we both know and deny these things. As children we loved to put our hands into 'lucky dips' for the surprise, not because it was worth having but because of the anticipation and excitement of it - for the thrill. We loved playing 'pass the parcel', 'musical chairs' and participating in 'sports day' events but they resulted in disappointment for all but the winner - who was sometimes disappointed too. We learn early on to cope with and accept setbacks that result in us feeling inadequate; we're not!

~~~

Advertisers tempt us into buying products we wouldn't want or need without their drawing our attention to them by making them desirable or fashionable; for example, novelty party foods, ice dispensers on our fridge doors and new 'specialist' blister-plasters that heal self-inflicted wounds from wearing *the* fashionable shoes - *and* allow us to keep wearing them. In some commercial sectors 'demand' precedes production; sales of products and pre-orders are guaranteed well in advance. Because of demand the markets are saturated with colourful and attractive goods for us to desire and as quickly as we buy them, we discard them - rather like children who open a longed-for present at Christmas time or on their birthday and never touch it again. Who are the people who produce and advertise these things for us? Humanity! Humanity is its own villain, victim and hero.

There's an underlying sense of something lacking in our lives - a pernicious discontentment; it's a black hole that can never be filled no matter how much we stuff into it. Little wonder we easily become addicted to smoking, alcohol, sex, snacks, shopping, gossip, television, laziness or excessive exercise. When we're 'hurt', offended, depressed or feeling unworthy we want to suppress those feelings - to desire something 'uplifting' in their place, and after the initial lift has dissipated, nothing's changed; we're right back where we started and feeling just as empty. Activities such as fulfilling an 'I need a drink' thought, exhausting ourselves with exercise, hibernating under our duvets or eating the contents of the fridge, provide only the coldest of comforts; they help us to cope with the surface of our woes rather than the root causes of them. Humanity is self-punishing, self-destructive and - with equal yet unused force - self-reflecting and self-healing.

How is it that we're caught in the loop of desire and disappointment? The problem is that we're reaching 'out' instead of 'in'; when we reach out, we place our trust in the hands of others that appear to be answering our *call*. We feel 'low', see something that pleases our senses and as we need a 'lift' we react in a way that brings a superficial gratification, even though we know the 'hit' is instant and leaves us feeling dissatisfied after the event - the so called 'anti-climax'. I'd suggest that we tend to suffer with *'Now Syndrome'* and that we're always looking for the next 'hit'. The actual *timeless* Now is never sad, lonely or depressing - these feelings require access to the past.

Despite remembering our painful past and looking towards our uncertain future, on a deeper level we always have and always will live in the 'Now' -

it's impossible to be anywhere or *anywhen* else. Time is an illusion obscuring the Now and it's this illusion that leaves us groping for what we can get in the aberrational *physical* Now, even if it's a re-vamped version of something old - we see it as 'new'. We're in the Now when we're crying, angry, depressed, can't stand another moment without him/her and the Now is when we self-punish because we see 'no way out' of a particular situation we've tightly wrapped ourselves in. It's when we can be offered no *immediate* consolation for our woes because it can only be offered in the future - everything *will* be alright. To deal with this lack of immediacy we turn to that which *is*; the first bite of the cake or junk food we convince ourselves to eat, the money we overspend (or borrow) or the excess alcohol we recklessly consume. We 'enjoy', yet at the same time hate ourselves for succumbing to these comforting temptations and pastimes; a hate we justify because of our circumstances.

Desire is so much more than just 'wanting' things. There's something about a wrapped glittering package, prettied with ribbons and a label with our name on it. We love new things and we love surprises so these packages - as assembled under a Christmas tree for example - hold great appeal to our senses; the surprise adds a sensational element that excites us more than the gift itself. Some small children prefer the wrapping paper to the gift; it could be because they're unimpressed with the present or that they love the crackling sound of the paper and feel of the silky ribbons. Have you ever felt the disappointment of having no further gifts to open on Christmas day (if any at all) or seen a child searching under the tree in anticipation of finding another present with its name on it? These gifts appeal to our selfish side that claims 'They're mine'; try taking a toy from a young child or preventing them taking a toy from another

- the result is a tantrum. Once opened, a gift can be cherished, admired or be a bitter disappointment, but none of these feelings can compare to the elevated sensations and concentrated delight we feel as we carry out the process of discovering what's inside. The gift stimulates multiple sensations that we enjoy feeling for reasons we don't give a second thought to - the adventurous expectation of what's inside. We love and can't live without sensations and in the case of gifts, the whole process of receiving them is over too soon.

We'd experience the same sensations and expectations even if a beautifully wrapped present contained no gift inside, provided we were unaware of that fact. We live in a multi-sense 'reality' so it's understandable that we seek to experience and re-experience these sensations in full. We love to repeat anything that brings pleasure, like a child shouting 'Again! Again!' to be thrown up in the air and safely caught in the arms of his father; unless we're exceedingly disciplined we say the same words to ourselves when we're grown up, to a packet of biscuits for example, until they're all gone. There are the five senses that tell us this world is 'real' - physical senses - but there are many more sensations that we like to experience such as excitement, elation, curiosity, pain, violence, misery and fear to name just a few; we have many more spiritual/abstract senses.

~~~

We harm ourselves when we watch the news, horror films or try to hold on to things that aren't good for us like bad relationships and painful memories. We resist good advice and hold onto a perpetual 'not good enough' feeling - carried over from our pasts and re-lived in various forms many times every day. Why do we do it? I'd suggest it's easier to 'go with the flow' of society than it is to resist it - even if it's painful and disturbing. You may argue that we don't 'like' these things but then it would be necessary to think about why we agree to suffer them all our lives and put up such a huge resistance to doing without them. I've said before "We claim not to like violence, yet accept it as entertainment".

Just as we feel the misery of others such as, on television, we can feel their excitement and happiness; we love to see pleasure on the faces of others. For example, we love to see the faces of those who've achieved their goals such as winners of races and competitions or those who've succeeded to climb high peaks or overcome seemingly impossible difficulties from a position of hopeless weakness to one of towering strength. These are our heroes or role models and this is one of the reasons we accept the authority/celebrity status of others; we feel they've overcome difficulties to get to their positions and therefore, we hold them in high esteem - they've 'succeeded' where perhaps, we've failed. It's impossible not to be caught up in the energy of these moments or to react emotionally; we're attracted to - and repelled by - each other's energy fields like magnets. When we don't feel powerful, we enjoy bathing in the reflected glory of others; in effect, we're living our lives by proxy. It's a spiritual/abstract desire that we seek to fulfil through others, rather than ourselves.

The more I focus my attention on this subject, the more I see how incredible a human being is. Incredible in the sense of us being a wonderful piece of bio-engineering, but more in the sense of our crass foolishness and immaturity. One of the most bizarre traits we have is the desire to be desirable - to attract a mate. Advertisers go to great lengths to encourage us to be attractive to others with perfumes, fabrics, skimpy clothing, makeup, alluring images of men or women, encouragement to 'behave badly' and much more; in doing so, they tell us that we'll be (and are) undesirable if we *don't* use their products. There are no shortages of places we can go to fluff up our feathers in order to compete with the 'competition' and no shortage of 'hopefuls' trying to attract our attention.

We tend to be more and more outrageous in our desire to keep up with - or exceed - the expectations of our ever-changing disordered society, but grace, humility and wisdom are left far behind us in this race to 'fit in'. Disorder can only lead to further disorder. The most undignified display of attention seeking I've ever seen was at a railway station when a member of a *teenage* 'hen party' of half-naked girls held up a stick with a sex toy on it and asked the ticket collector if Mr **** needed a ticket; 'in what way will these impressionable girls become more outrageous' is a worrying question and I doubt very much that it will lead to their eventual happiness. It's highly unlikely that the group member with the sex toy 'tool' would dare to behave in this way outside the group - she'd be far too vulnerable, at risk and afraid. Acting in this way will never make up for what's missing in our hearts, hopes or deeper desires; we're more than adequate without the assistance of commerce and it's 'highly recommended' degradation of ourselves. Under the façade and bravery of our outward behaviour and appearances - outrageous or otherwise - we know that there's so much more to us.

The suppression of our desires is an invitation for them to rise again at a later date - they can't be eradicated. Desire is innate and in particular the desire we suppress the most; the desire to know what our lives are really about; in its place we accept the desires of the commercial world that encloses us. It's natural, that when we suppress our true desires they *must* express themselves in a negative way; suppression holds us back and when that energy builds up inside us we must one day let it out. It's for this reason that our world is full of anger, depression, war and other negativity; we work in opposition to what we know is true and what we really want - this is how 'regret' is born. No matter how much we suppress our hearts' desires they will crop up again and again until we recognise them and we'll continue to suffer the painful consequences of our ignorance. Trying to ignore a desire is like pushing an inflatable ball into the sea, the more pressure that's used to keep it down, the more furiously it will one day rise up.

~~~

Desire is a human trait that can never be satisfied; the very meaning of the word denies fulfilment. By its nature, desire demands gratification that we seek to experience again and again. We enjoy the sensations of getting what we want because it feels like we've gained some sort of power over our lives by working hard for something or manifesting it - we believe we're in control. But in 'reality' we're not getting what we want because we don't *know* what we want; hence, readily accept distractions that bring momentary pleasure. We're always getting what other people want *for* us and what we receive has become so limited that we believe 'version II' of a game, film, gadget or new relationship is something entirely 'new' and desirable; we choose to ignore the ripples of these actions. Just like the baby who discards a new gift, we quickly tire of our new toys and anticipate owning 'version III' - we're easily bored. In our hearts we know these things are transient; they're merely a 'consolation prize' for something else - something that eludes us until we 'have the time' to start looking for it. Until then, we wipe out any notions about the 'truth' of our existence because we can't access it right 'now' - it's too concealed and been corrupted. Being 'too busy' is a way of distracting ourselves or allowing ourselves to be distracted by others; we fill the 'black hole' with possessions and empty pursuits. We look for contentment without even thinking about what it *means* to be content; it always means gratification of desire in our society. A piece of chocolate cake lasts for minutes, an ancient monument perhaps for thousands of years, but neither is permanent or ever can endure.

There are different types of desire - physical and non-physical (spiritual, metaphysical or abstract - whichever term you prefer). The pleasure we receive from fulfilling our desires is temporary - like trying to repair holes in the road with ice; it soon melts revealing the hole again. The succession of unsuccessful repairs to the road surface leaves us feeling frustrated and inadequate - so it is with any gratification of desire. Until we realise this it's impossible to live in harmony with ourselves and by extension, with each other. We look for completeness without knowing what it means - looking for it in relationships (with an individual or within a group) or on the stacked shelves of commercialism. Both of these are closely connected to the security we wish to find but neither can handle the task. There's absolutely *nothing* anyone can obtain outside of themselves that will cause them to feel happy or *complete* for the rest of their lives - nothing that will fill the void. We can only find this completeness by a process of negation; a process that first finds out why we 'desire' so much and why beneath the skin of our physical existence, we feel so empty.

Am I Good Enough?

Find out why you feel the way you feel ... about yourself.

The answer to the question 'Am I good enough' depends on who we ask. If we ask ourselves, then generally the answer is 'No'. If we ask someone else and they say 'Yes', we tend not to believe them. Am I good enough? Yes! Absolutely! We're *all* good enough. Then why don't we feel it? Because of continual encouragement and manipulation to believe otherwise. I could end this chapter here but I want to write further on the topic as it's a particularly difficult problem to overcome; I'm *still* working on it. It's not enough to be told 'Yes! Absolutely! We're *all* good enough' - words are a thin blanket against the cold. When society repeatedly hammers in 'not good enough' messages, like splinters, they have to be removed before they do more damage; however, we can't look to our 'tormenter' for assistance, we must remove them ourselves. To put this another way - because I want to *stress* the point - the path we trod to feeling not good enough was a tough one and it's just as difficult to come off it. Splinters hurt like hell when we try to remove them, particularly when we have to dig deep to get them out.

Every time we look into the mirror we answer 'No' to the question 'Am I good enough'; even though we spend hours putting on makeup and our hard-earned pennies on a new outfit or hairdo. We invest in looking good on the outside but rather sadly, in feeling bad. We go to great pains to make ourselves attractive and acceptable not just for the sake of others, but also to make ourselves feel better. This effort gets us through the day/evening but, in the morning - the beast is back - our hair is a frightful mess and we're our-*awful*-selves again; our faithful mirror confirms this. I know there are those of us who 'throw' our clothes on and don't bother with the rituals but most do; either way most of us would like to 'tweak' what we see whether it's to lose or gain a few pounds, have curly hair instead of straight, be a little taller, shorter, have slimmer waists or thinner thighs. Some of us aren't averse to having major surgery performed or even a 'total body transplant' (our own mind in the body of one of the icons we idolise). Several people have told me that they're perfectly happy with themselves and even that they love their reflection in the mirror, but they take the trouble to be *stylish* and wear makeup. 'Makeup' implies making up for a lack of some kind; it's a decoration that covers up what's beautiful and natural about us. No matter how well we dress up or how many layers of makeup we put on we don't feel any different on the inside. We return home after our excursions to face the same walls and ornaments; nothing changes behind the security of our barriers. Physically, we've become more comfortable behind screens and masks than we are in our 'natural' state. We feel increasingly safe behind our various electronic screens and don't need to get dressed to enter into our virtual world; safe in the knowledge that the images on our profile - out-of-date or otherwise - will adequately 'clothe' us.

However, on another level, we're at our most comfortable at home *alone* when we take off our disguises. We're much happier lounging around barefoot in joggers without the need to keep up appearances or conform to the expectations of society by wearing a suit - or other uniform - to work for example; not to do so is unacceptable in many workplaces. We pretend to be happy with our lives and in some minor ways we are; however, nagging in the back of our minds - like fingernails scraping on a blackboard - are doubts and questions about why we agree to behave in these ways. We spend our lives supporting beliefs that we're not good enough and we tend to surround ourselves 'subconsciously' with people who confirm it. One reason for this is that we love to fall into the fantasy of the different characters we're capable of becoming; we're brilliant at it but need a supporting cast or audience in order to keep it up. As new fashions are offered up to us, so are the complimentary labels that go with them; such as, hell's angels, punks, goths or whatever the latest genre is. Unfortunately, our cultures encourage us to veer more in the direction of *trendy* and *need*. The personalities that 'go with' new fashions - to those who *don't* follow them - are rarely *angelic* and usually to be *feared* when they're in groups; these groups cause further division in society. The costumes, traits and fears were created by someone else (through the media) and therefore, can't be natural to us. I added *need* to the above statement because we all need to find out who we are; we seek a true *identity* and the commercials play on this. I'd suggest that any *character* is a limited creation because we zoom into particular personality traits that become who we *think* we are; for example:-

- Free-spirited
- A workaholic
- Sociable
- A daredevil
- Law-abiding
- Criminal
- Sporty
- Tough
- Religious
- Adventurous

- Sophisticated (please research this word - it means impure/un-natural)

and many more. These are creations of the Mind and from them we've created our society. Besides choosing which outfit to wear each day (and how) they're *not* new and *not* our own creations but merely a 'mix and match' of what we already have. We can change a colour, add studs or cut slits in the knees of our 'jeans' but none of it is new; in Tudor times, for example, 'slashed' clothing was fashionable, revealing what was being worn beneath a particular layer. Once we attach ourselves to these personality labels they stick and become what other people expect us to be and subconsciously, who we think we are until, if ever, we decide to change our costumes. To put this another way, we're all walking along the catwalk modelling clothes and images that someone *else* has designed for us. It's rare that apart from very close friends we'd allow anyone to see us without our makeup or when we're wearing joggers. We keep up the façade but our true nature is divine - wide-angled and limitless - if it wasn't we wouldn't be able to act out these parts. For example, no-one is born *goth* or *punk*; we learn how to play these roles and we love doing it which is why we have things like fancy dress parties, theatres and cinemas. We're capable of playing *all* parts and we *do*; however, these roles are being cast *for* us; we're being 'directed'. To sum up this point, we have an innate need to have the question 'Who am I' answered and society tells us, you're a 'goth', 'rocker', 'bookworm', 'sex-bomb', 'nerd' or even a 'genius' and we go along with it. In truth, we fall into 'not good enough' mode when we stitch ourselves to one label and that label becomes the limit of our comfort zones -- those limits become our prisons. It's more worthwhile to find out who we're *not* than it is to believe any label - negation is highly productive; for example, 'what' or 'who' are these labels attached to is worth pondering.

In *On The Other Hand* I wrote about topics that we don't particularly want to examine; they're not pleasing to our ears, because they make us feel that we 'ought' to make changes in our lives and we don't want the disruption. However, we can't find truth unless we're prepared to question *reality* and in questioning reality it's important *not* to answer those questions. The reason for this is that we can only answer them from the same conditioning that gave us answers up to now; in other words, from the unhealthy Mind that is the river we all live in. Our education was never about *who we are* and it never encouraged us to find out either; it filled our heads with an abundance of information that was about everything *but* us and what would be expected from us in the future. As a result we're unable to find out who we are from our 'knowledge base'. It's no wonder that Humanity is puzzled about its origin and purpose; we don't have a clue who we are or how we got ourselves into this mess. As long as we defend a society that in our hearts we know is sick, we won't be able to see the possibilities that lie beyond it.

As I've said before, we try to answer the question 'Who am I' by looking outside of ourselves instead of in; it's a *spiritual* question. When we reply to the question physically we can never get the right answer and there are two ways in which we try to do this. Firstly, by altering our physical structure through leisure activities such as sports - particularly those that build muscles to a point where we become unrecognisable to ourselves or others; we also do this through surgery and at the minor end of the scale by changing the way we dress, having a 'makeover' or taking on some other persona. Regardless of the methods we use to try to disguise ourselves, inside we haven't changed at all - it's entirely superficial. Secondly, we attempt to succeed by climbing a 'ladder'. Who are the 'chairman', 'president', gold medallist or a 'scientist' without their labels and what is left for them to 'achieve' when they wear them? The trouble with the top of a ladder is that it comes to an end, abruptly. There are only three things we can do from the top of a ladder; stay there, climb down or fall off it - the ladder of society is a dead end. Okay, some may argue that you can jump off (or be pushed) but these actions lead to the same unhappy ending - an eventual fall from a powerful yet fragile illusion that our egos don't want to let go of. I'd suggest, we can never become anything other than who we *really* are (as opposed to who we *think* we are) and that we dabble with life by trying on different masks and living in ways that keep up and reinforce the pretence.

I had a friend who took these masks to extremes and her personality and accent changed regularly, even with me. We were reasonably well-spoken when we were children (I don't like these scales, but this was our conditioning). I can still remember the time I heard her speak using foul language in another accent altogether; she wanted to fit in with the friend she was with at the time and I was expected to go along with it, which I didn't. She perfected her styles to fit into any social environment she found herself in and, as is inevitable when we experiment to this extreme, became increasingly confused about her own identity to the point where even I didn't recognise her. For the record, I've no problem with anyone speaking in any accent or any way they want to but when these get mixed together - as with my friend - it becomes difficult, if not impossible, to relate to her. Surely our relationships with each other are confusing enough without increasing the confusion of the relationship we learn to have with ourselves. If you'd been born in England you'd think of yourself as English but if the same 'you' had been born in Russia instead, you would have become an entirely different person with a different set of cultural beliefs and expectations; the root is the same, but the branches are different. This concept is not just about accents; it applies to absolutely everything we attach ourselves to.

~~~

There's something nebulous about answering the question 'Am I good enough'. It has a vagueness we can't quite put our finger on. Missing from the question is *what* or *who* we ought to be good enough for. Interestingly, more often than not we tell ourselves 'I'm not good enough' and *that* - let's face it - slams our 'Don't go there!' door in our own face, eliminating the question altogether. Being '*not* good enough' was the root of what prevented me from writing for so many years; however, putting my mind to doing what I love became a cure for that. I'm good enough to do many more things too but they'd be half-hearted distractions that would prevent me from following what I now accept as being my 'path'. A big obstacle to overcome is the belief that we can't earn a living from doing what we *want* to do but it can be overcome - only fear constructs the boundaries that enclose us. We can never know what'll happen if we decide to follow our dreams *until* we take action, but we live in fear of the unborn and conditioned consequences nevertheless. This is like standing by a door and being afraid to open it, just in case there's something nasty on the other side waiting to pounce.

Who is the *tormentor* I mentioned earlier in this chapter and why would they want to hammer us with 'not good enough' messages; so much so that we feel terrible about ourselves and have to hide behind a cast of characters in a play that quite clearly we can't see we're not the directors of? That sounds like a loaded question - and it is - but please don't try to answer it without giving it a great deal of thought. There are many levels to this question, but as always I only look at what I can see clearly and have meditated on myself. When we turn our attention inwards and cease to look outside for answers then the identity of our tormentor becomes obvious - it's ourselves. We torment ourselves day and night - so much so that we have to keep busy in order to get away from the 'noise'; however, it's still going on subconsciously. I won't even try to answer the 'why' part of the question because we can't know the answer to it; nevertheless, it's a question we ask.

We need only observe our mind to see how negative and antagonistic it really is and how it leads us into states of mind that aren't at all good for us such as arguments, anger, aggression, low *self-esteem*, fear, shyness and addiction. I'd suggest that to some extent at least, our characters are *born* in us and further develop as we grow according to the environment we grow up in; in my case this was an orphanage and not very pleasant. When they stopped punishing me for my existence I took over, because I didn't know anything else; I wasn't conscious of this phenomenon at the time. We tend to take over the roles of our past tormentors or go on to torment others; either way is self-destructive and passes these habits onto future generations. We torment ourselves far more than anyone else ever did; we're self-punishing and our own harshest critics. All our pain comes from stored memories and if we observe this fact closely it becomes clearer and clearer. We can't erase the memories but we can put them into context and see them for what they really are - the past which no longer exists (personally, I question whether it ever did). When we try to locate - by closing our eyes and zooming in on - our painful memories, we can't; it's like trying to locate a dream. What we learn from these past experiences at the time or later and what we're prepared to tackle or change is entirely up to us.

If we want to change we can. The road is difficult because the Mind resists at every twist and turn; it likes to keep us on our familiar track of self-destruction. With honest reflection and close examination of ourselves this can be overcome; we need an unshakable 'will' *never* to give up. How many of us have bought self-help books in the past and felt on a 'high' after reading them? The 'hit' from these books can be temporary and this is because:

- They tend not to go deeply enough into what's happening inside our heads/minds.
- We don't realise that we have to do more than just 'read the book' and then shelve it.
- We tend to use the information to advise others rather than apply it to ourselves; we're very good at this.
- There's no quick fix and this can be discouraging - like a diet we give up on.
- A 'hit' is just that. When a ball hits a wall it must fall again at some point and we're not prepared for this. Life happens in waves, not just hits.

We buy them because deep inside of each one of us is a need to find out who we are and in self-help books we share these experiences with others in the hope that we'll find our way out of the despair and confusion that our world is full of. No matter how good a self-help book is or how full our bookshelves are with them if we're not ready to change, it's not going to happen. Generally, all we find is more confusion as self-help has become an 'art'; we try to get to grips with the thousands of - mostly recycled - 'infallible' systems for 'healing' ourselves. The determination and will not to give up come on their own when we can see that the path we're already treading leads to nowhere. When we can see this, changing paths becomes not only worthwhile but essential and with this comes our passion to keep 'walking'; giving up, is no longer an option.

~~~

When we try to reach unattainable goals they can only leave us feeling 'not good enough'. For example, we may see an image and want to become like that image, as when we go to the hairdresser and choose a hairstyle from a magazine that quite clearly won't suit us, because we don't have the same face as the person the hairdo is attached to. That feels like a knock-back because we can never look as great as the image we've set our sight on becoming. I remember when I was around fifteen and feeling particularly inadequate. I bought a blonde hair dye kit and - without reflection - used it; my hair turned orange (I really mean orange). My head looked like the top of a Belisha beacon when I'd finished. I looked such a fright that I had to return immediately to the chemist (headscarf on) to buy a bottle of black hair dye in an attempt to get back to my own colour. It's ridiculous to try to become somebody else based on an image we've seen. Another example of how we do this is to buy the clothes a model looks great in and then hit ourselves hard when we don't look as 'good' in the same outfit. We bring up our children to follow 'heroes' and 'success' images which is why they become as confused and insecure as we are. We can't walk in the *footsteps* of another person, neither along their path; we must each find our own way, but as long as we live our lives like obedient copycats or lookalikes we can't *realistically* expect to find out who we are or what we'd be capable of if we were *in* control. At this point, I find myself wondering just how many Michael Jackson or Elvis impersonators there are in the world. To walk along someone else's path is to completely disregard our own existence or purpose.

If we stop believing that there's something greater than ourselves that has led us to where we are now, what've we got left? We're tiny in the universe but have been given a great deal of 'responsibility' in it - at least on this *earth* (next chapter). We're so busy wallowing in feeling bad about ourselves and re-living our pasts that we can't see the wonder of our existence - a physical manifestation of something metaphysical and more marvellous than we're capable of imagining. The world suffers with low self-esteem because it insists on repeating - and ignoring the ramifications of - its past mistakes. We live in fear of change - thereby resisting it - and at the same time, we long for it. An argument or conflict only come into being when we have opposing agendas with ourselves or others. Two of these common arguments are 'I'm not good enough' or 'someone else isn't good enough'. We sabotage our happiness and peace because we don't believe we deserve it; we live on the edge playing in our 'one-man-band' with full knowledge that it's being orchestrated from the outside. We effectively destroy the opportunity to find a better life for ourself when we insist on remaining in 'not good enough' mode which is only a perversion of who we truly are. It's tough; very tough, but if we can see that the burden is spread over the whole of Humanity then that lightens our load. When we see this clearly then we feel the pains of others before feeling our own; in other words, we no longer see the world subjectively but realise that we *are* the world and everything we think and do is reflected in it. The only thing we believe we're not good enough for is ourselves and one reason for this is that we're not ready to take responsibility for our freedom. The path is long, dark and tough, but it *is* there and there *is* light at the end of it; beyond that light, who can really know what we'll find. We can overcome all hurdles by refusing to be distracted or deterred by society and it *will* attempt to do this. When we become the act instead of the audience many doors open, but we have to make the first move and to be serious about our *quest* as at first, it appears to be a hopeless task.

Responsibility

Everything is as it should be, but not as it could be.

Responsibility - as we tend to understand it - means being answerable for the actions or inactions of ourselves or others - such as our children, employees or neighbours. But in reality, responsibility has come to be understood as an ability to manage the 'obligations' that society has put upon us. Responsibility is a mantle we grow into when we're 'old enough'; old enough to look after a younger sibling, to earn a living, drive a car, buy a home, get married or start a family. Sometimes we're forced to assume the role of a mantle earlier than expected - perhaps due to the death of a parent. We become responsible for getting to work on time, driving safely and teaching our children to be 'well-behaved' so they'll fit in with society - keeping those cogs turning - the process is mechanical. In theory this leads to a happy and rewarding life but in practise our dreams lie unfulfilled, financial commitments increase, wages don't keep pace and our children's interests lie *outside* the family home either physically or online - leaving us somewhat obsolete in their eyes as they live in a world that we *apparently* know nothing about. Our societal responsibilities have become a heavy burden and once they're 'fulfilled' we tend to feel prematurely retired and rather at a loss. While carrying out our 'responsibilities' life has whizzed by and we've strayed far from the true meaning of responsibility - the ability to respond, as opposed to pre-conditioned responses that rely on thought and therefore, memory.

Though we complain about monotony and the problems in our world we tend to accept it all as an inevitable 'way of life'. Society expects nothing less and we accept the 'contingency plans' it puts forward for us; for example, retirement homes, pensions and bus passes. However, history teaches us that we are and always have been stagnant - psychologically - and despite the horrors that have resulted, we refuse to change our ways regardless of the cost of this apathy; the cost is to accept the authority of others no matter how they use or misuse it. Life has become a game of pinning our tail on the back of a donkey (blindfolded) and expecting that donkey to carry our load; but it never makes our load lighter - it increases its weight. It does however make our journey extremely uncomfortable and leaves us feeling powerless because under these circumstances we *are* powerless. By accepting the authority (guidance) of another, by definition, we make them our 'Master' and alleviate our right to think for ourselves - we lose the ability to reason and to know that there are other choices. We leave our burden on the back of the donkey who is quite willing to carry it, for a price.

Throughout taught history Humanity has been violent and willing to fight in what we know to be immoral wars that leave a trail of devastation; we learn nothing from them and have no idea what we're really fighting for anyway. The order is 'Shoot' and we obey; this is madness. We're far removed from taking responsibility for the damage and wave of destruction the fragmentation of Humanity causes; in a twist, we shed responsibility while claiming to act in its cause; however, the action we take is superficial, in a way that society has made *correct*. Mostly that 'correct' way is to take no action and leave everything to our elected 'authorities' but it's also to apply dressings to the wounds of our victims and environment whilst crying over them; our tears falling into collection boxes of one sort or another. How much easier it is to cry about something we can do nothing about than something we can. We look to the society that created our problems to solve them because we don't want to take on that responsibility ourselves for more than say, picking up litter or recycling our waste; we're far too busy being busy. However, we *are* that society. In the above two examples it makes more sense to put our litter straight into bins and more importantly, not to create so much waste - the solutions are always easy if we take responsibility and we can do this under our own authority - it's empowering too. We can get so cross with the dustmen when they go on strike and don't pick up *our* rubbish; it's worth thinking about this. We produce far more waste than the 'authorities' can cope with or will take away, yet still we demand increasingly efficient 'services' for our increasing volume of landfill material. Our responsibilities surely must go further than this - to at least *think* about what happens to this rubbish after it's out of our sight. Just because we can no longer see it, doesn't mean that it's no longer there.

It's absurd to think that we're powerless to create a better world in which the whole of Humanity has enough food and is happy; we don't even have to *create* it as there's already enough for every one of us. To believe that suffering is inevitable is a limit put forward by the voice of our egos, not the voice of rational or compassionate thought. Even more absurd is that we agree to live in a world filled with violence, greed and apathy - dumping responsibility for it onto elected governments that we hope will change things for us. We can't hope to become responsible whilst placing responsibility in the hands of other people who are also irresponsible. Governments are a part of our unhealthy society and made up of human beings - just like us; they don't know any more about the nature of the world we live in than we do and they're certainly no wiser. We've been diverted from our beautiful world and lured into the worlds of others - worlds that are highly immoral and far from benevolent. It's Humanity who complies with this diversion and sits quietly watching and crying about the destruction seen either on news broadcasts or as an eye-witness in so-called third-world countries - then we move in and clean up the mess. However, we only create more mess, hatred, bitterness and division in this process. Imagine an enclosed room in which we dust and sweep the floors; all we really do is move the dirt from one place to another; the room can never be cleaned until someone opens a window and allows in light and fresh air. We've lost our ability to reason and are living in a world of common nonsense, rather than common sense.

~~~

The intention of this chapter is not to 'tell off' Humanity - there would be no point in that. I too am part of that society and see clearly that for the most part of my life I did nothing to change it - nothing to change 'me'. However, now that I see this I can't sit by and do nothing; more importantly, I know I can't rely on others to change anything for me. We were *born* into this mess and therefore it's hard to see how we can get out of it; it's also difficult to see how we got into it. This chapter is more of a plea to Humanity to - at least - begin to see the folly of our ways, how we've inherited this 'mindset' and how we're leaving it as a legacy to our children. One tiny footstep towards understanding the mindset of Humanity is a huge step in the right direction. We can't make plans to live in better ways because they won't work; the plans would be made by the society that created the problems and we know that when society makes plans things get more complicated, rather than simpler. This is because we're re-formatting old information to try to find out something new; all we can find inside a haystack, is hay. We only need to recognise what's going on - in good conscience - and the rest takes care of itself. If we take those 'Huh' and 'What the heck' moments one step further when something seems to be odd or ridiculous rather than brushing them aside we start a process that picks up its own momentum; it is, however, up to us to either stay on that path or ignore it. We need to recognise and consider why our world is being abused before casting aspersions about who's responsible for it.

We live in a world where good news is not welcome, where those who spread love and morality are ostracised; a world where everything is up-side-down and impossible to comprehend or get to the bottom of and a world where the bottom of the ladder (immorality and corruption) is considered to be the top. This situation is not 'new' - it's been spoken about for millennia and *still* we aren't listening. We feel helpless, unworthy and are in pain to the point of despair; only fear keeps us rooted to the spot - fear of the things we believe we can't change and fear of things we can. In other words, we fear 'change' itself; we don't want to upset the apple cart. There's little for us to do for our 'entertainment' other than watch programs (social media too) that mock others, offer prizes, bring bad news, promote violence, immorality, ignorance and stupidity - dumbing down a willing and obeisant society. Alternatively we can drink or drug ourselves into oblivion, act outrageously, become obsessed with our bodies, shop ourselves silly or compete with each other. The greatest entertainment of all comes from our own mind - our true elected authority. We can protest about what's going on but a protest is only a request for somebody *else* to change something. It's no wonder that 'hope' holds no power over us, let alone faith; it's not a good position to be in. We tend to work in directions that increase our salaries - if we have a job at all - in order to pay our increasing bills; this is a material world. We work in pointless jobs that serve the system we complain about - and rely on - because we can't see the way out of all the confusion and kerfuffle that get in the way. In this world, we're *for* or *against* the system but whatever our preference we tend to believe ourselves powerless to change it. We're not powerless at all; it just feels that way when we look at it from a subjective and 'locked-in' point of view; when we don't want - or know how - to take responsibility for our own lives.

~~~

The first step to becoming responsible is to realise how much responsibility we've put onto others; such as, governments for bringing peace to the world, teachers for the education of our children, religions for 'guidance', science for 'solutions' and a 'justice' system to keep law and order. None of these would be necessary or even exist but for the fragmentation of our world; the cause creates the effect *but* the effect doesn't bring an end to the cause; it generates more of it. We don't have to look far to see that there's no peace, that society is largely being dumbed down and that we live without 'guidance' or justice; none of these are heading in a positive direction. None of the above 'authorities' are healthy themselves so we can't reasonably expect them to solve the problems of Humanity; they *are* Humanity. The world is different when we look at these scenarios from a distance. Becoming responsible is a process; a process of self-observation and examination that leads to a better understanding of ourselves and therefore, what it means to be responsible; it's also realising how irresponsible we actually are.

The biggest argument *against* becoming responsible is that we believe if one person changes, they can't change the whole - an 'everybody's doing it' excuse - so we drop out of responsibility and join the masses; I had *big* issues with this one. The problem needs to be faced before we can see the bigger picture and before we realise what a huge difference a change of perspective can make. Too often we want to know results before we even look at problems and this is the result of learning by rote; when we learn by rote we don't learn at all, we memorise. I can't tell you how it feels to reach the age of fifty because you wouldn't be able to relate to my experiences; we have to wait for our own birthday. In so many ways reaching the age of fifty changes our lives - mostly because of conditioning - regardless of what the rest of the world is up to. Humanity is arrogant to think that it already understands, knows and believes itself to be in control of the universe it lives in. One person changing the 'whole' only *seems* to be impossible, until we make more than a passing effort to try it.

~~~

I infrequently refer to, but never discuss religion or politics in my books as these subjects are responsible for so much of Humanity's pain and confusion. Instead, I prefer to erase all conditioning - by seeing it for what it is and looking at the world through unveiled eyes. I've had several responses to my 'Thank You' page in, *On The Other Hand* and *Just Around The Bend*, regarding my 'thank you' to God and it's caused some people to say 'She's *God Squad*'; how closed-minded we can be when we accept the conditioning of society and judge others inflexibly without seeing the whole picture. This is a trained mechanical reaction; it lacks independent and rational thought. These rejections are our resistance to letting go of our problems; we tend to refuse to hear or see anything that *might* help us. This may be because we've been let down by society before and even though our reaction isn't good for us, it's all we have for security; we know - only from our own perspective - where we stand with it. Look closely at this and it's easy to see that 'God Squad' is nothing but a well-worn cliché and that these three letters (God) are enough to break up friendships, start wars and drag us into the realms of so-called *darkness* where we can live safely in fear; just three letters can do all that and more. Another friend of mine associated the word God with 'organised religion'. God, on my 'thank you' page is short for Godfrey - a friend that gave me so much encouragement to finish my books. I've now changed 'God' to 'Godfrey'; I changed it because I want to reach as many people as possible and if they close the book without getting past the front matter then I'll *change* that front matter - this is my responsibility and obligation, but only if the hurdle agrees with my reason. I don't feel responsible for other people's problems or for picking up the pieces of their lives, but I do feel responsible for doing what I can through my books; it's *my* world after all. The alternative was to dig in my heels and allow myself to be controlled by my ego and pride which is always counter-productive. Many years ago I would've done just that as then I felt responsible only for sustaining the tightly enclosing illusions that defined who I believed myself to be; these are the 'notes' we pin on the walls of our minds and refuse to remove. Does God exist? This is a question worth pondering but only if we get rid of every thought and belief about it currently pinned on our minds; we can never find truth in subjects that have been influenced by others and consequently, labelled 'taboo'. We're far more powerful than we dare to believe. No matter how rich or poor, how educated or how many books we've read, we can know all we'll ever need to know, only by searching inside ourselves.

If we're old enough to say 'Yes' to something, then surely we're old enough to say 'No' as well; however, we tend to make these decisions based on conditioning rather than wisdom, which is why we make so many 'mistakes' in our lives. When I was seventeen I married for the first time; the decision was made based on fairy-tale happy endings, parental/societal consent and a need to leave my family home; no wisdom, responsibility or reason came into my decisions and I most certainly wasn't ready for such a commitment or subsequent ones many years later. I was playing life 'by the rules'. We tend to take our first 'drink' when we 'come of age' - sometimes pretending we've reached it earlier - and it can't be denied that this and other minimum age limits are entirely conditioned. We're told when we've reached 'grown up' status and generally, we're far from responsible when we reach these milestones. I'd suggest grown up status isn't at all grown up if by 'grown up' we mean 'mature' psychologically; coming 'of age' in no way implies becoming responsible.

Becoming responsible begins with an honest 'change of mind' - our mind. When this happens it's amazing to watch it in 'action' and catch ourselves out when we're up to mischief; when we look at and judge another person, when we're about to tell a lie to ourselves - or someone else - or when we get a glimpse of our reflection in the mirror and recognise a familiar moment of vanity. We become aware of our contradictory and irrational behaviour; we also become deeply aware of our surroundings and of the same *true* nature of every human being, without any division or judgement. We're quick to speak about the repeating horrors in our world but at a standstill when it comes to seeing the origin of the problem - separation. Everything falls into place in its own time, but only if we want it to. If we remain self-observant and self-critical riding the inevitable ups and downs of these activities, then we're allowing in that welcome "light and fresh air" and inviting grace, humility and wisdom to guide us.

Consolidation

Before becoming One with Humanity we have to become One with ourselves.

The title for this chapter came to me in the middle of the night. I woke up remembering many years earlier when I'd so many different email addresses and messenger nicknames that I had to be very careful about *who* I was speaking to and *how*; it could get rather confusing when multi-tasking or talking to more than one person at a time. I'd frequently send my messages (by mistake) to the wrong people. I think we've all done that at some point in our lives and these momentary lapses of concentration can be 'awkward' in some cases - like when we dial a wrong number on the telephone. These were in the days when instant messaging was relatively new for the general public and we were *encouraged* (more so now) to be fearful of the people we'd encounter online; we could only message from desktop computers at that time. I kept notes of my nicknames and passwords because there were far too many to remember. I could *hide* from some people while showing online to others and have to admit, it was rather fun and 'empowering'; I had some bad experiences but I also met (physically) and still know some very lovely people. Not much has changed as we can still do all these things but now, on many different devices and websites; the charade is now more wide-angled. Naïvely, many still believe that if they keep things private online then no-one will know who or where they are - this is a clever illusion by the major operators of the internet; we may think we're hiding, but we're easily seen, increasingly so as we're 'permanently' logged in with our mobile devices.

The illusion of 'anonymity' is rapidly changing as social media websites tend to *encourage* us to use the *better_known@email_addresses.whatever* to any that may be more personal such as those connected to our own web addresses. As we 'log in' our personal details and contacts are ripped out of our - what we thought to be private - contact list and added to the new site; the larger websites are becoming more and more closely connected to each other, resulting in us logging into multiple sites with just one click. Whether we like it or not the cloud is expanding and enveloping us, by our acceptance of its invitation. We're not *explicitly* asked if it's okay for the people who run these websites to copy our contacts but it may well be hidden in those brilliant long-winded 'terms and conditions' that we click 'ok' on; who has the time or inclination to read them? To add to the intrusion, these websites then make suggestions for further contacts we might like to add based on the contacts of the contacts they copied; what other information have they gathered? It's all part of a long-term process of 'consolidation' (control) on the internet (and off) and this type of consolidation is not what interests me as I'm always interested in things I *can* do something about rather than things I can't. For those of you who do wish to research the above, it's well documented and just as contradictory as any other type of research. I mention it because it's the apathy of the 'general public' that acquiesce to this control and this agreement ignores something far more important - the journey that each and every one of us will one day make. Becoming One with myself and Humanity interests me but becoming one with the insane and immoral society we've created, doesn't; we can say 'No'. In both cases we don't know *who* is in control but in one case, we *can* find out. There comes a point when we can no longer deny that the madness exists - *or* that we accept it - and it's at this point that we can continue to ignore it or change. I want to reiterate that Humanity is *One* and it has become separated; whichever side of the fence you live on (or hide) you're *still* Humanity.

~~~

Some of the things I was told as a child left me puzzled, like 'Snap out of it', 'Get a grip of yourself', 'Pull your socks up' or 'Pull yourself together'. The latter in particular left me somewhat bewildered as it seemed to me that I wasn't in pieces. Looking back, it now makes sense; more so, I would imagine, than it meant to the people who used to say it - the ones who delighted in taking me apart at such a tender age. As a child, teenager and young adult - way into my thirties - I played many roles for different audiences. We all do it (some more than others) as it's in our nature; our *conditioned* nature. There was the 'me' that spoke to family, to friends, another to work colleagues, another 'me' to my doctor, father, self in the mirror, people I didn't like and a 'me' reserved for the complaints departments in shops; I took pride in each one. There were also the me's that developed the characters for my online aliases but in those cases I gave them monikers too. All these me's were like the branches of a tree - reaching out in different directions, from one trunk. I was 'personally' divided and had no real idea of what that meant. I didn't even give it any thought; the concept is 'alien' and irrational; it can leave us confounded.

We play different characters to other people but we're not doing it for fun; in most cases we do it subconsciously and automatically as we're so used to it. We're hiding parts of who we think we really are and developing the parts of who we want to be - from the various role models we've encountered. For example, I was very good at complaining in shops and getting refunds for goods I was returning, but knowing what I know now, my immaturity was obvious and I probably got the refunds just so they could get rid of me. In order to do this successfully I must have watched others doing it and tried to assert myself in the same way. My new characters concealed a far deeper insecurity that was afraid of the world (my world) and I hid behind them, pretending that the insecurity didn't exist - giving the illusion of me standing up for my 'rights' - 'the mouse that roared'. It seems strange that I could act the part out but not make it a part of my 'private' self; however, it works because when we act out these parts we reinforce the walls we don't wish others to see through; we don't like the traits we hide about ourselves so we cover them up with layers that please us more. I don't believe we do this to deceive, but rather to survive and also because deep down we've come to love playing 'let's pretend' - literally losing ourselves in the new characters we create or rather, assemble. I created what I believed I lacked and at the same time, protected myself in case it went wrong; I kept what I believed to be my true self 'Private and Confidential' - well hidden.

Gradually, new personas are created from our assembled traits, including our body language, speech and temperament. We spend many years tweaking these until who we really are becomes so deeply buried under personas, conditioning, wishes, hopes, pains, fears and frustrations that we don't know who we are anymore, if we ever did. If you give this some thought for a while, with an open mind, it becomes apparent that our multi-faceted characters have been entirely created and are being maintained, by us, or rather by our minds and egos. Behind all the layers of 'pretence' lies some*thing* else. For this reason 'Who am I' is the most important question we can ponder and generally, it can only be approached by being prepared to remove *all* our artificial coverings and stripping ourselves back to bare plaster, as it were.

Like layers of old wallpaper, these layers of conditioning aren't easily stripped off. One reason for this is that there's no reward for doing so; 'What's in it for me' is a non-starter and nothing can replace the layers or prevent our inevitable resulting vulnerability. This might feel like a waste of time but I can assure you it isn't. It's these layers that hold us in our 'prisons' and therefore, when we remove them we remove fears, pains and frustrations - it sets us free. For those of you who have long hair you know how difficult it can be to remove the tangles. You can't begin from the top of your head because the lower tangles get worse and the whole process becomes very painful. We have to begin from the ends and gradually work our way up; it's much easier in the long run and when we do this regularly our hair shines and is in much better condition. There are times however, when we reach particularly stubborn tangles or particularly awkward pieces of wallpaper and it's easy to become disheartened. It's the same process for *removing* our layers; begin with the ends (last added) and gradually our pains and frustrations peel away with them - it's these layers that have caused all our confusion. I say 'gradually' but in reality sometimes we let go of a great deal all at once. It takes concerted effort and determination to 'come clean' with ourselves and at times this can be hilarious and humbling. For example, if I have a disagreement with a friend (my editor) and our 'layers' reveal their ugly heads again, we now tend to burst out laughing in recognition of what's happening and just let it all pass over. It's much more fun than being two angry bulls head-to-head in the middle of a no-win argument, which only serves to create more layers of grudges, anger, hatred or whatever you will.

~~~

Hair-brushing and removing wallpaper layers are useful metaphors to help explain what's involved in a process of consolidation, but on a practical level they leave us rather baffled; they are 'outside' physical actions that we need to apply to a spiritual concept. The difficulty comes in trying to translate these metaphors into a metaphysical 'action' for a mind that has never given it any serious thought and in my case at least, it took many years to see. As I said earlier in this chapter the concept is alien to us - we haven't been conditioned this way; on the contrary, we've been taught that outside action brings results. We've been taught that the world is physical and our spiritual nature has been ignored; we're not encouraged to think about what life is about, what we're doing here or why we're always at war - nothing changes.

I mentioned a friend in my chapter 'Our Cluttered Mind' in my book *On The Other Hand*, who cleared out his attic; letting go of some memories at the same time. Now, perhaps this is going to sound insane to you, but there's nothing we *need* to physically do; observation and recognition of how we constructed ourselves and society are what's needed to start the process. Society is a reflection of our layers and what we've buried beneath them; our world is a reflection of the mind of that society. The insane mind created our insane society and society, the insane world; surely it's time to put this vehicle into 'reverse' by *unlearning*. Once we see through the illusion it falls away by itself. However, it's generally difficult for us to see how to make changes to anything *without* physical action. For example:-

- Our house will remain dirty unless we clean it.
- We can't get anywhere without moving our feet or on some other mode of transport.
- We can't get a worthwhile job unless we pass our exams.
- We can't buy anything without handing over money.
- We can't have full stomachs unless we eat.

We're in the habit of having to *do* something in the physical world in order to see the 'results'. Our characters hang on our branches which hang on a tree trunk and our lives are dependent on a social conditioning system that's controlled by our apathy; we blame this control on so-called 'fat cats' but they only get fat on what *we* agree to feed them. Our desires feed our society and we'll sacrifice a great deal in order to satisfy them - like our spiritual journey or a debt-free life in order to buy something like a house, a car or the latest mobile phone. The physical is a projection of what's going on in our minds; we're separated, in pain, sorrowful, confused, proud and angry. These feelings lead to the wars in our world but the wars never end because we're fighting each other rather than thinking about why we won't stop doing it. The first war that needs to be brought to an end is the one going on inside our head.

Our conditioning makes metaphysical exploration difficult; we can't conceive of anything outside of the physical other than what we've been taught, shown in films or read in books. There's so much (physical) that we refuse to let go of because of fear that - for example, we might need it one day. All this has to be put out of our minds if we're to see a bigger picture. We don't have to leave our homes or give up our jobs; we only have to begin to look at things in a different way and become aware of the conditioning that influences our thoughts and actions. If our lives are meant to change in the process, then they will without any help from us; the universe works in strange ways that we don't yet understand and maybe never will. Though we don't need to take physical action there are ways in which it helps. We can take a look around our homes and see how much we've accumulated over the years; this can be shocking when we realise that the inside of our homes - to a large extent if not entirely - represents the inside of our mind. All our memories and sentiments surround us and we're reluctant to let go of them - so it is with conditioning. We mirror our minds in our homes and now also on the internet and the contents of these, mirrors the baggage we're not prepared to let go of. We're reluctant to let go because our conditioning, homes and belongings represent who we think we are; they serve to *define* us and therefore are the boundary between the physical and the metaphysical, or if you will, our spiritual nature. There's nothing wrong with having things - it's when those things have *us* that the problems begin. The strength and fight we put up to keep these things secured in our homes and memory are equal to the force we use to push away the Now - to push away what's true.

It's the act of recognition of our behaviour, lifestyle and the various characters we portray that release us from our beliefs that they're a part of who we are - they're all in the past. The layers won't peel away easily but they *can* be removed if we're serious about it. For example, bringing our multitude of media pages together as one; this process begins to set us free from our multi-faceted characters. I'd suggest that only two are needed and then only if we need one professionally - if not then only one. As long as we behave in different ways for different audiences and keep secrets from same we can't expect to keep our balance while we hop from one to another like bunny rabbits running in and out of different burrows; it's desultory. It's important to see that our social media accounts and walls are an accurate reflection of our minds - we have different 'faces' and 'names' for each one. When we have multiple accounts we increase the separation of Humanity and lock people into the categories we separate them by; for example, family, friends, best friends, work only, drinks pals, ex-boyfriends, people I know, people I don't, or whoever else you can think of. All these can be brought together as one; if not then it would be prudent to find out *why* we want to hold onto them so badly. I wish to specify that this consolidation of accounts has to come from us personally, not from corporate/social websites who've decided - on our behalf - that our accounts should be *merged*; these conglomerates have their own *agenda* and it isn't in our best interest. It's not a tragedy to have a few friends that we know and *like* on a page but it's rather sad to collect thousands that we don't; the numbers and the charade become more important than the people. We love to accumulate things whether it's memories, 'friends', followers or clutter; none of these will ever bring Humanity together; they're attachments and they bring only an illusion of popularity. We live in a world - physical and projected - of 'private', 'business', 'social' and 'none of your business' and this will never lead to our peace of mind or to Humanity coming together as One; on the contrary, it creates further separation and therefore, more conflict.

Louder than a Whisper

Our hearts are the loveliest landing place for truths that are hard to face.

Without reflection, we do little to serve the psychological advancement of the Human Race. Instead we serve or function as a human resource whose only purpose in this world is to advance an antiquated ritualistic societal system that chooses to remain ignorant of its true nature; a system that abhors benevolence and seeks to complete its own agenda - total control, at both ends of the scale. In other words there are those who want to control and those who don't mind being controlled; you can't have one without the cooperation of the other. We fight, argue, hate, gossip, envy, judge and abuse each other so much so that we don't recognise that we're doing it; ironically, harming ourselves more than the recipient of our sentiments. We poison rather than nourish our bodies, minds, land, air and water. We harbour guilt, grudges, conditioned negative responses towards others and carry the weight of our pasts on our shoulders whilst wearing a superior mask. We retreat to the safety of our cocoons while pointing the finger of blame with a 'What can *I* do about it' attitude; mentally assembling jigsaw puzzle pieces that we trim, re-colour or squeeze into place to suit our loves, jealousies or prejudices for whatever we choose to believe. I find that when I confront anyone with any of the above their kneejerk reaction is 'denial' swiftly followed by the immovable 'I don't want to talk about it' wall. More often than not people respond with 'Why would anyone want to do that' Come on! We know that hurting each other is so in our faces that we can't see beyond it. Peace doesn't come out of conflict - only power and submission - and in our hearts we know this; it won't drop out of the sky or come knocking on our front doors either. Some people often repeat 'World War III is coming' messages and this concept really needs to be thought out with something greater than compliant activism. We're always waiting for peace in our world, which means 'war' itself has never actually ended; there's a great deal more to war than guns and explosions. What's it all about? I can't answer that question but I can certainly think about it as living with this level of insanity has become unacceptable to me. Our world is seriously out of balance and heading towards its own destruction.

Why do we do it? In my case I've had to completely change my romantic notions about what a human being is. We can be confrontational, spiteful,

233

violent, aggressive, egotistic, confused, selfish, judgemental, needy, inclined to be pessimistic and dishonest with ourselves and others, even amongst friends. One of the reasons is because we're frightened. We live in a world of fear exacerbated by the never ending stream of war, terror, lies, sickness, suffering and the underlying threat of the destruction of our planet pouring from the media 'social' or otherwise. We can't make head nor tail of the information we've been fed and don't know who to trust or what to believe in, if anything at all; we've created a society that's full of doubt, suspicion and judgement, about itself. Yet another reason we don't change is due to the loss of our loved ones (human or animal); we frequently see and feel the pain of *loss* and mourn those that have 'moved on'; the clear message here is that whatever we become attached to we will one day lose and this makes 'death' dark, inconsolable and undesirable because even while we're still alive, death hurts too much and there's nothing we can do about it. I'd suggest that this is one of the reasons we cherish our personal belongings and beliefs so much because to some extent, we *can* hold on to them until our bodies die - it's comforting.

Language and images are the tools we communicate with and have come to understand; how we interpret them is another matter altogether. Horror, dystopia, science fiction, fantasy, thrillers, adventures and time and space, are just a few of the genres that we love in games, films and books - frequently they're homogenised. We find it hard to see these as having any real substance; they're seen as entirely fictional by the majority of people which makes them hard to conceptualise as anything *other* than fiction, yet they're worlds that we love to live in. Our inability to ascertain the truth or to know fact from fiction leaves us feeling helpless and vulnerable. We like to see these genres as fictional because the pain of there being any fact in them is too horrific to contemplate and too complicated to fathom. There's a philosophical thread running through all these entertainments that we don't tend to notice; mostly because we're not looking for it but we do recognise it otherwise we wouldn't be able to make sense of any of it. Imagine a nice big fruit cake; the mixture has been thoroughly blended and the cake slowly baked in a hot oven - we can no longer identify the ingredients, save for a few. We love the appearance, taste, texture, softness, aroma and richness of the cake but rarely consider how it was constructed because 1. we can't and 2. we're more interested in consuming it. That this cake is amazing is what we consider to be the truth; how it was created doesn't interest us past being able to reproduce the product - and many variations of it - in order that we might enjoy it again.

~~~

Each morning we wake up from a sleep that we either feel rested from - or don't. Our lives are habitual and mundane regardless of what day of the week it is; weekends are also routine; naturally there are a few variations to this. For many years the first thing I'd do every morning was reach for a cigarette (now stopped), rush to the kitchen for a cup of coffee and listen to the news. Suitably *drugged*, I took a shower, got dressed, returned to the kitchen for breakfast and then the rest that invariably followed; work, shopping, meals, commute, television, laundry, social life and sleep again. We perform these routines so often - perfectly timed - usually because our focus is on the next scene; we label our actions a part of 'daily life'. For example, alarm call at 6.00am, snooze button, alarm again, coffee, shower and dress, kids up, breakfast at 7.00am; we're always watching the clock and routines demand this; even 'running late' is a routine. Some days these routines are harder to perform and this is often because we didn't sleep well or went to bed too late, tired, stressed or maybe drunk - making it impossible to 'unwind'. We're unable to re-charge our energy for the following day and therefore, we function less efficiently - something we've come to accept so well that we're unaware of it. Even holidays are routine and often more exhausting than our working lives - they're like moving home, temporarily. Routines are unavoidable to some extent. We need sleep, our meals and at least some form of work/passion to keep us occupied - a *raison d'être* without which life means very little.

We'd serve Humanity much better if we could see that society is our elected master; a master that saps our energy, is self-destructive and at the same time afraid of its own destruction. There comes a point when the folly of this unsustainable way of life can no longer be ignored and then we've a choice - start thinking about what we're doing here or continue living with our eyes closed. For me this was a no-brainer choice and once I got my head out of the sand there was no way I'd ever put it back in again. The whisper was loud and the sound of the bell - crystal clear; more than enough to get my attention and make my head ring in confusion. The decision to change does leave us rather disorientated for a while and those bells keep ringing and resonating and that's perfectly normal. When I was very young I'd love to spin round and round until I felt giddy and then I'd have to sit down until I recovered my senses - it's confusing for our brains/minds. This is rather what it can feel like to retire or to be made redundant; the pressure of work is suddenly off and unless we're one of the super-planners (which few are) we can be rather at a loss for anything interesting or stimulating to do - unless we've already found our passion and purpose, in which case we're more than happy to have more time to pursue them. We get confused when we break cherished habits whether we enjoy them or not; *any* habit is an addiction and therefore, hard to break.

When we begin to question *everything* the fog starts to lift and things become clearer; not crystal clear because what we see is so unfamiliar. It takes time to clear the clouds of conditioning and to change our point of view. Think of it as walking without knowing where we're going; there's no GPS, map, road signs or compass; however, despite being unclear about our destination, *something* keeps us going. The *drive* is powerful and our energy increases with each step. It's not that we didn't have this energy before, but rather that we expended it elsewhere. Energy is a bit like money; if we waste it on useless things we've nothing left for the things we really need; however, our own energy is more valuable than money can ever be but we can't know this until we start preserving it. If you're struggling with the concept of money being energy then just change perspective a little; think about how much power it has in our world.

The road mentioned above probably seems a bit silly and I can see that. Why would anyone want to think about walking along a metaphorical road that may lead nowhere? I can't tell you where it goes but think about this; where does the road you're on now lead to? The answer to the latter question is known by everyone; *absolutely* nowhere unless you consider the graveyard to be your only option for a choice of destination. This alone - illusion or not - was enough for me to change direction; there's not much point in continuing along the road if it's not heading where we want to go and when we realise this, our fear of changing dissolves along with our will to continue on the same path. Okay, so we might not *know* where we want to go but that's not important at this stage; what is important *is* that we know where we *don't* want to go. Yes, our bodies still end up in the graveyard and if we believe this 'material' world is all there is then that's rather discouraging; however, material is *not* all there is and despite the beliefs of some people 'something' else *does* exist and I'd suggest that's worth thinking about; we know it very well.

~~~

In this world, as we understand it, we have to live with 'time' and telling you that it doesn't exist would generally be unacceptable; it was to me for a long time (pun not intended). More often than not this idea leaves us feeling inadequate and frustrated because we may not understand it straight away;

please don't give up on it. We've had *time* in our lives since our 'births' and we're reluctant to let it go; the mind and ego want to hold onto it and they're powerful, influential and unyielding. Society reinforces the illusion of time by putting clocks and watches just about everywhere we look. It's almost impossible not to know what time it is or what we should be doing at any particular time; for example, working hours, tea breaks, lunch breaks and holidays; 'life' is always 'arriving' and 'leaving' via various timetables whilst we plod on. On this 'journey', some days feel good and can leave us feeling as though we're floating on air, but some feel bad; the bad can drag on for weeks, months or even years. Nothing really changes other than how we cope with day-to-day problems as they present themselves; however, this is a necessary part of our journey and therefore, not wasted. It's only wasted if we don't keep moving and what doesn't move is effectively, dead.

~~~

We live in a dualistic world of all possibility and that means we can turn it all around; one way to do this is to observe our own behaviour and change it according to how we want our world to be. We need each other and we're all a part of a greater whole. All of the above traits I mentioned regarding Humanity can be changed; we need only make this choice and the process begins. Yes, yes and yes, it's *hard* and feels contradictory but our lives are hard and contradictory anyway - as is to be expected in a dualistic world. One of the wonderful things about dualism is that we have choices; there's a 'yes' and a 'no', a 'this' and a 'that'. All we have to do is choose to change and when we make this choice something different evolves but, not if our decision isn't in earnest. If we change we'll find that there's so much more to us; for a start, that the Human Race is One, life is worthwhile and wisdom, grace and humility are worth striving for. Our focus needs to be on, not what others are doing but on what *we're* doing. We need to make a decision to be *done* with pain and suffering (my continuous affirmation) *and mean it*. We've everything to gain and absolutely nothing to lose. When we see this, the layers of beliefs we've created for our 'characters' fall away and that's very revealing. There'd be little point in just looking at a box covered in wrapping paper and ribbons; we'd never find out what was inside if we didn't remove them. Life *demands* something from us but we continue to ignore this and instead, we take more and more from it; returning to its river only our anger, tears, refuse and frustrations.

We make decisions to change our lives all the time; for example, when we:

- Go on a diet.
- Make a new year's resolution.
- Start a new hobby.
- Decide to get fit.

- Move house.
- Begin writing a book.
- Join a group.

But these days, in most cases, they're only temporary pastimes or more accurately, passing fads. These make us feel great at first but they soon get pushed to one side when we get bored with them or find something else to fill our lives with - our homes and garages are full of unfinished projects. I see these fads as being rather like fireworks; they look impressive in that first skyward rush that explode into enthusiasm but they soon lose their sparkle and the burnt stick of 'reality' falls back to the ground. We can easily mistake these fads for our true passion, but passion doesn't burn away or fizzle out. Passion is the fuel - it drives itself and once ignited, it can't be extinguished.

The closest physical and psychological relationship we can ever have is with ourselves - from birth to death. We can never leave this 'home'- not even for a second. This is so important to contemplate. Problems have arisen because we believe we're the person in the mirror, the personality we created, the slob, the professional, the big man, the small man, the characters in films, the beauty or the beast. Our pasts define us. For example, I am who I am *because* of my past and therefore can't let go of it; this is just an excuse not to remove its stubborn stain. These beliefs are like the tethers of a hot air balloon preventing it from going on its adventures - until the stakes are pulled out, the balloon isn't going anywhere.

238

I know of some people who work well past their retirement age because they're terrified they won't know what to do with their time; however, once the chord is cut most people wonder why they didn't do it earlier. The real terror here is that when we retire there's nothing left in our lives that defines us so we refer to ourselves as what we used to be; I *was* a doctor, a secretary, an engineer etc., and these tend to be what we like to talk about with other people in later life - reliving our past glories. It's important to see that these professions aren't *who* we are; they're what we *do*. We also allow society to define us with its various labels and divisions; such as, unemployed, professional, white collar, labourer, academic, elite or lower class, to name but a few. We have no boundaries unless we choose to construct them, or allow others to forge them for us. When we were young children we had very little control over this but now we do. Yes, it's true that we are where/who we think we are because of our past and when we realise this we have the opportunity to break free from its grip. Why do I say "opportunity"; wouldn't we just 'break free'? No! When push comes to shove and the enormity of what stands before us becomes apparent we start to make excuses about why we can't change; fear kicks in and we're held in place by our comforting pasts until the 'right moment', the 'right tool' or the 'right person' present themselves - safe in the knowledge that they never will.

Betrayal

No-one can let you down, unless you depend on them.

Unlike the rest of the chapters in this book I was *asked* to write about the subject of betrayal. I skimmed this topic a little in my chapter 'Completeness' in *Just Around the Bend* but here I want to focus more on betrayal itself. This request was the first I ever received and for a while I felt reluctant to write it because I saw it as a part of someone else's journey and therefore, it didn't belong in my book. However, on reflection, the topic came into my field of vision for a reason so I decided to examine it and now, it fits rather nicely right here. Often, the things we put up the most resistance to are *exactly* what we need to focus on.

My initial thoughts about betrayal were to do with disloyalty, particularly with regard to personal - non-familial - relationships, because this request was put to me in that context. However, like all things, when we zoom in closer to any topic - not relying on conditioning for explanations - a new and clear understanding of it evolves. Betrayal is 'breaching an agreement' and we're betrayed every day in one way or another by:

- A stark contrast between an image on a packet and its contents.
- Financial *chaos*.
- Things we expect but never receive.
- The betrayal of confidences.
- Political manifestos and promises that don't deliver.
- The infidelity of a trusted friend.
- Ourselves for 'believing' in things we *know* to be false,

and much, much more. With this new understanding comes simplification and responsibility*. When we hold onto the aches and pains of betrayal, simplification and responsibility are the last things we want to hear about; we prefer to hold others accountable.

More often than not we already know who's going to betray us well in advance; we prefer to gloss over the indications that we first noticed. Some of the very things I once found endearing in other people proved to be 'early warning signs' that I chose to ignore; one example of this was the alcohol habit of one of the men I married; his drinking began several hours before lunch and ended at bedtime. At first he didn't drink too much but it quickly became apparent that his consumption of alcohol had been reduced/hidden in order to *secure* our relationship. Other examples of advanced warnings of betrayal are a 'roving eye', flirtatious personality and various excuses we somehow *know* are lies. We've been taught that no-one is perfect and therefore, we don't expect perfection; we're happy to accept a person's 'down-sides' and can initially convince ourselves that these are 'charming' - because we *want* them to be. If we think back far enough to the beginning of these relationships we realise that what we now call betrayal - more often than not - was anything but a surprise when we first discovered it. Still, we feel 'let down', again and again.

~~~

It's impossible to talk about betrayal without talking about trust. Trust is something that grows, rather like the construction of a spider's web and gradually its delicate threads build up into this beautiful thing we call trust. However, if that web gets damaged by betrayal then we can never restore it to its original form - try as we may we'll always be aware of those broken threads - giving rise to suspicion and the expectation of further betrayal. Suspicion (mistrust) is something that increasingly pervades our society in all walks of life; business, private, social and personal - so much so that we don't even trust *ourselves* and therefore, faithfully rely on the *authority* and consequently, the guidance of others. A great many people are reluctant to reveal their identity online and I've had many refuse my offer to send them free copies of my books - some didn't want to reveal their addresses. Even when the intention is kindness, people feel threatened in some way and find it difficult to trust. This is because of the excessive stories in our various forms of media that focus on betrayal, violence and other negativity.

These stories include the shattering of an illusion; for example, in someone famous we once trusted - our apparent 'fallen heroes'. We can't trust the stories and because suspicion has been planted into our minds, we no longer trust the person concerned regardless of whether or not they're innocent; suspicion and judgement are powerful condemners - with or without proof. More importantly, we believed in these people and what they stood for - we 'loved' them - and it *seems* as though our trust in that was broken; repeated stories like this leave us unable to trust or believe in anything at all. Because of this we're more likely to accept the *authority* of those 'in control' in our world; they so often remind us 'never to give out our personal details' and to 'check the credentials' of just about everyone we come into contact with; the 'authorities' offer us a protective parental arm to snuggle into; to accept and rely on this 'snuggle' is unwise. We continuously hear stories of broken trusts so it's no wonder we live in a world where we're suspicious of each other.

In this mixed up world it has become necessary to lock, double or triple lock our doors and windows and in many cases, to live in 'secure' blocks that have more than a hint of penitentiary about them. Security is a highly profitable business which translated means; the creation of communities that live in fear is profitable. Despite so much betrayal and suspicion in our world we *still* tend to jump straight into new relationships or one night stands and in some cases believe that this makes us 'free-spirited'; what it really does is misleadingly make us feel as though we're in control of our lives - it injects a little artificial and temporary *freshness* into them, but on a deeper level, these relationships confirm what we believe - that we're 'not good enough' - and leave us feeling more insecure; mostly, they don't contain anything worth holding onto and we know it.

Misplaced trust is like a walking stick we believed could stand our weight and one day whilst we're still holding onto it, it cracks and we injure ourselves when we fall over. We can repair the stick with glue or tape it together but we'll never be able to trust it to support our weight again. Trust is something we give to someone else and when they betray it, it can hurt more than we've ever been hurt before and leave a deep, ugly and *unforgettable* scar. To give someone our complete trust is to invite them to betray us one day; it also means we rely on them to treasure that trust as much as *we* think they should. A broken trust is the shattering of a firm expectation - with full confidence - that we can rely on someone or something outside of ourselves. The problem with this expectation is that it doesn't allow for the fact that we're all fundamentally the same and - save for our different experiences - destined to experience the same 'ending'. The walking stick we leaned on cracked because there already existed a weakness in it that couldn't take our weight - it was flawed - and though we knew it, we still chose to trust it; whatever we entrust to another human being or organisation we run the risk of losing one day.

The betrayals mentioned in the above list come about because we live in a fragmented world; we're divided (and sub-divided) from each other - in hundreds of ways - and therefore, as individuals, we reach out to others for what we believe we lack. We reach out because we feel incomplete and we feel this because we *are* incomplete; Humanity is One. There's a thought that lives in the back of our mind; 'There's more to me than this - I'm missing something important' but every time it pops up we push it right back where it came from; it's called a *Hintergedanke* in German, which means a 'nagging unconscious thought' - but we don't trust it. To ignore it isn't very different than refusing to open the mail that's delivered into our letterboxes. One person I know told me there's no point in changing the way he lives because no-one else will and this is the number one reason that the insanity of this world persists; this idea also demonstrates how we prefer to place ourselves in what we think of as 'safety in numbers' situations. Trusting ourselves - and our instincts - involves a great deal of sacrifice and determination. More importantly, it involves a lot of self-reflection, which is not one of our favourite pastimes; we keep ourselves busy in order to avoid it. If we can't trust ourselves then we can never trust in anyone else; no-one will ever think more of us than we're able to think of ourselves. When we question everything, then by definition it follows that we must leave everything we believed in behind, including our suffering, pain, mistakes and regrets. This process includes all forms of 'security' in our relationships with others and yes, that includes family; relationship implies attachment and subsequently the risk of betrayal; the greater the attachment, the greater the injury we sustain when the walking stick cracks. No, I'm *not* saying anyone has to leave their home or their family; all that's needed is to examine the subject, observe the world we live in, how we interact with it and accept whatever follows those actions.

The betrayal of a child is caused by the same fragmentation of society. For a long time I hated my father for putting me into an orphanage, particularly at such a young and tender age. I was unable to protest or defend myself against the staff and I saw the world as an unfair place to live in. I was unable to complain to anyone or report incidents as I never had the language or knowledge that it was possible to protest against mistreatment; for me it was both terrifying and normal and more than likely the reason I decided to forget about it all (most of it anyway). I felt terrible in the orphanage - as though I were something worthless that had been discarded. I now see this differently. We can't expect our parents - whose lives have been as painful and problematic as ours - to be loving towards us; they simply don't know how. This new understanding doesn't make what happened 'okay', but it does help to see how a particular situation came about and more importantly, how not to dwell on it. We tend to be pretty bad parents to our children; we give them 'too little' or 'too much', tell them scary stories, threaten them if they don't 'behave' and after they reach school age have very little to do with their upbringing. When they begin school, we lose whatever influence we once had over them; it passes into the hands of our various forms of education and media, who are people just like us. While this book is being written and beta read I've already had feedback from a friend on my "bad parents" comment so I'll elaborate a little. Are we looking after the planet and eradicating violence for our children or future generations? No, we continue to destroy it - and ourselves - in many different ways. This is also a form of betrayal; we're damaging and poisoning the world our children must live in and making them afraid - very afraid.

~~~

Let's get back to that stick for a moment. Sometimes the stick cracks because it was leant on too heavily. Too much trust can be a heavy burden for another person to carry and I'd suggest that this trust can be broken, not always with the intention of hurting another person but because the weight is too much to bear. The trust of billions of people is in the hands of an untrustworthy minority who head political, religious and commercial organisations. This gives them enormous power - *our* power - and we don't even know who they are, yet rely on them to sort out the mess our world is in. It's *us* who need to take care of our own welfare; we're the light *and* the shadow in this world and therefore, accountable for our own predicament. Any way you look at it, giving trust and risking betrayal of that trust are the prices we have to pay for relying on something or someone else. Trusting in someone else leaves us vulnerable and that means powerless and in fear. We'd prefer to walk through a 'minefield' after someone else has 'cleared the path' ahead and then we'd be more than happy to join them. There's nothing to be learnt from following in someone else's footsteps; they can't clear *our* path for us because they haven't lived through our experiences. Because most people want to live a risk free existence, nothing changes. Most importantly, our reluctance to change is one of the greatest betrayals of all; the betrayal of ourselves and consequently, of Humanity - it's also 'spiritual laziness'.

* Discussed in earlier chapters; 'Responsibility' and 'Consolidation'

The Abyss of Loneliness

Loneliness is what happens when the connection between ourselves and our source is broken.

As a child, I can't remember exactly at what age but it was over a period of many years, I used to watch one of my sisters closely. I saw her as a role model, because she was the only relative around at the time; in some ways, I saw her as a surrogate mother though I know that was the furthest thing from her mind. I'd try to dress like her, mimic her walk, talk and copy some of her other well-rehearsed traits, but these attempts to 'become' her only left me feeling more confused than ever about my place in the world. I depended on her for my happiness and wanted to share her friends because I never had any of my own; this always backfired and I don't think I meant any more to her than a pat-on-the-head 'little sister'; an act that made her feel good about herself and left me feeling betrayed and humiliated on many occasions. I was a means to an end, as was she. I'd allow her to choose my clothes as I'd no idea what would or wouldn't suit me and she looked good in anything. My sister always chose something unflattering for me, knowing I'd wear whatever she suggested. The nearest I can get to explaining how I felt at the time is to say that I'd been born on the wrong planet, into the wrong body, to the wrong parents and had the wrong siblings; I was effectively, lost.

This sister, in later years had many 'friends' and a busy social life. I was invited to go out with her but I was still introduced to her friends as 'my little sister' and ended up feeling alone at parties, pubs, or bars; they held only more emptiness for me because no matter how hard I tried, I was unable to fit in; for the life of me I couldn't see the attraction. Years later, I realised we'd been looking for the same thing (acceptance) and - ironically - she'd wanted to be as much like me as I'd wanted to be like her, which came as rather a shock when I first realised it. We both needed to 'belong' somewhere and to be 'loved'. Despite her popularity, she was as unhappy and lonely as me; the parties, alcohol, drugs and crowds only served to numb the pain of her loneliness.

~~~

My perspective on loneliness has changed over the years and I now see that loneliness is not the same as being alone. Loneliness is a deep longing for completeness, which we search for in companionship, friendship and our need to relate to someone on the same level as ourselves which is why we need to go out socialising and the like. 'Alone' doesn't need any of society's attractions and is free from the struggle of trying to 'fit in'. What was really happening inside my head was a resistance to partying my life away - counting down the minutes to an 'acceptable' time to go home yet dreading the same loneliness that drove me to the party in the first place. However, the happiness we seek *can't* be found in this way; it's like trying to draw water from a well with no bucket on the end of our rope. It's important to see that just about everyone is doing the same thing from an innate longing to 'connect'. This need can't be met by anyone or anything else because the only 'agenda' at these social events is to curb the loneliness that lies in our hearts. I needed something that held deeper meaning and in later years this led me to challenge what I'd come to know of as 'reality'. It wasn't that I was unable to express myself but rather that my expression was met with indifference; yet I kept on trying and kept on failing, which increased my feelings of inadequacy leaving me feeling lonelier than ever. It's easy in our loneliness to try to find happiness on the 'outside' through social activities because this is how we've been taught to do it through clubs, groups, teams, classes and of course our parents and siblings.

Loneliness causes us to hide - from ourselves and others - behind self-constructed barriers and it's terrifying to think about taking them down. The power of our loneliness is much greater than our ability to overcome it and hits us hard from every angle (inside and out). No matter where we go, what we do or how busy we keep ourselves there's no way to escape our loneliness other than to seek out its cause. I mentioned to a friend that I was writing this chapter and when I asked what loneliness meant to her she replied "I don't like to think about loneliness because it makes me feel so lonely". Another friend said "You can have a huge family and lots of friends but behind closed doors you feel lonely because it's always you that makes the effort, which is upsetting, so you create a distance between you and *them* which results in you feeling lonelier still". For my part, I started writing this chapter many times because I was both drawn to and repelled by it - I also procrastinated. In all three cases, it's clear to me that loneliness is something we struggle to understand, face, live with or talk about and for this reason, I've written this chapter.

~~~

In general, we tend to consider anyone who's lonely to be socially *unacceptable*. The lonely feel that there's something wrong with them because they're unable to 'play the game' *correctly*. We're labelled as 'loners', 'misfits' or given some other belittling title. In truth, the lonely would like to connect with people but in a way that's more meaningful than having a 'good time', fitting in with a crowd, discussing the latest bad news or following a particular fashion; the lonely resist these 'guided' definitions of themselves. 'Loners' are *deep* and I'd suggest that it's for this reason most people choose to stay away from them - 'deep' is not our idea of 'fun'. People who are lonely see possibility; they see the beauty in how we *could* live, rather than how we do. Somehow, the lonely know true friendship but are unable to find it and they tend to hate themselves far more than they think others do. The more we see that isn't good in our society, the more space we put between ourselves and those who choose not to. The trouble with things like parties is that they're someone else's idea of fun (the organiser); we're expected to fit in and all there really is to do at them is listen to the problems people want to tell us about, feel frustrated that no one wants to listen to ours, behave badly, eat party food, compete with each other or drink alcohol - formulaic and meaningless activities. These social gatherings are often a distraction from the pain of reality, memories we'd prefer to forget and an uncertain future; a temporary escape from the mind for everyone who 'succeeds' at enjoying them. We put each other under pressure to *develop* fashionable social skills and appearances, which are nothing more than prescribed antidotes for loneliness and we do this in order for Humanity to fulfil a need for company and 'excitement'. Popularity is something that's subjective and superficial; it's abstract and requires someone to be admired and, a trail of admirers; all of whom must play out their roles until the party comes to an end, which ultimately it must do. One modern example of this scenario is the plague of 'selfies' that has hit social media websites; selfies that scream out 'Look at me!' Where is the wisdom in this sort of lifestyle; is wisdom something society intends to eradicate?

The lonely know something's missing from their lives *and* also from the lives of others who suffer the consequences of our 'partying' and demands for more toys and excitement; they find parties painful rather than enjoyable. No-one sees or hears us screaming; we're effectively, invisible and that leaves us with a deep and inexplicable feeling of 'out of placeness' or if you will, an inability to be comfortable with our surroundings despite the fact that we can't go anywhere else. We don't so easily escape the knowledge that so many in the world are suffering on our behalf and we can't live with the weight of that on our shoulders. We're left staring at a reflection that we don't want to look at - let alone think about - and consequently, keep ourselves busy in order to keep our gaze averted.

We vacillate between our loneliness and the pull of the world of 'excitement' and social gatherings in the hope that they might bring an end to it; for example, if we happen to meet Mr or Mrs Right or a new 'best friend'. We're not at all comfortable in this 'ping pong' situation because deep down all we really want is a permanent end to our loneliness rather than a respite from it. We're the frontier between the two worlds; as the mind sharpens, it's possible to see that this frontier doesn't actually exist. It's not possible to see this clearly until we're prepared to remove our walls altogether, which leaves us vulnerable, but how else will we ever be able to see the 'whole' picture. Deep down we all want the same thing - inner peace and happiness.

Aside from when we're feeling lonely at home, it's not just at parties that we feel this loneliness, but also at school, work or in any other place where human beings are gathered together, regardless of their age. Just take a look around a crowded train or bus next time you're on one; no-one speaks to anyone else but rather they're absorbed in their own worlds. The deepest feelings of loneliness aren't just felt when we're alone but so often in public places where we want to reach out to others but our arms aren't long enough - or strong enough - to break down their resistance. I'll go so far as to say that this includes at 'spiritual' meetings; most people have only their own deepest agenda on their list and if we say something that contradicts what they *want* to hear, conflict follows and more barriers are raised instead of removing existing ones. Mostly - deep down - we're thinking 'I don't want to listen to *you*, I want you to listen to *me*'; often we're not listening to what the other person is saying and waiting to cut in to the conversation with our 'take' on things. These gatherings can leave us feeling that no-one knows or understands us. However, we can take some consolation from knowing that they don't know or understand themselves either.

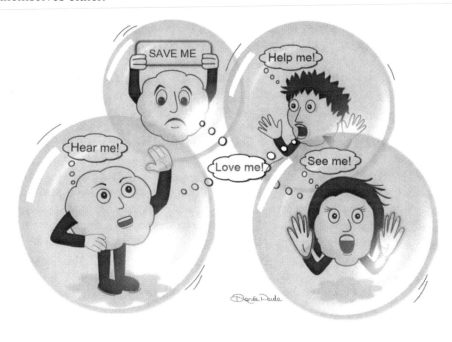

Perhaps it's our fear of loneliness that's created so many homes for the elderly; before they'd remain with their families but now more and more of us have our *own* lives to live and can't handle the responsibility of others. It's possible that we see our elderly family members as being lonelier and more isolated than we're willing to imagine or live with. Society takes up all our waking time and therefore, we don't even *begin* to reflect on these important matters until we close our eyes, but by then we're invariably so tired that we fall asleep. Where can this situation end though; if our children become too difficult to handle will we, in the future, also think about giving them up to some other 'authority'? It's already necessary in many families that children are cared for by childminders so this isn't such an alien concept for the future; it's been woven into literature for a long time now. From who or where will these children ever gain their wisdom?

Loneliness can cause us to feel as though no-one knows or cares that we're here. Some of the deepest forms of loneliness we can experience are; for example, when we've been out all day and despite crowds, not managed to speak to another soul, or when we're checking to see if our telephone is broken because no-one has called. Other examples are when we:

- Watch the clock to see if it's time to go to bed.
- Pass our time *staying* in bed.
- Make a cup of tea before the last one we made gets cold.
- Flick through television channels and never really watching anything.
- Nip out to the local shop for something we don't need just because we want to see another face.
- Check for messages when we know full well there aren't any.
- Feel as though we're the only person in the world.
- Comfort eat, drink alcohol or take drugs.
- Look to others for our security.

There are some people I know of who are so desperate to connect that they read, and reply to, their spam as though it were from a friend; this is a dreadful state of affairs for Humanity to find itself in and no-one should have to suffer like that. There isn't a human being who can make us feel better in these situations; we lock people out because they don't understand us and ourselves in because *we* don't understand them. However, all of us want to be seen and heard by somebody else and because we want the same thing, we can't find it. In other words, we can't hear the cries of others while we're crying out to be heard. Interestingly, when I was feeling lonely I never thought about or noticed anyone else that felt the same way; this is how deeply loneliness penetrates and we can't see further than our own agony. No matter how awful loneliness feels, it doesn't have to be that way; we can find all we need within and now I see that my loneliness was in fact a blessing. For many years I didn't use the time wisely or realise that I was my own greatest friend.

In all the loneliness situations I've mentioned above, the barriers we put up serve to prevent honest communication. The conflict is both external and internal and has a deeper meaning than is at first apparent; it ignores the innate *need* that I mentioned earlier, to connect with each other, not only on a physical level but on a psychological one as well; understanding this is pivotal if we ever want to bring an end to conflict. Serving one 'side' can't bring any balance into our lives, but only more struggle; isn't that what happens in war? Each side fighting each other and each person fighting their own internal battle and from that we kid ourselves that we can bring about peace. As mentioned above, the walls of both worlds (internal and external) must be removed or else it isn't possible to see what's actually going on. The apples of one tree are its fruits and there's no conflict between them or the tree that bore them - that would be ridiculous. Likewise, we're all the fruits of Humanity and it's equally ridiculous to think that we're not *or* that one of us is more important than another; we're One and unlike the apples, we're not only physical; we're conscious and therefore have a great deal more responsibility in our world than we're prepared to - or do - take on. Like the apples we have an origin and connecting to it when we're feeling lonely is the best and wisest thing we can ever do. We feel lonely because we're disconnected from our source and resist reconnection - for whatever reason. This causes us to seek solace in the company of others, who are as lonely as we are and therefore, cannot help us. When we figure this out and reconnect to our origin - by deconstructing our barriers and examining how they were erected - we'll better see what's magic and permanent; what never has and never will change.

Personality, Pride & Other Tough Stuff

Pride is the pedestal we climb up onto; shame and humiliation, what we feel when we fall from it.

To understand what pride is we need to know what it is we're proud of and how we came to be proud - or ashamed - of 'it'. In furtherance of this, it's necessary to put together some of the things I've previously discussed and to examine how they relate to us, personally. If we want to strip ourselves of our illusions we must first understand how they've been woven together over the course of our lives and how we became so attached to them and to other people; we can't see the truth while we still believe the deception. It's a process of 'unpicking' the weave and we resist because we don't *want* to be unpicked, but these traits were not with us when we were 'born' and are not part of our true nature. We're possessive and protective of our 'identities', convictions and contradictions - though we tend to be dissatisfied with how we see ourselves. We find a sort of comfortable security in our attachments to the familiar; rather like a child holding on to a torn and ragged favourite teddy bear that no other 'teddy' can replace. Our creations are our 'pride and joy'; who - after all - would we be without them?

Human beings are the most cunning of creatures and skilful at assembling character traits and appearances that are nothing more than a metaphysical photofit of what we call 'ourselves'. These traits make up our character/personality and we continually tweak them for any given situation; wearing them proudly - as though they were works of art - for works of art, they are. We pretend, in the main, to be interested in others by calling ourselves generous, hospitable, kind, charitable, respectable, compassionate and approachable, but usually we're nothing of the kind; how could we be when we live in such a mischievous world that's obsessed with self. Generosity for example, can't exist without a need for it and surely for us to behave kindly towards someone, implies unkindness in the first place; we're full of contradictions. One business example of this is a answerphone greeting that the creator probably thinks is funny 'Your call is important to us ... please hold the line'; the call can't be important at all as often, some thirty minutes or so later we're still holding on - so they get away with it. If we all hang up immediately after hearing the message the companies would see how important our call actually is and would have to adapt their system to become one that values rather than wastes the time of its clients. We're master imposters and pranksters trying to con and outwit each other with just about every breath we take and we're only interested in - on a conscious level - what's going on inside our particular 'bubble'.

The concept that our personalities are woven can be a difficult one to grasp. We tend to see ourselves as being entirely physical, ignoring - or having no curiosity about - our 'spiritual' nature; we think in 'ego' mode. We take great pride in our 'creations' and nurture them until we become exactly what we want to be; professional, social, downright miserable or whatever else we choose to make of our lives. More threads are interwoven over the course of time; for example, at the age of five, we've no idea about things like romance or how we'll relate to it when we're older. We do however, begin to formulate this trait through fairy tales and other stories building up our dreams of what it would be like to be 'grown up'; for example, how we'll interact with the different people who cross our path. We wrap ourselves up in these 'dreams' and if anyone attempts to expose them, we lash out in one way or another in order to keep the fabric of our *imagined* world intact.

The difference in our reaction when we see the innocence, beauty and the miracle of a new born baby and an adult is stark. The adult is the baby who has grown into everything we've added on to it over the years including jealousy, hatred, judgement, opinions, fear and pride; the innocence, beauty and the miracle are no longer recognisable behind our hardened hearts. As a baby our character begins to be formed according to our environment; everything we see, do, taste, touch, smell, hear and everyone we meet influences and shapes our personality; society is our 'parent'. Society is the mould that shaped our characters and we hold on to the accumulated memories that parented us because we'd be unrecognisable to ourselves without them. We however, add to our 'egos' with every thought, gradually building up a wall that's so thick we can't see through it; we get caught up in the illusion and change - where possible - our appearances to fit (metaphysically and physically); I'll be a brunette, a missionary, or a judge for example. We tweak what we see as our faults through 'new year's resolutions' or 'fads' but these rarely amount to any change because they tend to have no more meaning than a change of clothes. On a deep level we don't like who we become but as our 'personality' is 'apparently' all there is to us, we hold on to it tightly in order to survive; our inner character is very different to our projected one which to all intents and purposes, is the shield that protects - or hides - our true nature; the two are in conflict.

One of the features of living in a dualistic world are the contradictions present in each of us; these are the internal arguments we can't get any peace from. Rather than living in a way that prolongs our lives making them happier and healthier, we generally live by a 'death wish' and in order to make this wish come true we poison our minds, water, land, air and bodies. Despite increasing laws on 'Health and Safety' there's little evidence that we care about them until we're personally affected; for example, when we - or someone close to us - becomes ill or has an accident or perhaps if dirty water comes out of our kitchen taps. How can we have so many concerns about health and safety on the one hand and cause so much devastation and illness with the other? We know the risks and damage caused by smoking and alcohol for example, yet corporations make enormous profits from them; we're paying for our own destruction in the name of a 'good time'. We rush to support charities in a crisis, but generally, make no effort to eradicate the need for them. We far too often prefer things just as they are; things that are bad for us as opposed to good - becoming addicted to them as we turn to them for 'comfort', which is really 'escape'. If you don't agree that we like the 'bad' just take a look at any given week of yours regarding; food (unnatural), cleaning the house (chemicals), television, newspapers, fuel consumption, gossip, waste, judgement, thoughts, spending, smoking, alcohol, mind dramas and pride. We can't be perfect in this world, but we can become aware and that in itself will make a huge difference, which we can't see or benefit from, until we earnestly put our minds to it. The only possible reason I can think of for Humanity to live this way is that we all know, deep down, that our true nature is infinite; so we play for high stakes believing that there really isn't any risk at all. Does this argument have any substance? Only we can decide that, as individuals; not in groups.

~~~

Pride is an inflated sense of achievement and superiority that allows us to hold our heads up so high that we can't - and don't want to - see where we're going. We award it to ourselves in the form of self-congratulation, while bathing in our pool of glory and achievement. Society encourages us to take these 'bows' with a host of awards and certificates that we aim for in one way or another because with them, we become 'successful' and are considered to be 'upright citizens'; in other words we get the approval and respect of the 'authorities' that set *their* standards for us to achieve. One of the most serious side effects of this ballooning of our egos is that it leaves others far behind in our wake of gratification - causing division and resentment. Another effect is that we become what others want us to be (copies of our predecessors) and can therefore, never discover who we really are. I mentioned in an earlier chapter - 'Am I Good Enough' - that there were three things we can do from the top of a ladder; stay there, climb down or fall off it and 'staying there' has surely got to be the least stimulating of options and because of this boredom, the most dangerous. We need things to do, see or think about - things that are exciting, new and challenging, no matter how meaningless they may appear to be.

The mind needs continuous action and it doesn't want to be quiet even for a moment; a so-called 'couch potato' is still stimulating his mind by watching the television - or rather having it stimulated for him - regardless of what he's watching or how many times the program has been shown before; repetition is not boring for the mind and our lives are full of it. Our mind seeks stimulation anywhere it can get it and this, I'd suggest, is why we keep ourselves so 'occupied'. Television, radio, newspapers, commuting, work, shopping, chores and our social lives feed the mind's need to feel all sorts of emotions like fear, sadness, happiness, despair, frustration and anger; our world has become so noisy that what we can't bear - more than anything else - is silence. Whatever we do with our daily lives - regardless of where we are on the 'ladder' - we want or strive for more and more and more of it, but the stimulation comes from something external and therefore, it's nothing to do with self-discovery and, nothing new.

It's possible to watch our pride in action; it's one of our ego's treasured facets. The ego is the star of our 'show' and it doesn't want to leave the stage even for a moment. The mind is always scheming to maintain and increase its hold on us and it's highly efficient and very much 'on the ball' - it's as sharp and as dangerous as a dagger. Pride comes into being when we identify ourselves with our 'achievements' or in some cases, achievements we claim to have made and also when we polish our appearance/character - rather like shining up those medals. But pride isn't just about medals and ladder rungs; it's the sharpest tool that separates us from our true nature and from others. Pride is:

- Apparently, the number one sin.
- The need to win an argument - though we may not know what we're talking about - and also to shout louder than our 'opponent' in an attempt to intimidate them into submission.
- A refusal to pick up the phone when we want to speak to someone but are unable to bring ourselves to dial their number.

- Boasting.
- Refusing good advice because *we* know 'better'.
- The belief that we deserve the respect and admiration of others.
- A control mechanism.
- All about 'Me'.
- The wall that refuses to ask for help when we need it.
- The refusal of help that's being offered.

First we have to come clean about our world and then we'll be able to take responsibility for all that's going on in it. Our intention in these cases is to stand our ground - no matter what - even when there's no solid ground to stand on; pride prevents us from retreating or admitting error. We know full well when we're doing this but refuse to back down; watching our pride in action brings that to an end because just in watching it, we become more self-aware and also see how ridiculous pride actually is. If you wish to see what pride means to the collective mind just do an internet search for the word and see what comes up both on the *web* tab and on *images*; you may be surprised at the results - they are there because *we* put them there. As our awareness increases it becomes very difficult to maintain the façade and increasingly, we're able to admit 'error' without feeling humiliated and with this change our pride begins to subside. Before blaming society for being a 'bad' parent we must first ask ourselves if we've been 'good' children in it.

~~~~

Society is an accurate reflection of the human mind; proud, stoic and resistant to change - though we collectively agree to live in it and to uphold its practises and regimes. It's what we do every day and each one of us is put through an educational system that demands the continuation of this proud society; it's a generational loop and it's an unhealthy and unworthy one. Despite society being unhealthy and destructive were proud to be a part of it - flying our particular flags. We tend not to want it changed or criticised - particularly by those who think differently, seemingly posing a threat to the status quo which we fight to maintain; a status quo that's resulting in a 'hive mind' mentality. The world is the way it is because the majority of people like it this way, despite their protestations to the contrary. It's important to discern that we can't find our *centre* when our 'walls of pride' are up or when we're following somebody else's directions, because we're relying on an unhealthy system and an unhealthy mind to do it for us, which they're incapable of doing.

When our pride takes a 'hit' a wave of mixed emotions washes over us, ranging from anger to fear. It gets hit when someone thinks they could've done something better than us, effectively deprecating us. We don't like criticism regardless of whether it's constructive or not. We see what we do as excellent - even if only by effort - because we've rehearsed it for a long time and to have someone not see us as we want them to, hurts our pride very much. One example of this is when we invite some friends to dinner and one of them comments - across the table - that we added too much salt to the meal, or that they'd let us have their perfected recipe for what we spent all day preparing. Pride is wobbly and easily offended, particularly when it's met with such rudeness. I'm sure that every one of us knows that feeling of vulnerability when whilst walking down the high street we trip over a paving slab and everyone who saw it watches as our face reddens and we self-consciously struggle to get up again; believing, if not knowing, that all eyes are on us. This is also how it feels when attention is unfavourably drawn to us in the company of others, such as with my "pat-on-the-head" big sister in the previous chapter.

Men feel vulnerable if they leave their trousers undone and women if they're caught with their skirt tucked into their knickers as they come out of the public toilets; particularly if someone points it out before we realise it for ourselves. In these moments of discomposure we feel humiliated and exposed because one of our walls collapsed in a momentary lapse of concentration; we dropped our guard and our ego *never* likes that. Two of the layers behind our pride are 'shame' and 'embarrassment' and we feel these when our wall of pride shows cracks leaving us exposed because of our 'failure' - usually a failure to keep up expected appearances. Imagine, if you will, an actor whose moustache slips or he forgets his lines in the middle of his finest performance; he's no longer fully 'under cover' and shows his infallibility as he struggles to straighten the moustache or to remember his lines - in front of everyone. Even if we correct the error before anyone notices we worry that someone *might* have seen us because we're so self-conscious about the things we do. In the reverse of this situation we get to keep our wall up when we watch the misfortunes of others and I'd add that we're happy these didn't happen to us. If something unfortunate happens to someone we dislike or disapprove of then we may get a certain amount of enjoyment from the incident and consider that justice has been done; a rather judgemental and superior attitude to take, but we take this stance often and state that 'it served them right' or if we don't know them we may think that they 'must have deserved it'; bad is okay as long as it's happening to someone else and unfortunately this attitude has reached pandemic proportions.

In order to cope with the world and the society that we find ourselves living in we build up a shield of pride and this helps us to feel acceptable - by gaining respect or a good reputation. But, society doesn't reward our achievements any further than to 'stamp out' another appropriate medal or title before moving on to the next in line. Are these rewards really worth anything at all or do they fill a hole with something temporary? Heroes are soon forgotten as others wait to step into their 'still warm' shoes; no-one is indispensable in the society that we've created. We can find ourselves at a loss when our services are 'no longer required' and all we're left with are our memories, a crumbling past, and a future in which we can clearly see the *finish* line that we'll soon have to cross - "Now Syndrome"* then takes on a whole new and less exciting meaning. Because our lives are relatively short, we become selfish and proud - taking what we can get from them. Because we can't see the results of any effort to change within our own lifetime there's little motivation to change anything for the benefit of 'future' generations - as evidenced by the way we treat our world now. Our personalities are masks - personas that we're proud of and love to defend - and if we can see this then what's actually happening becomes clear as day. Problems occur when we don't want to strip off our masks any more than we want to walk down the street without our clothes on. If we *want* to find Truth and the New, then we must accept *unconditionally* the necessity to leave behind all our illusions, personalities, titles, certificates and medals. I'd suggest, that 'Now' - *before* we 'die' - is a good time to begin the process.

* Discussed in 'Sensation, Desire & Relevant Reflections'

Hidden

I listened to your lies of all shapes and sizes
Of colours and words in your master disguises
I never knew the centre could be
The infinite roots that you'd hidden from me

So fare thee well
And good-bye my friend
The truth must come out in the end
The clouds are dispersing
They're almost gone
And now is the time …
To sing out my song

I lived with all your fears, tears and maddening abstractions
Like love, lust and your comical actions
I never knew the centre was free
This heartfelt Love that was always in me

So fare thee well
Adieu my friend
It will all come right in the end
The lying is over
Your treachery clear
It took me a while
To breach this frontier

So fare thee well
Au revoir my friend
The truth is out; now the light won't bend
This night has passed
And it's almost day
I'm not sure where I'm going
But I'm sure on my way

Deep Thoughts: a Symposium

If you're following me and I'm following you then we must be going round in circles.

~ Suffering ~

I'd suggest that there isn't a 'soul' alive who can state for certain what the true nature of a human being is, how we got to be here or what we're supposed to be doing with our lives. There's no doubt that what we're doing to our world isn't in our best interest, nor that of the wonderful creatures we share it with; everything is suffering unnecessarily in one way or another - physically and psychologically. This suffering is 'alive'; it passes between us from generation to generation, government to government, book to book and from film to film, like a mutating virus passing through the physical and metaphysical veins of humanity and for the foreseeable future - there appears to be no respite. Humanity is the cause *and* effect of its own adversity. The media is so full of the suffering going on in the world that we're becoming immune to it; so much so that it takes a horrific image - of perhaps a disaster victim - to catch our attention, but even that image can't hold it for long. We talk about suffering for a moment or two and then get on with our daily lives expecting various 'peace' organisations to get their act together and bring it to an end - turning our backs on it after the initial outcry. We feel safe and comfortable behind our walls and borders and believe that these events are nothing to do with us, *personally*.

Suffering - of humans, animals and the environment - is entertainment on our screens; we decorate our online walls with horrific images kidding ourselves that this will help to eradicate the problem. Advertising these images doesn't alleviate the problem; it serves to increase levels of fear, hatred and division. There isn't one of us who doesn't know this though with some, it's buried so deep that they can't see it. To put this into perspective: we go to war, glorify and reward the 'heroes' of that war and *then* declare horror at the images of the resulting devastation - we applaud the cause and subsequently condemn the effect. We then make films - and games - about these horrors (even re-enacting battles on their anniversaries) and they become highly profitable best sellers; as if the horror itself isn't enough, we're willing to *pay* to see more of it.

Images - of suffering are more powerful and influential than most people realise and we put them everywhere arguing that we need to be informed, yet despite being regularly 'informed' these things keep happening and we keep passively discussing them. How will the nightmare ever end if we don't take responsibility for it? We claim that the corporations, governments, army, navy and terrorists etc. are responsible, but they're human beings just like us; they're no different to you or me except that they're willing and know how to take advantage of our fear and we allow them to do it; one gives the order and the other obeys. Human beings commit these atrocities and that's what must stop. If we don't want war, we won't have it. The process *must* and can *only* begin within each of us but when we want to make everyone *else* stop what they're doing then nothing will ever change. Who after all, would you allow to change *you*?

There's a sense of great unfairness that occurs to all of us at some point in our lives; a feeling of being cheated out of our chance to live in peace because we were born into a world full of cruelty, horror, war, hatred, racism, violence, politics, religion and sickness. There's also a sense of limitation and a lack of control; we find that we must comply with regulations in a world where it's impossible to find justice. We're encouraged to make the most of things and accept 'that's life', by someone else's standards rather than our own. We inherited these regulations from an unhealthy society and they must be changed or in some cases, abolished. Very few people question this 'powerless to do anything about it' situation or choose to examine it further but if we do, it becomes obvious that we're not here by 'chance' and that things aren't all they seem to be. Together, we *can* live joyously rather than accept suffering as not just our only option, but as something we must endure in order to find peace; this is as preposterous as taking a lethal dose of poison in order to live. In *On The Other Hand* I talked about a feeling I once had about life feeling pointless, but since then my view has changed; life isn't pointless, only what I was doing with it.

I recently met a lady who believes that 'this life is it' and although she sincerely believes that, she's content to 'accept' the struggles of our world until she 'comes to an end' and, as is the case with most of us - quite bizarrely - we prefer that end be delayed as long as possible which is somewhat masochistic. Surely it's wiser to ask why we're living in a 'back-to-back' horror movie world than not to question it at all. There's something absurd about an innocent baby being born into this mess with 'no way out'; in this scenario, being born can be compared to being thrown into a dungeon with no idea why and no chance of getting out again - a life sentence. No! No! No! This is *senseless* and surely invites at least a little investigation on our part. If anyone of us *were* thrown into a dungeon surely we'd - at the very least - attempt to find our way out again rather than accept our 'fate' and give up?

A reviewer for *On the Other Hand* said that the book "... won't suit everyone, especially if you don't like thinking" and I've heard similar comments many times before. It's true that many people don't like thinking for themselves; we're fatigued by the pace of life and already have enough to think about. However, what's the point in having the capacity to work things out for ourselves if we don't use it? If we don't use our ability to think - preferring to be 'entertained' - then someone else will do it for us and consequently, make our choices and take on our responsibilities. In my opinion, we each have a responsibility and obligation to act in a way that's guided by our conscience - to work with it rather than against it. For example, dropping pennies into a charity box and then walking away may salve our conscience leaving us feeling satisfied that we've 'done our bit'. Perhaps it would be wiser to ask why these charities exist in the first place and why we allow ourselves to do so little to eradicate the need for them; in our hearts, we know how to achieve this and all we have to do is listen to and act on this wisdom. Often we prefer to push aside and ignore our conscience but a little reflection tells us that we *have* one for a reason. Only we, as individuals, can begin to understand this when we reflect on it; to reflect on how we live our lives and why we tend to prefer what isn't good for the whole of Humanity, rather than what is.

The difficulty in ending the suffering of Humanity is that we must begin with ending our *own* first - as an individual. We must literally, change our mind. We don't think changing ourselves will make a difference, because it seems too simplistic an idea for such a big problem. How can changing 'me' change what's going on elsewhere in the world? Because it removes the walls and masks that separate us from it - psychologically speaking. As long as we focus on the suffering happening 'elsewhere', the whole will remain dysfunctional and we'll continue to maunder. Keeping our attention on what we can change, instead of what we can't, will make a big difference to our world; the mouse *can* overcome the lion, if it will just try and each generation has the opportunity to do just that.

~ Impermanence ~

There's a sense of 'life is temporary' amongst us; it lies in our hearts and consciences. Years of pain and struggle have pushed the importance of this sense to the back of our minds; we choose to lock it away where we don't have to think about it again. That we'll die one day is too awful to contemplate, particularly as death - due to conditioning - is frequently painted as dark, morbid and terrorising; it's something sorrowful to be feared and life, something to be held onto at any cost. Thinking about these things is considered by many people to be an act of rebellion or anarchy rather than intelligence but more than that, it's thought of as *risky* and we tend to prefer to live in fear rather than take risks. Just about everywhere we look looms a sense of impermanence, of time corroding and wearing out *everything*. No matter how robust we make them, a tower block will erode just as a straw house will - though the time taken for the process varies enormously - nothing we can do or make will last forever.

Though time is abstract and an illusion, we must live by it so surely it's prudent to use it wisely whilst we have the opportunity to do so, rather than living in a way that tosses a 'heaven or hell' coin up into the air hoping for a glorious outcome when we catch it again, if - and only if - we behave ourselves.

There's a big difference in the timescale of something like a pyramid crumbling and the lifetime of a human being. Because we can't relate to a human being living for thousands or millions of years, it's hard to put this into perspective. Over one, two or even three generations there's very little visible difference in the deterioration of a pyramid, which makes it more difficult for us to see the transitory nature of them. Historically, these constructions have been here much longer than we have and will remain long after our deaths. When one archaeologist dies, another takes over where he left off and another after him. Still, we continue to study and preserve death and history as though it could bring us to life - to save humanity from destruction. This is impossible. We're alive *now* and it would be far more intelligent to stop digging into the graves of those who died a long time ago; it's impossible to find something new in something old, or something new in something that hasn't happened yet (future). We have a dream to go into 'outer' space one day in a hope to find another world, but space exploration is also a 'relay' occupation and each of us knows that we won't be alive - or going on the trip - when 'or if' it ever becomes possible. Knowledge of this is a reminder of the nature of our impermanence and also that while we're delving into our pasts and possible futures there could be something far more important that we're supposed to be doing, realising or noticing - Now.

We assign great value to our belongings and want to hold onto them for as long as possible, even if that means passing them on to our children who we hope will value them as highly as we do and subsequently, pass them on to theirs. Just like us, our ancestors lived a 'smash and grab' lifestyle, accumulating as much as they could in their own lifetimes and even trying to take their wealth with them into their next life. In a desperate attempt to live on after our deaths we try to 'immortalise' the things we've accumulated over the course of our lifetimes; but these are memories that we'd be better off losing our attachment to while we're 'living'. If we don't then we're merely passing on a legacy of the misery of the world yesterday, to the world of tomorrow. These things - that we'd like to hold onto so much - are the spoils of a world that has known and *still* knows great suffering; they can't be used to change it. We don't just pass on objects to the next generation, we pass on their energy too. Whilst we're occupied with our pasts and futures, rivers flow, waves break on the shore, eggs hatch, the wind blows and the sun 'rises' and 'sets'; what doesn't change is far more important to contemplate than what appears to.

A friend of mine once lost their mobile phone and they were very upset about it; not about the phone itself, but the deepest secrets it held about them that could now be discovered by someone else. This information will survive long after our deaths, even if we do wish to believe it's private. We're not only concerned with our pasts, we're also occupied with passwords, logins, electronic privacy, speedy up-to-date technology and fast free delivery of our purchases; these are the things that concern and control our world now, but life can't continue at this pace without self-destructing at some point; this message is very loud indeed.

It takes determination and effort to cover the ground between the starting block and the 'finish' line. There are times when our heads spin with all the confusion and this is inevitable when we set our intention to 'de-condition' our mind; we're trying to hold onto what we've got but at the same time, radically change our lives. We have to clear out that jam-packed dirty and dusty attic after many years of storing our memories up there with one vital difference; we discover that it's not just our clutter up there; it's the clutter of Humanity and we've been collecting it for a *very* long time. Many can't see the point of deep thought on these subjects and from asking quite a few people I know, the general consensus is that we'll find out what life is all about 'all in good time' and that we should just enjoy it while we can, but are we really enjoying our lives or simply opting out of anything that requires us to use our capacity to work things out for ourselves - thereby merely keeping ourselves occupied or if you will, filling the gap between what we think of as our 'births' and 'deaths'. We'll find out 'in good time' implies that we already know we'll *survive* this life so surely it's worth a moment or two to think about what we're doing here, rather than taking our time for granted? Time is impermanent and therefore, cannot be relied on for anything other than it *possibly* 'running out'. Time decays, time rots and time passes by.

In summary, we think of death as something to be avoided and can go to a lot of trouble to pretend we're younger in ridiculously superficial ways; for example, wearing younger clothes or having plastic surgery. Neither of these - or any other way - will prolong our lives; they serve our vanity and attempt to cheat nature, but the clock still ticks. We don't know the difference between 'reality' and imagination and what we've come to think of as reality we continually reject in the hope that we can conquer life itself; we'll settle for nothing less. This attitude is misguided and the likely cause of many of the world's problems and more than a little arrogant for we each are, effectively, temporary residents.

~ The Journey ~

There are times in our lives when something makes us stop in our tracks and wonder where exactly we're heading, but such thoughts tend to be forgotten about as quickly as they occur and the 'moment' is overtaken by the pressures of daily life; for example, we have to cook the dinner, get the kids to bed or keep an appointment. These thoughts remain lost in the 'garage' of our minds amongst all the other clutter that we accumulate, like an old car we've been promising ourselves that we'll 'do something' about, but never quite get around to.

In the physical world, a car left standing for any length of time won't start without 'shock treatment'; for example, by having its battery charged. It needs help as it can't get going by itself. Deep thinking helps us to start our *own* 'engine' but it takes a while to get our motors running smoothly and confidently; our engines have been left standing all our lives. Just like the car, which needs to be taken on a long journey in order to fully charge its battery again, so we need to follow through with anything that comes our way after a 'What the heck' moment or perhaps a 'push' from this book. If we choose to shelve this opportunity then our battery won't charge and we'll remain 'parked'. Leave a car for long enough and it'll refuse to start altogether and could be costly to get going again, if at all. It's the same with us; the longer we wait the more reluctant we become to embark on our journey.

Imagine sitting in the back of our cars expecting that by some miracle a driver will appear out of nowhere and take us to our various destinations such as the shops, work or the cinema. The idea is ridiculous and we wouldn't even consider it, yet we do this with our journey through life, based on the beliefs of our various authorities (our drivers) and our goal is to earn enough money to pay our bills and buy enough possessions to keep that same society going, or rather sections of it called 'Me' and 'Mine'. Ironically, every time we embark on any kind of journey, we leave everything we cherish behind anyway. Each time we leave our homes there's a chance we may never return to the belongings and people that we believe define us and are reluctant to let go of - yet our lives can end at any moment, without prior notice.

Yet we wait ... and wait ... and don't get around to thinking about the true meaning of our lives. Perhaps we're waiting for scientific 'evidence' to tell us that this 'invisible' journey really *is* important, or maybe for the arrival of an anticipated saviour. But this inaction puts the onus of our welfare - and our very existence - onto something or someone else. Meanwhile, we - Humanity - believe there's enough time to discover what's 'true', but until we do it's 'business as usual'. It's quite a gamble to wait for the unknown and waiting isn't exactly an odds-on favourite, especially considering the direction we're already heading in - disaster. Only we can walk on our path and only without holding the hand of another, otherwise we're just following someone else in the hope that *they* know where *we're* going.

Once when I was driving - in the days before we had satellite navigation - I got lost after being diverted from my route. There was a car in front of me that I'd naïvely followed since the beginning of the diversion. The driver seemed to know the area well because he wasn't glancing around, as we do when we're looking for a sign of some sort; he didn't appear to be lost. For this reason I decided to follow him - if you drive, I'm sure you can relate to this. It wasn't until he turned into a driveway several miles later that I realised my foolish mistake; more importantly, I was still lost and as it turned out, further away from my destination.

When we water ski in the wake of a power boat we can get into all sorts of difficulty after its engine stops; whereas we were 'walking on water' our skis and bodies then sink into the sea again and to use a cliché, we haven't a leg to stand on. We rely on the speed and momentum of the boat to keep us afloat and it's a lot of fun; dolphins have fun swimming in the wake of a ship, but fun is *all* it is and there's no deeper meaning to it or permanent change in the life of the dolphin. It's the same on dry land. Take for example a popular self-help book whose momentum carries it way up the best-seller charts; we may feel so lifted when we read it but that feeling is temporary. Primarily this is because we're *reading* about how someone applied self-help to their life. It's a different matter altogether when we try to apply it to our *own* life because it doesn't account for our individual experiences; we can't walk the same path the author is treading.

'Self-help' is exactly that; we must help our-*self* and remove ourselves from the belief that we can plug into someone else's energy field and expect it to power our lives; our journey isn't theoretical *or* physical. If we were given a blank canvas, paintbrushes, paints *and* instructions by Leonardo Da Vinci, we still couldn't paint as he did. At best, we can create a *copy* of his work and however good that is, it will always be only a copy - a *fake*. Where's the value in that? We must create our *own* masterpiece.

We would however, feel good about having received Leonardo's gifts and instructions. If something makes us feel good, it's prudent to find out why because more often than not that 'good' is nothing more than what we want, rather than what we need. For many years I avoided the best advice I was given because the *best* advice is never the easiest to swallow and neither does it make us feel good; the application of good advice involves effort, sacrifice and risk - a big part of our journey. Good advice can sometimes be recognised by the force with which we reject it. There can be *no* permanent change unless we're prepared to make permanent changes; we have to want those changes, more than anything or anyone else.

Keeping our 'sights' on a target - our journey - isn't an easy task. The mind distracts us at every opportunity and it's easy to become disheartened. I used to feel frustrated when this happened and it can feel like a hopeless task to get back on track. But all we have to do is raise our bow, hold it steady and repeat this process until we're no longer distracted by 'Upgrades', 'Free Beer' or '50% off Sale' signs. Through this repetition the mind begins to lose its control and with this comes the revelation about how much control it has over us and also, a clearer understanding about our *two* voices; we built the 'wall' between them and only we can take it down again. It's a gradual process and we can't speed it up any more than we can speed up the flow of a river as it returns to its source. All we really have to do - though tough - is to keep our eye on the target; say 'Yes' to truth - whatever that may be and at whatever cost - and 'No' to the illusions. This is the only way to remove our conditioning unless we're one of the few 'blessed' by a rare 'Eureka' awakening experience. When we watch our mind closely we see how it loses its hold, it's worth thinking about 'who' realises this; *'Who am I'*, *'Who am I'*, *'Who am I'*, is our journey, and the journey is a miracle.

~ *Miracles* ~

The world can cater for all our needs. No-one needs to be thirsty or to go without food or shelter, yet our cities, towns and villages are full of various 'institutions' set up to provide these basic necessities for those who *do*. Our desires and their numerous divisions; greed, selfishness, competition etc., are the cause of the problems we delay solving. Dependent on a corrupt and menacing system to supply us with silly things we can well do without, we're unable to see the miracle of our world as a self-sufficient, wondrous and generous 'planet'; we take it for granted and abuse its gifts. The miracles have to be looked at, seen with increasing clarity and deeply contemplated. Then, because we change perspective, we begin to see things in an entirely different light. Take for example the miracle of water; we fill our kettles, wash our dishes, scrub our floors and protect ourselves from getting wet with umbrellas - never noticing what a miraculous process is taking place. We can't know where water originally came from or why there's so much of it but we can think about the wonder. Water floats on itself when frozen, expands, crystallises, flows, reflects, cleanses, dilutes, dissolves, evaporates, quenches thirst as well as fire, falls as rain, snow, hail, sleet or dew, hangs in the air as mist or clouds, returns to its source and so much more - all without any help from us.

We're surrounded by miracles but can't see them and therefore, are unable to appreciate them. When we stay focused on the wonders of the world our lives can't help but be transformed and we see things differently - we change channel. A crumbling building looks very different to me now compared to the way I perceived it twenty years ago. The difference is nothing to do with measuring the further deterioration of the building but in the way we observe it; for example, seeing that there exists a natural 'automatic process' that over time, returns everything to its source. I can't tell you how to do this, but you can see it for yourself if you're determined enough. That determination involves seeing the futility of the way we live now and realising that we're powerless to change anything unless we change ourselves; as I've said many times before, it's a process of negation; we must all change sooner or later - no exceptions.

A new born baby is a miraculous reminder of how far from innocence we've drifted and continue to drift away from. A toddler, a reminder of how much we don't mind that these babies lose their innocence and how foolishly we prepare them to become 'streetwise' so that they can live *successfully* in the complicated, violent, decadent, threatening and competitive world we've created for them - rarely, if ever, to notice the miracle of their own existence. As they grow they become mirrors of ourselves and then - because we don't approve of what we see in them - families become more and more divided by children who complain about their parents and parents who complain about their children. Parents compete with parents for the best dressed and equipped children; providing them with the masks and toys that society wants them to have. It's difficult to know how to break the chain and very few people have the energy to think about it; we've become disheartened and frustrated by this inherited chain of psychological disorder because we feel powerless; however, we *are* that society and only we can change it. Each one of us in our turn was once the miraculous innocent new born baby and I'd suggest that thought is a valuable one to ponder.

One of the greatest miracles that we ignore is the miracle of our own existence. From the joining of a sperm and an egg we become a single cell; we don't think about where the sperm or egg come from. The sperm and eggs are somehow produced by our bodies and most of them go to 'waste'; not all of a woman's eggs become part of a human being and out of *millions* of sperm cells produced by a man, only one at a time - under the right circumstances - gets to fertilise an egg. The miraculous process of procreation has become little more than a joke and a highly profitable business; we've turned the beauty of human reproduction into an immoral multi-veined industry - advertising, porn, violence, degradation and 'a relay society' are just a few examples of these veins. Many miracles take place during the creation of a baby and continue after it's born; a baby grows, changes, learns and in due time apart from its nails and hair, stops growing. The above is highly simplistic compared to the rest that goes on in this process but my point is that we don't see or think about how the hair on our heads can grow so long, but not our eye lashes, any more than we think about where a supermarket gets its apples from. We tend to see things that our senses attract us to but never think about the miracle of these senses or the fact that we have them in the first place. Mostly oblivious to the miracles that surround us we continue in our acquisitive lifestyles, forgetting that without prior notice we can lose everything we value so highly in the next moment. Still, we cling to our delusional arrogance that we can conquer 'outer space', control the universe and believe that we're in control of our lives. We each have a time limit in these bodies, ordained or otherwise. There's nothing to lose in thinking about this, so why are we so afraid to do so?

~ Nothing for Nothing ~

I've written a great deal about Humanity in my books and on many subjects that ultimately lead to *the* big question; 'Who am I'. On the way to that question many thoughts arise that challenge our existence and purpose - showing the futility of the way we live and how it leads to further suffering. One example of this is how we destroy the beautiful creatures that share our 'home' with us; elephants, tigers and other creatures we hunt down; we destroy them and then set up institutions to protect the few that are left; if this isn't insane then I don't know what is. Apart from the excessive consumption of products and information that lead to the rapid advancement of a technological evolution and a psychological devolution, we're inactive. Each of us is one of billions who passively observe this horror unfold and this makes us miserable as everyone 'on the stage' appears to be in control while *we* feel powerless to change what's happening; we accept this powerlessness and at the same time, complain about it. Rather than ask the question 'Who am I' we're more interested in who or what we can become on that 'stage'; for example, free, rich, healthier, attractive, famous or even infamous - thus adding to our problems. We enjoy applauding, criticising, comparing ourselves to and 'rating' others - one of the reasons we enjoy films, news, comedies and reality shows so much.

We seek a 'high life' - an *easy* life - not to have to work or *think* about a lack of money for the duration of our lives and we call this state 'success'; this success requires a great deal of either hard work *or* 'luck', but no matter how we achieve it we must still leave it all behind one day - it's superficial. It's not because we're *innately* lazy that we look for this 'high life', but because we're weary and resentful of the treadmill that supports a system that serves no good purpose whatsoever. 'Deep down', we want 'out' of the 'rat race'; we *know* it's fruitage is poisonous; however, this is the 'highest' life that society has to offer, so we 'tread-on' hoping to achieve it knowing that there are too many applicants for the few positions available and consequently, 'slump onto our couches' in frustration. It's because of this boredom - and loneliness - that we succumb to any sensational pleasure we can find - in many ways it's our 'reward'. No matter how much money we may accumulate to live 'higher' we'll never find happiness, contentment or more importantly, the security that we seek because we'll *still* be all we have for company if we get 'there' - the same face looking back at us in the mirror, only much older; the same conversations going on in our head, only more bitter. There isn't any place we can be in the world or any level of 'success' we can achieve that will change how we feel about ourselves.

There are times when we may feel a surge of energy to change something because we've had enough; like when we decide to make a stand against something in our life that has been problematic for a long time. We may, for example, write a letter of complaint to our employer about being over worked or the laziness and incompetence of our colleagues that lead to an increase in our own workload, while they take it easy. Those of us who find ourselves in this position tend to 'unwind' once we've written the letter and then spend hours editing it, until we talk ourselves out of handing it over at all. Our motives for editing the letter are many and varied; for example:

- We fear upsetting people.
- After writing our letter our anger has dissipated and we may even feel regret.
- We take the blame and convince ourselves that we're being unreasonable and making too big a deal of it.
- We're not ready to let go of the problem.
- We walk to the edge of change but then fear the change we seek.
- We fear the unknown.
- We fear the fallout of our 'betrayal'.
- It's not team-spirited.
- We'd prefer that our employer realise what's going on for himself.

So we back off and allow resentment to build up and the problem to continue. The new version of our letter doesn't resemble the original in any way. In fact, often it ends up more like an apology for our inadequacy rather than a complaint against our colleagues; for example, 'I'm sorry, but I just can't cope with this workload'. The familiar may not be *much* but it feels secure in some perverse way nevertheless. The fact that we're doing the work of others arrives because we feel it should be done and we assume responsibility for it. We were never forced to do somebody else's work and therefore, not accountable should it not get done. The whole drama however, is *entirely* of our own making and stems from a will to change others to our way of thinking, rather than change ourselves. Importantly, this drama is known only to ourselves; no one else is aware of our anxiety and *more* importantly, the problem remains unresolved.

~~~

It's no good acquiring thoughts from self-help books or wise men and women; this knowledge is worthless unless it's applied. I read a one star review of a random self-help book and the reviewer said "There isn't treasure here … just the promise of it". This reviewer was looking for answers, which are impossible to get from a book, or its author. We must do the work ourselves and know that there *is* work to be done. Imagine, if you will, holding a bottle of medicine and expecting to get better just by reading the instructions - it isn't going to happen. Similarly, whoever wrote the above review was obviously disappointed that the author's 'prescription' didn't deliver its promise. The reviewer was looking for 'quick-fix' answers outside in order to heal what was hurting on the inside - little wonder in a world of 'instant-on', 'no-effort-required' lifestyles. When the reviewer didn't get what they wanted they attacked the author. The ability to do so makes us feel empowered, but in truth, we do it because we *lack* any 'true' power of our own and in its place, accept the illusion of it. Our lives have become convenience lives; they're formulaic and organised and we're fast losing our skills in favour of the 'industrial-led' lifestyles we created. Without a cause (consumerism, for example), there can be no effect (industrialism); without the effect, there can be no cause - a chicken and egg situation. Without changing, there can be no change - nothing for nothing.

~ Promises ~

A promise is an assurance that we *will do* what we have said and the promisee expects it to be carried out; this commitment has been greatly diluted over time and has become no more than a 'throw-in' word that we have little faith in. We make plenty of promises to ourselves and others - too often without matching intentions - and these become 'heavy' reminders on our minds, refrigerators or notice boards, because we know we're expected to keep them. A promise - regardless of who it's made to - is something we hang on our 'to-do-list' or more frequently, on our '*not*-to-do-list' - which is usually much longer. These promises tend to consist of things like sticking to a diet, drinking less, spending less money, studying more, returning something we've borrowed or doing a favour for a friend. They get pushed to one side in favour of the things we kid ourselves are more important and these tend to be our 'habits' like going shopping, doing the housework, watching television, doing the laundry or any other mundane routines we may have.

Promises get forgotten about until we meet up with the 'promisee'. We tend to feel worse than they do about the unresolved issue and the subject hovers conspicuously between us in that awkward familiar way that never gets mentioned, or 'forgotten'; it's there every time we meet up again and it won't go away until the promise is fulfilled or we become immune to the reminders. Today's world tends to feel a responsibility to fulfil legal contracts rather than personal ones, perhaps because we fear fines or being sued more than we feel guilt or shame. Whatever the reason we tend to give promises, or handshakes, no more importance than we would a 'white lie' - not keeping our word is *very* acceptable in today's world of expediency over personal responsibility. These things matter if we want to improve our world and to find peace-of-mind - to stop the incessant chattering that haunts us day and night. The voices are there for a reason and I'd suggest that - if we've had enough of the nonsense, contradiction and mischief in our world - it's time we started listening to them.

~ *Procrastination* ~

It's said that procrastination is the 'thief of time' and we don't have to think very hard to see how this is true - that 'putting off' doing things that require our attention in favour of those that don't. The truth is, that the longer we put those things off the less inclined we are to do them; often they're replaced by those 'more important things'. We feel that as long as there's a 'tomorrow' we may not have to think about should've', could've or ought to've as we'll have time to do all the things we promise ourselves, but is this wise? Unfortunately time has a habit of catching up with us and when it does all those things that once begged our attention, now *demand* it.

The possibility of existing - even in the minutest way - after this life can make it bearable; it gives us a hope of the permanence we're unable to experience in this world - a chance at 'immortality', or perhaps a hope that science will find a way to stop us aging so that we can live on. We know of this 'chance' through education, literature, spiritual teachers and films - conditioning; yet we treat what we've been taught as *truth*. A truth based on hope, fantasy and weak optimism that are born from fear - from the words and actions of a corrupt society. Even with this 'chance' at immortality we tend to be reluctant to reflect on the purpose of our lives before our 'deaths'; we want someone else to do it for us. Who, or what, wants to survive this life is worth reflecting on, and why. That our life is temporary and driven by our ego is beyond question. The ego is *born* when we are and *dies* with us which makes it also temporary. Wherever there's a modicum of doubt about the purpose of our existence, surely the subject is worth reflecting on without referencing the past experiences and conditioning of others - continuing a cycle. After all, the problems of Humanity can't be solved by referencing the past; it can serve as a 'reminder' or spark our 'curiosity' that can motivate us to find our own path - to find our own power. Instead of heeding this reminder, we look to others for guidance, reassurance or confirmation of what we already know.

We tend to use 'guides' for spiritual comfort, for a vain hope in times of need, more than anything else but there's a danger that we become reliant on them so they're no longer guides but our leaders and we cease to think for ourselves. However, if we require this level of comfort then it follows that we have issues we lack the courage to tackle; why else would we need comforting? We seek it when we're feeling low; when we need a 'pick-me-up' or can't stand the mess we've gotten ourselves into any more and look for someone to kiss it all better, be it a priest, guru or 'best friend'. Comfort comes after an event, therefore it's required to make us feel better about the past, but it doesn't eradicate it - it fixes the past in place together with all its pains, sorrows, beliefs and insecurities. The past is something *dead* that we want to hold onto despite the certainty that we can't. Comfort tells us that it's okay to hold onto all our baggage as it's not our fault that we're carrying it; it denies responsibility and expects a miracle that will make everything better with no effort on our part;

I'd suggest this miracle *won't* arrive and that we must learn to leave our beliefs behind us in order to see the falseness of them. The past doesn't 'exist'; it's a memory and we hold onto it and treat it as something precious as we believe it defines who we are. Sooner or later we must let go of our pasts; we *all* know this on one level or another and we know that the challenge to do so is enormous, yet we leave ourselves no 'time' to reflect on it - we procrastinate.

~ Positivity ~

There's a great deal written and said about positivity and much effort is put into promoting this phenomenon with almost religious zeal believing that it will solve all our problems, if we just stay positive!

Positivity however, can't last the course and though we feel great for a time whilst looking 'on the bright side', no psychological change has taken place. All we've effectively done is look the other way, while someone we'd rather not see passes us by. There's a promoted form of positivity that tells us if we think positive everything will be alright, but positivity isn't a cure for negativity; they go hand in hand. Thinking positive is a deliberate action of recognising and ignoring a negative situation in the hope that it will go away; very different from having a positive attitude about dealing with that same negative situation. Positivity, in itself, serves to make others comfortable around us and to distract us from truth; if we're looking in one direction, we can't see what's going on in another and more importantly, we can't see the whole. If we ask someone 'How are you' we don't want to hear their list of problems; we want them to be positive and tell us that they're 'doing very well'. Try advising someone who's just lost a child or partner to be positive; there's no empathy or compassion in that guidance. In some cases, we want them to be positive because *we* can't cope with - or don't want to know about - their sorrow; we have enough of our own. No matter how positive they may try to feel, on a deeper level they're in terrible pain and positivity attempts to suppress that pain rather than to deal with it. Positivity and negativity are imbalances of the 'whole'. Like the volume on the radio, if it's too low we strain to hear it and if it's too loud we cover our ears; we need the sound to be 'just right'; we also need to be able to listen without noisy or visual distractions - without any distortion.

~ In Our 'Humble' Opinion ~

We want everyone to agree with our opinions, but they're rather busy with their own.

When I was designing the cover for my first book, I put up six different designs on a new website and asked everyone I knew to help me choose one for the final product. I already knew which of the covers I liked best but to my dismay, no-one chose it. There were no shortage of conflicting opinions and I tweaked the covers accordingly, until they no longer resembled the originals. In the end, I scrapped the lot and designed a new cover altogether. This time I *didn't* ask for opinions and put it on the website as my definitive cover. No-one disliked it or suggested any changes and I was happy. Had I added this cover to the previous ones, it would've been subject to the same process and likely ended up following the same fate. By asking for opinions, we're 'passing the buck' onto others to make our choices for us and to approve of what we do; we care what people think. The more choices we ask others to make for us, the more confused we become by their subjective opinions; there can never be an 'outright/overall winner'. Interestingly, everyone liked the final cover despite not having been asked for their opinion. The problem it seems is choice. When there's no choice put forward we accept the only option. This has enormous ramifications in our competitive and self-serving society, the biggest of which is that our choices are going to be made for us and our opinions formed, based on those choices.

We ask for the opinions of others but do we *really* need them? I'd suggest that we ask because we don't have confidence in ourselves or our choices and that we're looking for approval, in its many guises. Mostly however, we want other people to like us and to see things our way; we value our *own* opinions and would generally like others to value them too. Our world - particularly online - increasingly encourages 'likes' and 'dislikes' and these get us into a muddle as we become confused by the differing opinions and conflicting suggestions; it becomes impossible to satisfy everyone - or *anyone* - and that leaves us feeling frustrated and as in the above example, without a book cover.

Further examples of this confusion are easily found on any forum or online video that allow reviews or comments; the same applies to books, films or other online purchases.

The world is absolutely bursting with opinions and for this reason they're often given *without* being asked for. Everything we put online is asking for the opinion of someone or other - whether we want them or not - and it *will* get them. Online is our 'showcase' and it will be criticised, both online and by those who choose *not* to air their opinions publicly. We want to be noticed, validated, appreciated and we want *this* from a world whose mind is volatile, debauched, quite mad, full of violent imagery, irresponsible and consequently, highly unstable. It's from within this world that our opinions, comments and creations are both given and received. This situation didn't begin with the internet however; we've always been more than generous with our opinions - asked for or not. We give them when we look someone up and down, when we listen to gossip, when we want to agree with somebody else in order to be in their favour or - in some cases - when we just want to be plain nasty.

Nowadays, we rate and review just about everything before we buy it and like to 'try-before-we-buy'. Often we buy products based on the experience and opinions of others, yet we've no idea who they are. We also rate and review things we *haven't* bought based on our preferences and prejudices - we have many of those. The result is a world that criticises everyone in one way or another; a world where we fear to show our masterpieces in case they're negatively criticised. We fear our efforts and dreams being torn apart, which - if we look at it from another perspective - means we live in fear of our own creativity and in particular, of it being marked down by others. Reviews, likes, dislikes and ratings are different names for 'judgement by others' according to their own 'impeccable' standards. This causes chaos and further division which can - and often does - lead to anger and other negative emotions being vented online. These judgements are used as successful and easily corruptible marketing techniques; for example, companies can - and do - set up multiple accounts in order to negatively rate or review the products of their competition, whilst positively rating their own.

~~~

Dishonesty plays a large part in our opinions and *correctness* has hijacked 'diplomacy' and 'tact' - painting them in its own colours of self-importance and expediency. Apart from the obvious antagonists waiting to pounce on anyone who cares to listen to them, we don't want to 'offend' with our opinions so we tiptoe around the truth in fear of waking it up. Dishonesty therefore, becomes acceptable - and even creditable - if it appears to be in a 'good cause' like in an 'appealing' political manifesto. However, dishonesty, can never be a good thing no matter what disguise it wears. For one thing; we're highly intelligent and we generally know when someone's lying to us or being 'diplomatic'; we know a sham when we see one. We also know when *we've* lied and then things like guilt and superiority can come into play; one thing always leads to another. If we ask a friend 'Does my bum look big in these trousers' we expect them to say 'No', but the very question implies that *we* think it does. What's happening is, we're asking our friend to lie to us and generally they'll comply; the corollary of this is our bum becomes bigger than ever. The lie then demands continuity; so it goes ... on and on. People don't always lie about their opinions but when they don't then we tend to strongly resent what we hear; this can be a great way to lose friends.

What do *you* think? Is asking for an opinion courting disaster? It depends on our intention and usually that's to hear what we want to hear, which isn't always the truth. It also depends on the intention of the person we're asking for opinions from. We'd be better off asking ourselves *why* we need someone else's opinion or why we think they may need ours, and watch - *closely* - our responses to that question. Often we look for approval because we lack confidence in our ability to make decisions for ourselves; we look for the 'green light' (permission granted) and gratification. Gratification that tells us we're good enough, or confirms that we're *not*; yes, some of us want this confirmed too, as it lets us 'off the hook'. Our minds may sometimes be changed by the opinions of others; we may not like those opinions but often go along with them anyway. We end up feeling frustrated by our lives because we don't live them as we want to, but rather as others think we should. As always, we can't change what's happening in the world but we can better understand it by taking a closer look at ourselves. This is how we become empowered and grow in our ability to think for ourselves. This is how to change the belief that we need the opinions of others.

~ Hypocrisy ~

If you tell a lie for long enough, it becomes your truth.

We often betray our thoughts with our actions. Sometimes these are well intentioned - like when we don't wish to offend anyone - and sometimes not, lacking in sincerity for the sake of expediency or keeping up appearances. Take as an example a person who 'lovingly' strokes a dog, with the sole intention of getting to know its owner. He's betraying the owner of the dog by acting in one way in order to impress her, but whilst he's pretending to like the dog his thoughts tell another story altogether; perhaps by thinking about kicking the dog the minute the owner isn't looking. I've witnessed someone do this when its owner's eyes were diverted and then pretend to like it again. Should a relationship develop between two people in this situation - or a similar one - it won't stand much chance of being healthy. How could it when the first communication was hypocritical and therefore, dishonest?

No good can come out of any situation where we behave in one way but act and speak against it. I'm sure that - just like me - you've had friends over for dinner or a social gathering and had a great evening, but later criticised the things they said or did *after* they'd left, despite having been in agreement with them at the time. If you haven't been in this situation then perhaps you've spent some time in a discussion with one person and immediately telephoned a friend to tell them about it, 'You'll *never* guess what so-an-so just said', from an entirely different perspective. We're dualistic in our lifestyles, particularly when we're out to impress others. This is just another way of expressing a lack in our character that we feel obliged to make up for. We also make up for this lack in other ways, like when complaining about someone who hasn't telephoned us for a few months. We feel increasingly bitter about it and create a drama in our minds about what's really going on. What we don't see is that *we* haven't bothered to pick up the phone either which we could easily do if we wanted to; we project our criticism and hypocrisy onto others when we don't want to examine ourselves. When we fail to live up to our *own* standards we can never be free or complete.

There's a lot more to hypocrisy than we allow ourselves to talk about; it doesn't only arise in a 'do as I say but not as I do' situation. It's an attempt to deny our dualistic nature; a cover up. Hypocrisy, for example, is at the root of pomposity; of those who raise their noses skyward refusing to recognise that they walk on the same ground as every human being - it's delusional. It's a false sense of superiority developed in order to cover up a true sense of *inferiority*. If we have to 'think' ourselves superior, then we can't be. On the deepest level, hypocrisy is the betrayal of ourselves; the betrayal of our heart and we do it all the time - it's a mask.

Who am I?

At the core of the fire, lie the spoils of desire.

Every moment, every minute, everything that we put in it
Every thought, every deed, every flower, every weed
Every muscle we expand, every blow that we withstand
Every place that we dwell, every rat that we smell

Every mask that we wear, every colour of our hair
Every film that we watch, every point that we notch
Every turn of our head, every place that we're led
Every cake that we bake, every pleasure that we take

Every need we fulfil, every blush, every chill
Every wall we defend, every tale that we bend
Every nose in the air, every time we don't care
Every scar that we leave, every ace up our sleeve

Every tear that we cry, every rule we apply
Every word that we spread, every dream in our head
Every face to the ground, every idol that we crown
Every smile, every pout, every legend that we doubt

Every truth that we taint, every sinner, every saint
Every shoulder that we chip, every stiff upper lip
Every morsel that we eat, every innocent we cheat
Every tactic we employ, everything that we destroy

Every person that we hurt, every call we avert
Everything we ignore, every tally, every score
Everything we despise, every view through our eyes
Everyone that we mock, every door that we lock

Cont.

Every man we detest, every time we know best
Every bubble that we burst, every person that we curse
Every cut, every mile, every step, every trial
Every stone we have thrown, every seed we have sown

Every fear, every frown, everyone that we put down
Everything we create, every heart we vacate
Every song that we sing, every touch, every ring
Every moment, every minute, everything that we put in it.

Afterword

We're brilliant - often too brilliant - but we're not yet wise; we don't even *wish* to become wise. Throughout my books are many thoughts, ideas and self-reflections; none of which haven't been thought out before and each one of them is a part of Humanity studying of all things, itself. We're somehow aware of our own consciousness and able to reflect on many things about our existence and evolution, though more often than not we choose not to. We walk without thinking about how we put one leg in front of the other and eat without considering how we digest our food. We do these in much the same way as we drive our cars or use a washing machine - mechanically. Incredibly, we're able to think about how our bodies work and our thoughts too and the implications of that are worth pondering. As individuals, each one of us can think these things out for ourselves and find - if we're sincere - that nothing is what it appears to be.

All we really *need* to see is right in front of us when we observe our world and what we're doing with *and in* it; *none* of it is - or can be - hidden from us if we want to discover it. As an example, we follow orders every day; orders that we don't realise we're being given because we've followed them for so long. These imperatives come in many forms such as 'Stop', 'Go', 'Give Way' and 'Keep Left' - orders we're unaware we're obeying. Other common imperatives in our daily lives are 'Open Here', 'Push', 'Pull', 'Click Here', 'Queue This Side', 'Up' and 'Down' - there are hundreds, possibly thousands more - little wonder some of us live in fear that someone will 'push the button'. We can argue - and do - that we need imperatives for things like 'organisation' or road safety but would we *really* just crash into other cars and run people over if the signs weren't there - of course not. On the contrary, we'd pay more attention to what we're doing and stop looking for instructions on how to do it. For goodness sake, even our text is predictive and corrected for us; when did we become so dependent? It's through these observations that illusions begin to fall away, and very many must. It's also through observation that our minds sharpen because they're not being used *for* us but *by* us - we begin to think for ourselves again.

This 'life' causes us so much anxiety or if you will, dread; dread of what we (as a society) created with the imminent possibility of the self-destruction of ourselves and our 'planet' or, dread of the mysterious 'void' we fear entering.

We don't know what's in store for us after we die and we generally have only fables, myths, legends and 'history' to guide us and not enough time to read all the books they're written in, let alone know if there's any truth hiding as ghosts between the lines. More often than not we don't have the energy or will to search for 'guidance' as it's hard to know which books are worth reading; the market is saturated with conflicting information and biased reviews of that same information. We're not keen to work things out for ourselves as we live in a world full of 'experts', instructions and reference manuals and from them we expect to find out all we need to know.

We seek gratification rather than wisdom or good advice. We're prepared to take our chances on whether or not we need to become wise, perhaps because we've as much to fear in our futures as we do the events in our pasts or perhaps because on a deeper level we're frustrated about working so hard in this world for things we know we can't keep. In the world as we now know it - as we've always known it - there seems to be little need for wisdom. We know that no matter what we 'achieve' we must give it all up again and we don't want to; it can be felt - or seen - as 'failure' and no-one *wants* to feel that way about themselves. However, failure and success are illusions that must die when we do; still we want so much to hold onto them because it's what we know so well. Bearing this in mind, it's understandably difficult to 'take a chance' embarking on a 'metaphysical' journey that may *also* lead us nowhere at all; if we have to give up who we think we are and everything and everyone we know when we die, then why would we want to give it all up earlier?

Whether illusory or not, our lives begin with our births and end with our deaths. I'd suggest that we've a great deal to achieve between the limitations of these two markers. We take a chance that everything will be okay 'on the night' but this surely invests all our eggs in one basket and places a low value on our lives as individuals. It's worth remembering that this basket isn't ours 'personally' - it's society's - and any decisions we make to put our eggs into it are based on information we receive from that society. These decisions originate from the past with all its horrors and as such can never solve Humanity's problems. We can't repair today's fractured society with the pieces from yesterday's fractured society. Our 'spirit' has been broken; we've no enthusiasm, energy or even the will to try to pick ourselves up - we're disheartened, disheartened by the wall to wall daily dose of Humanity's insanity with no end to it in sight. We're resigned to our circumstances and need to stop and 'take stock' if we want to see change. Without self-investigation we limit our possibilities and remain reliant - for guidance - on the corrupt and mischievous system we created. Because self-investigation *exists* as an ability within each of us, it's worth reflecting on how important it is to explore it and also about in how many ways we're being diverted from our purpose by senseless and unintelligent influences, pastimes and attractions. We have - after all - nothing to lose.

"And in the end
The love we take
Is equal to the love … we make."

Golden Slumbers
John Lennon & Paul McCartney

NOTES

NOTES

NOTES

NOTES

NOTES

NOTES

NOTES

About the Author

Renée Paule was born in London and was brought up in an orphanage, despite having two living parents. Subjected to mental and physical cruelty, the trauma she suffered left her with twelve years of almost total amnesia. Six marriages later (four official), she chose to 'take stock' and began a process of questioning everything in her world.

Her take on life changed dramatically following a profound experience revealing the connection between herself and the Universe; there's no separation. With this realisation, she no longer accepted the 'face value' world she'd once thought of as the norm.

Renée Paule wishes to share this knowledge and show how a change of perspective can provide an alternative to the topsy-turvy world that Humanity, on the whole, accepts as an inevitable way of life.

She now lives in Ireland.

www.reneepaule.com

CPSIA information can be obtained
at www.ICGtesting.com
Printed in the USA
LVOW10s1352120117

520729LV00001B/28/P